IMAGES
*of America*

# LONDONDERRY

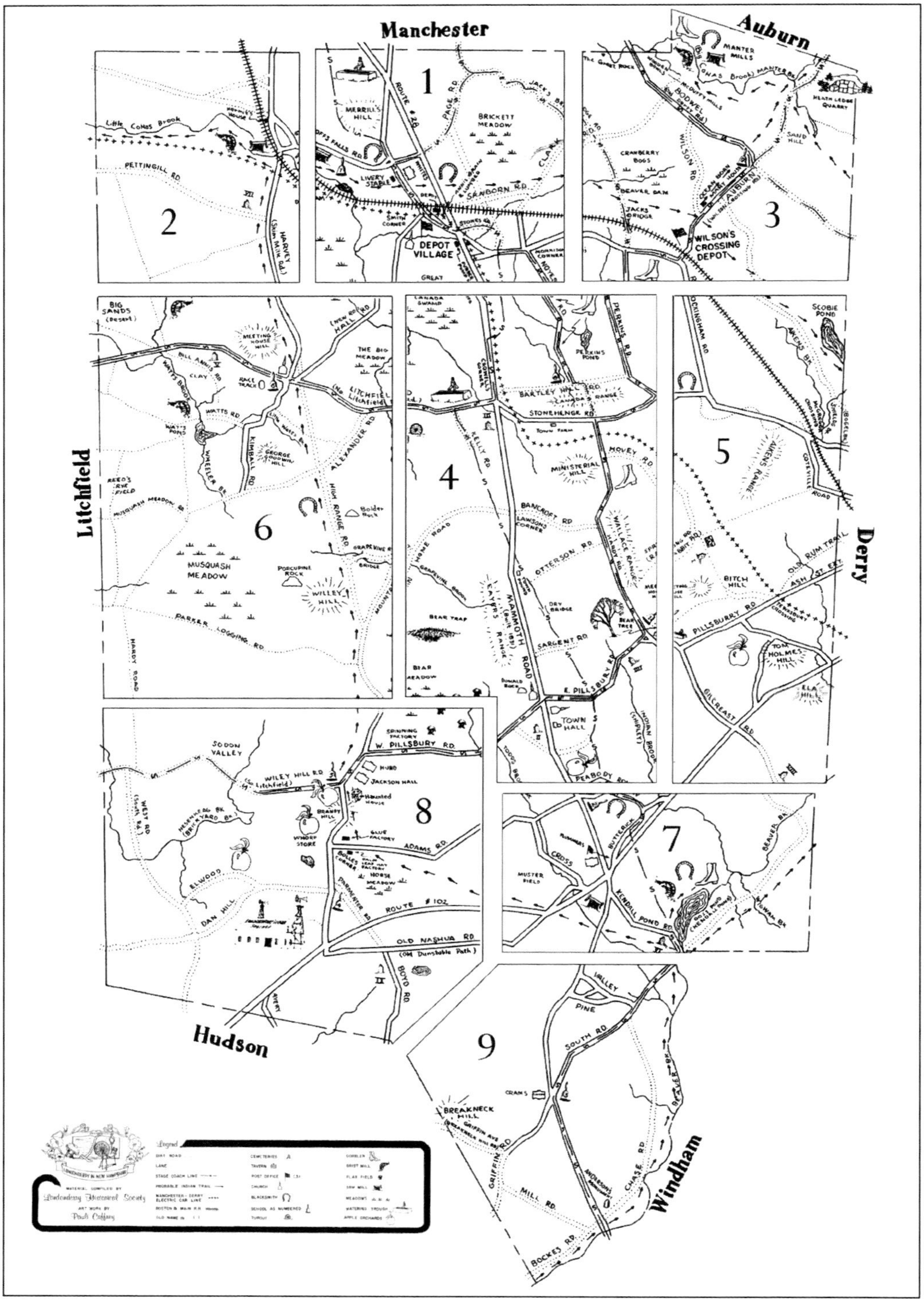


**Map, c. 1960.** This map was prepared by the Londonderry Historical Society with historical points of interest. It has been broken into nine areas of town that will be explained in each chapter.

IMAGES
of America

# LONDONDERRY

Londonderry Historical Society

ARCADIA
PUBLISHING

ISBN 978-0-7385-3557-9

Published by Arcadia Publishing
Charleston, South Carolina

Printed in the United States of America

Library of Congress Catalog Card Number: 2004100861

For all general information, contact Arcadia Publishing:
Telephone 843-853-2070
Fax 843-853-0044
E-mail sales@arcadiapublishing.com
For customer service and orders:
Toll-free 1-888-313-2665

Visit us on the Internet at www.arcadiapublishing.com

*Special thanks to the researchers and composers, Virginia Dahlfred, Patricia Deneault, Marilyn Ham, William Longmaid, Anne Rozmovits, James Schwalbe, and Penny Webster.*

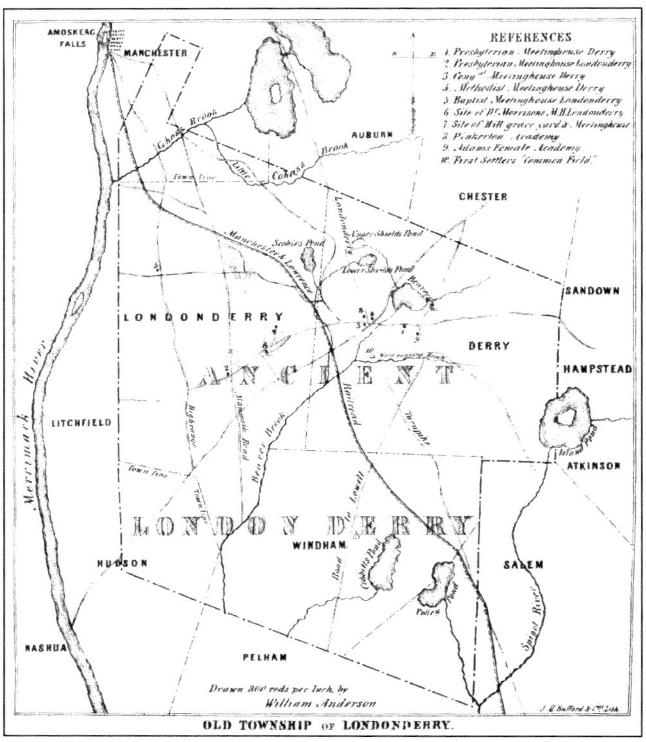


**MAP, C. 1850.** This map of Londonderry is from the *History of Londonderry*, volume I, by Rev. Edward L. Parker, published by the town of Londonderry in 1974.

# Contents

# Acknowledgments

The members of the Londonderry Historical Society who have worked so diligently and tirelessly on this book are to be commended for their efforts. Due to the encouragement of other like-minded individuals within the society, we believe we have succeeded in producing a photographic history for all members of our community to enjoy. The families and friends of these individual members also need to be acknowledged for their patience and encouragement.

The historical society would also like to acknowledge the members of the Londonderry community who shared their photographs and historical information. The society's collection of photographs and postcards, reproduced here, has been greatly enhanced by the contributions of the Clark family, Eleanor Barton, Dorothy Ela Ross, Emily Foley, John Gilcreast, Marilyn Ham, Rick Holmes, the Joudrey family, Priscilla Parmenter Lockwood, the Londonderry Presbyterian Church, William Longmaid, the Mack family, Betsy McKinney, Ken Merrill, Margaret Mortimer, Bob Perry, Hank Peterson, Martha Pinkham Phillips, Kit Plummer, James Schwalbe, Gerry Van Grevenhof, Ada Wingate, Vera Wingate, and Mason J. Young Jr.

We would be remiss if we did not thank all the individuals who were instrumental in researching and writing the *History of Londonderry* and *Early Londonderry*, which helped immeasurably in compiling the text for the photographs in this book. They are Jessie Beckley, Marge Nissula, Lennie Ogden, Helen A. Reynolds, Ferne Schmidtchen, Junie Vickers, and Melvin E. Watts.

Profits from the sale of this book will benefit the Londonderry Historical Society, which strives to preserve its historic buildings and artifacts for future generations. The society encourages readers to visit their website at http://www.londonderryhistory.org.

The historical society asks the indulgence of all readers for any errors or omissions.

# INTRODUCTION

Colonial Londonderry came into being in 1719, when 16 Scotch-Irish families from Londonderry in Northern Ireland settled here. Part of what was first called Nutfield (named for the many native nut trees growing in the area) is thought to have been the earliest inland settlement in what is now New Hampshire. The original boundaries included a large area of present-day Londonderry and Derry, along with parts of Auburn, Hudson, Windham, and what later became the city of Manchester. In 1740, Londonderry was the second-largest town in New Hampshire. Not quite a century later, its physical size had slimmed some, but it was still too large to be efficiently managed as one town. In 1824, it split in almost equal parts into the towns now known as Derry, on the east, and Londonderry, on the west. For most of its life, Londonderry was a town made up primarily of farms, most of them self-contained. Domestic animals, notably horses (448 in 1900) and cows (758 in 1900), nearly outnumbered the people who depended on them.

By the 1850s, the decade just before the Civil War (when the scope of this book begins), Londonderry had experienced momentous change when the Lawrence & Manchester Railroad (later absorbed into the Boston & Maine system) connected it to Boston and well beyond. The rail link was analogous to the coming of Interstate 93 a bit more than a century later. By the mid-1800s, the Industrial Revolution was well underway in the area, including neighboring Manchester, which by then was producing steam locomotives.

At the same time, the invention of the camera helped put the town on the map. Photography had been added to the recording of history throughout the country and the world, and Londonderry's own photographic story began. By the end of the 19th century, postcard photography became an inexpensive way for people to send short messages to distant friends and family. Such postcards are part of our visual record.

The Londonderry of the next 100 years was a far different place from the one most of us today would be familiar with. The people living in the community—farmers and their families, tradespeople, merchants, teachers in the 10 district schools (9 grammar schools and 1 middle school), pastors in the few churches, and a handful of doctors and lawyers—numbered only 1,408 in the 1900 census. We can try to imagine this country town at the time of the Civil War, with the help of the few photographs we have of some of the men who served. We can see families posing in their dooryards or scholars (as they were once called) and their teachers looking at us from the schoolyards scattered around town, each within walking distance (sometimes up to two miles) of the pupils' homes. The photographs let us see some of the many horses that pulled wagons or buggies and helped the residents attend community and social functions. Some other farm animals also have their place in our pages.

We can see something of what Londonderry was like a century or more ago, but we need to use our imaginations to hear what it must have sounded like. Compared to life here today, the town would have seemed very quiet, maybe blessedly quiet, but there were sounds all around of things that today's traffic din would easily drown out. Neighbors knew one another and could call to each other and converse without a phone before there were any of the multi-party crank phones of the 20th century. They could discern the distinctive sounds of farm animals or people at work in the fields. They could hear the cracking and snapping of pond ice in the winter and the rushing of brooks after the spring thaw. In those days, a country person would have had an intimate feel for the immediate landscape because, for most people, home and work were the same place. Londonderry was a place of life, but life at a slower and perhaps less stressful pace than life today.

We hope that those who peruse this book will let this collection of images, from a time beyond the memory of most, reach out and speak to them and treat them to both an eyeful and maybe even an earful of a town not quite as remote as it might have been without these pages.

*One*

# DEPOT VILLAGE

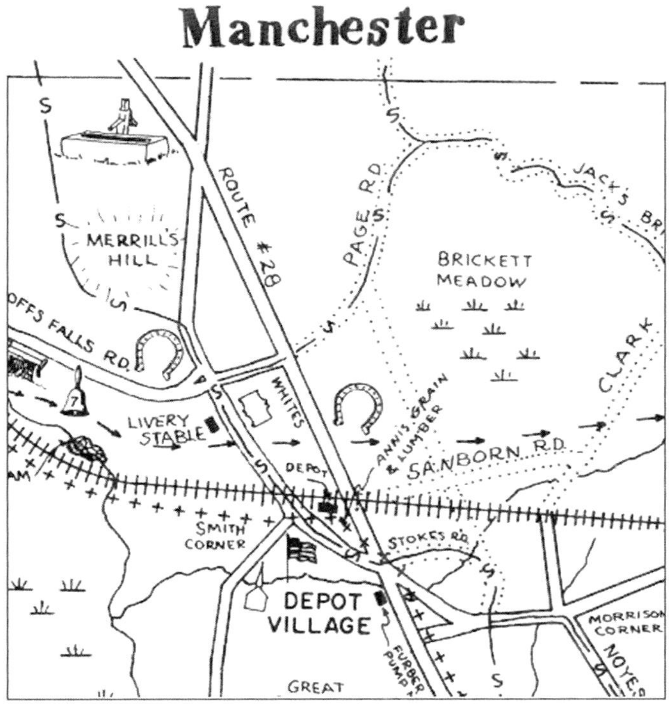


**NORTH CENTRAL.** This area of Londonderry was once known as Depot Village and contained Schoolhouse No. 7 on Grenier Road (formerly Goffe's Falls Road) near Mammoth Road, as well as Morrison Junior High School on what was called Morrison's corner on Rockingham and Noyes Roads.

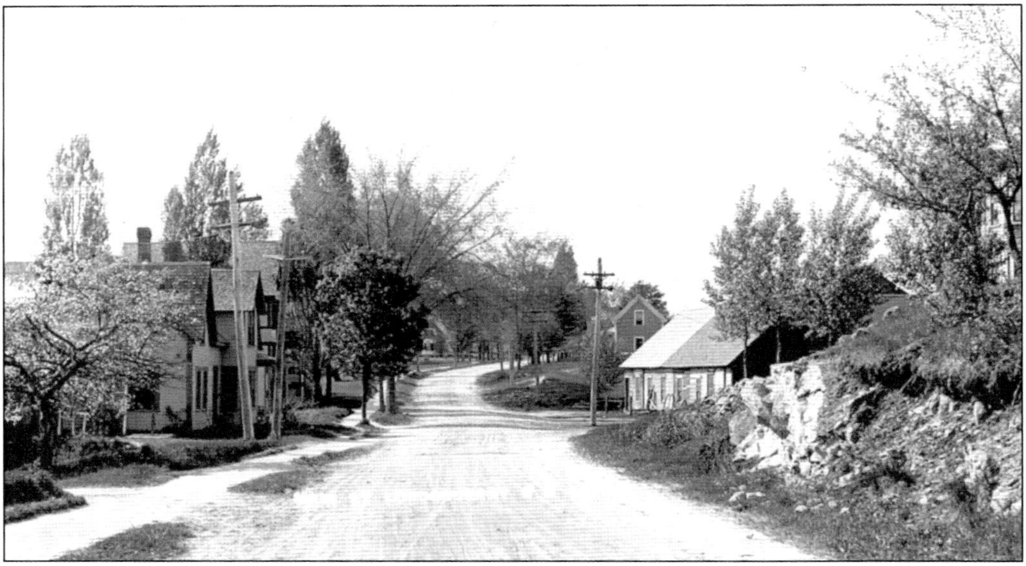

**Mammoth Road, Just North of the Depot.** This photograph of Mammoth Road, taken about a century ago, shows a Londonderry hardly recognizable from the same spot today. It is possibly a fresh spring day for the many villagers living near the Boston & Maine train depot in the years before World War I. The many wagon tracks in the road, the wires overhead, and the well-kept sidewalks and yards indicate a town of industrious, busy people. The one-story Smith-Merrill blacksmith shop on the right was an important part of the community.

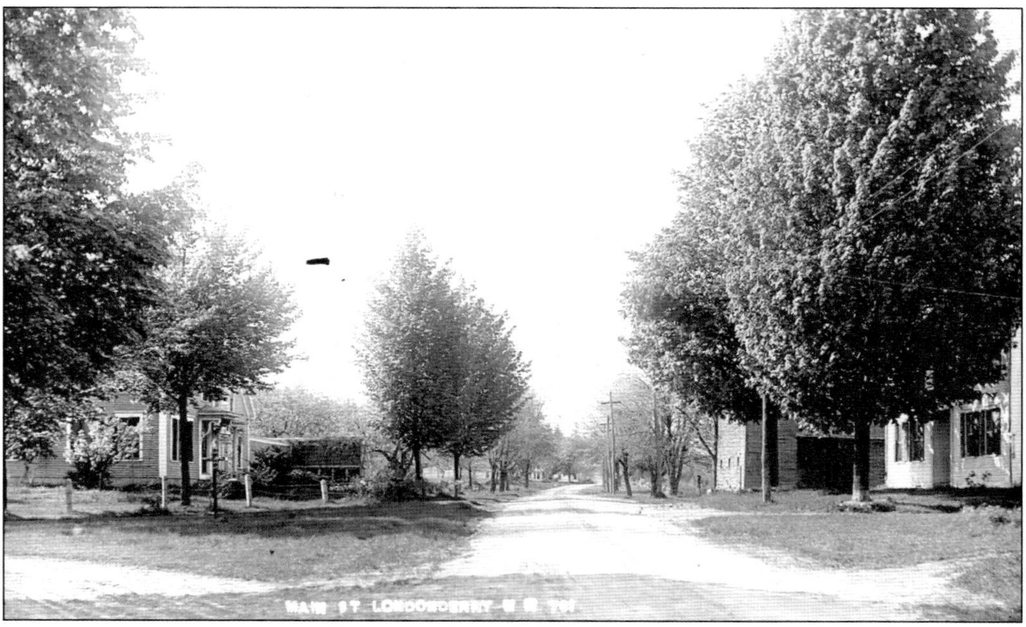


**Mammoth Road, Looking North from White's Corner c. 1907.** This scene includes the present intersection of Grenier Field and Mammoth Roads. The Brooks house on the left still stands, but the Tuttle house and the White's Tavern barn gave way to the road connecting Route 28 to Mammoth Road. In the distance is the farm of Oliver Merrill, who put up his own power poles, some of which may be the ones visible on the right side of the road.

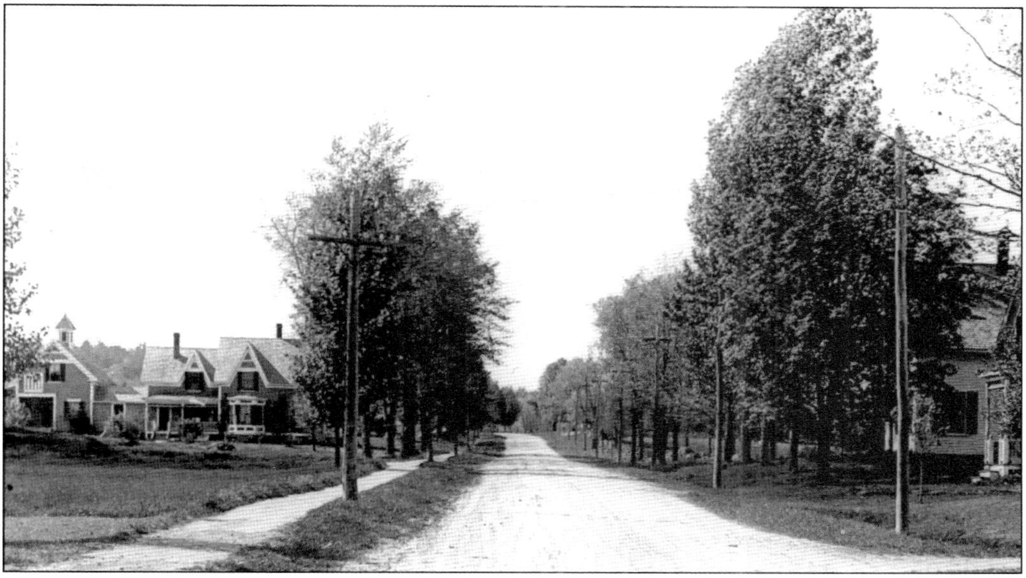

**Mammoth Road, North Londonderry, Looking North from Smiley's Store.** In the late 19th century, the village grew, and houses sprouted on a group of side streets. The house on the left, located on the corner of Buckthorn Street and Mammoth Road, was built in 1894 by shoe-shop proprietor Frank Benson. It also housed families named Watts, Ray, Brooks, McLane, and Thibeault, among others. The arrival of the railroad and Annis mill brought on a modest building boom, followed in the early 20th century by a new forest of power poles.

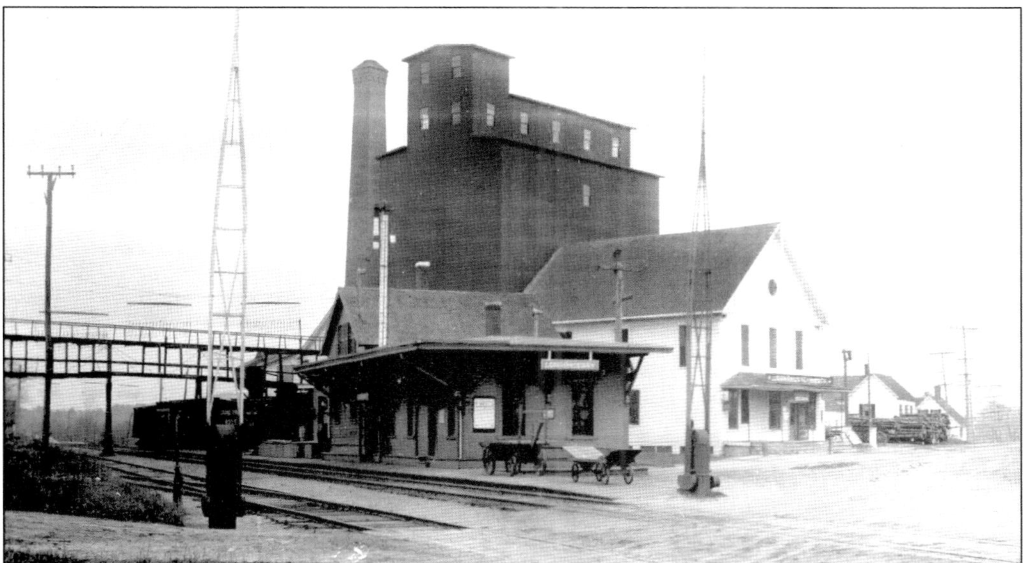

**Annis Mill and the Boston & Maine Depot, North Londonderry.** The Boston & Maine Railroad served the commercial and passenger needs of Londonderry for a century with a station and two tracks. It also served the grain elevator and the lumber mill of the Annis Grain and Lumber Company. In this c. 1900 photograph, one siding holds three freight cars. To the right of the white company building is a pile of logs waiting to be milled.

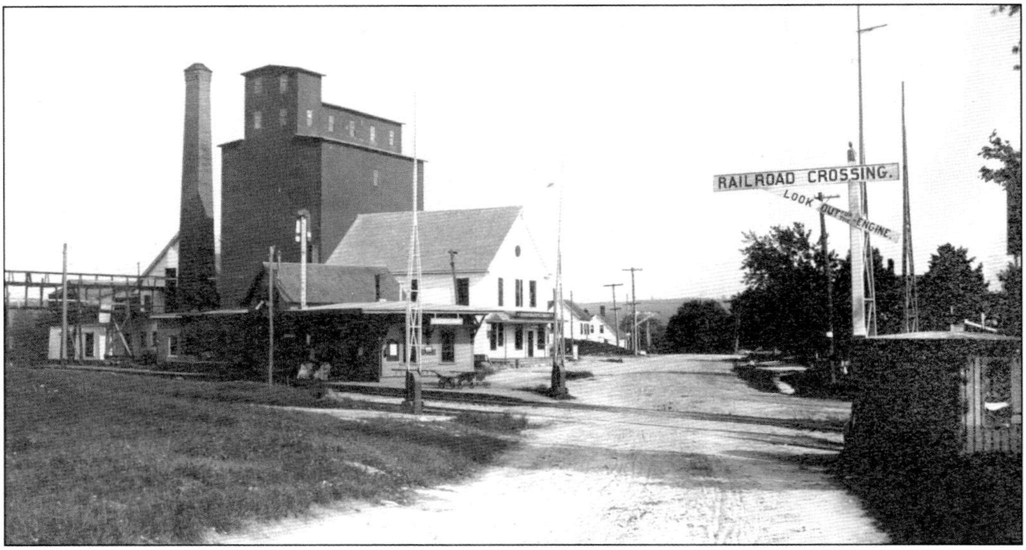


**THE RAILROAD STATION AND THE ANNIS GRAIN AND LUMBER COMPANY, LOOKING SOUTH, C. 1910.** The Annis elevator, next to the still-standing chimney for the wood-fired boiler, stood at least five stories tall. The company produced lumber and grain and was the business center of town. The railroad depot served passengers going north through Manchester and south through Lawrence. Trains also carried mail and railway express packages.

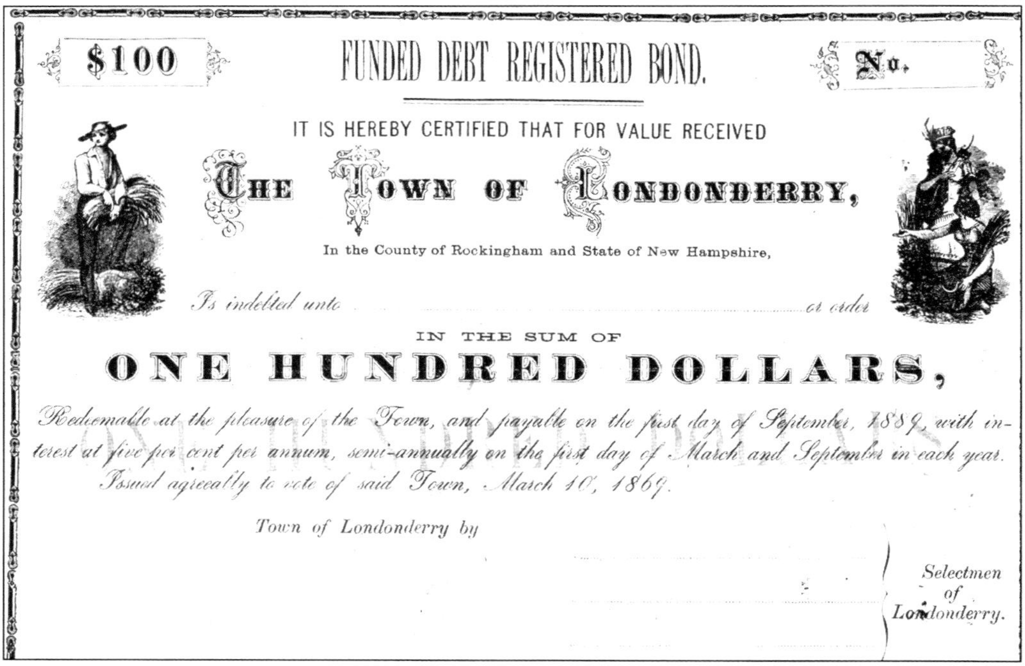
$100 FUNDED DEBT REGISTERED BOND. No.

IT IS HEREBY CERTIFIED THAT FOR VALUE RECEIVED

The Town of Londonderry,

In the County of Rockingham and State of New Hampshire,

Is indebted unto ................................ or order

IN THE SUM OF

ONE HUNDRED DOLLARS,

*Redeemable at the pleasure of the Town, and payable on the first day of September, 1889, with interest at five per cent per annum, semi-annually on the first day of March and September in each year. Issued agreeably to vote of said Town, March 10, 1869.*

*Town of Londonderry by*

*Selectmen of Londonderry.*

**A LONDONDERRY $100 BOND, 1878.** Judging by this certificate, the people of Londonderry, like residents in most towns, have been borrowing money for much longer than one might think. The purpose may have been the need for funding for a new school or some other building or for roadwork or other capital improvements. The terms were 20 years at 5 percent per annum. Oddly, the bond has no certificate number.

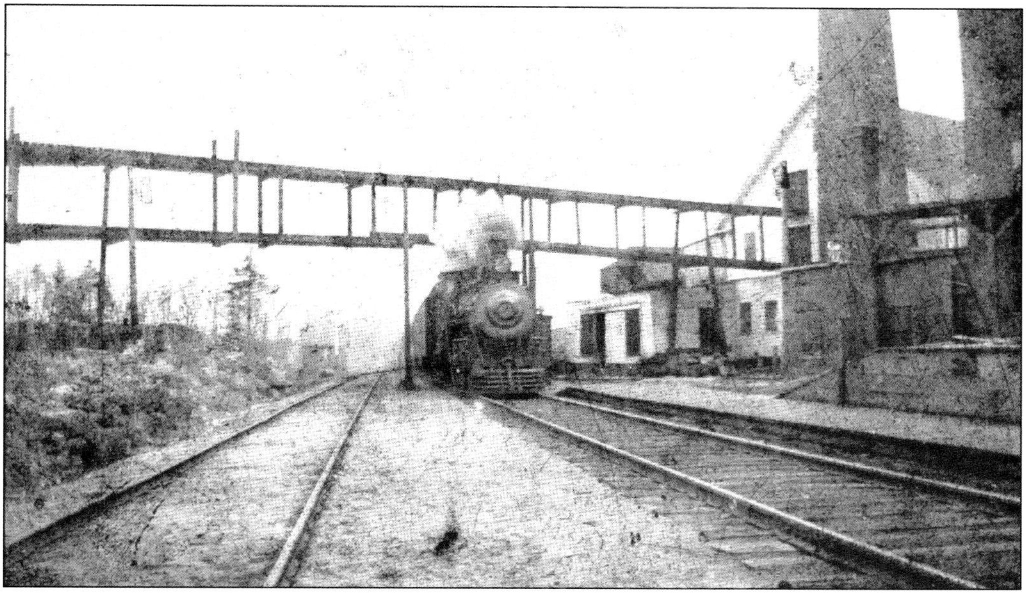

**A Boston & Maine Train Coming into the Londonderry Depot.** The notation on the back of this photograph, in keeping with the railroad timetable, gives the exact date and time of the train's arrival: May 7, 1899, at 2:07 p.m. This line, torn up in the early 1980s, began as the Manchester & Lawrence Railroad in 1847 and ended as the Boston & Maine. Passenger runs ended in 1953, and freight runs ended *c.* 1980. Workers used the walkway above the locomotive for moving freshly milled kits and staves to drying sheds to the left.

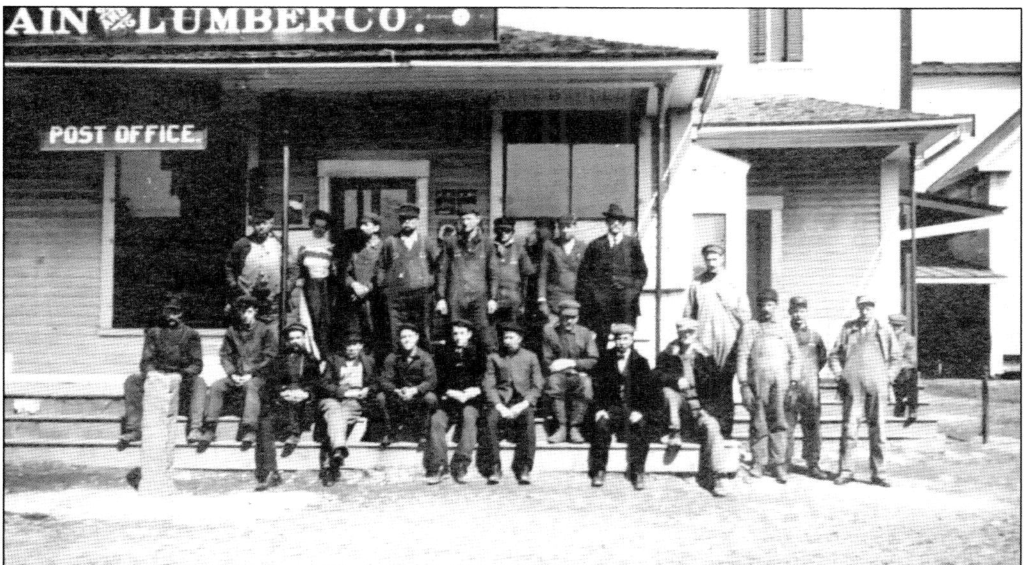


**The Post Office and Store at the Depot, North Londonderry, c. 1910.** This group posing on the front steps of the Annis Grain and Lumber Company store near the time of World War I is most likely a gathering of people who made their living in the building complex.

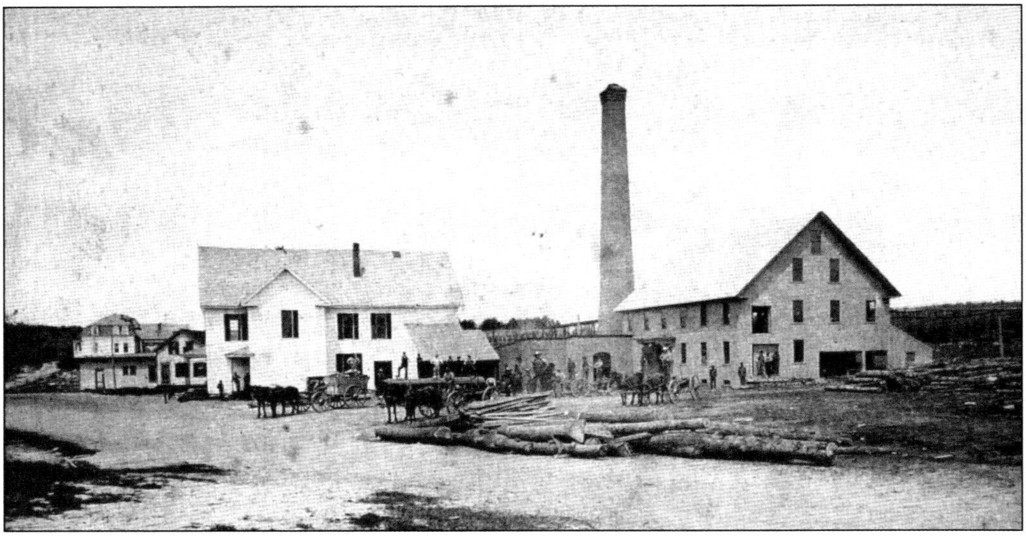

THE ORIGINAL DEPOT AND THE ANNIS GRAIN AND LUMBER COMPANY C. 1882. The buildings that Daniel and Roswell Annis erected in 1878 burned in 1880. This early photograph shows what they rebuilt. The large store on the left stocked flour, groceries, and grain for livestock. The low brick building in the middle housed the steam boiler to power the machinery for turning logs into lumber. Treetops and branches became staves for kegs and barrels. Bark, shavings, and sawdust fed the furnace. The large building to the right housed the horses and storage areas.

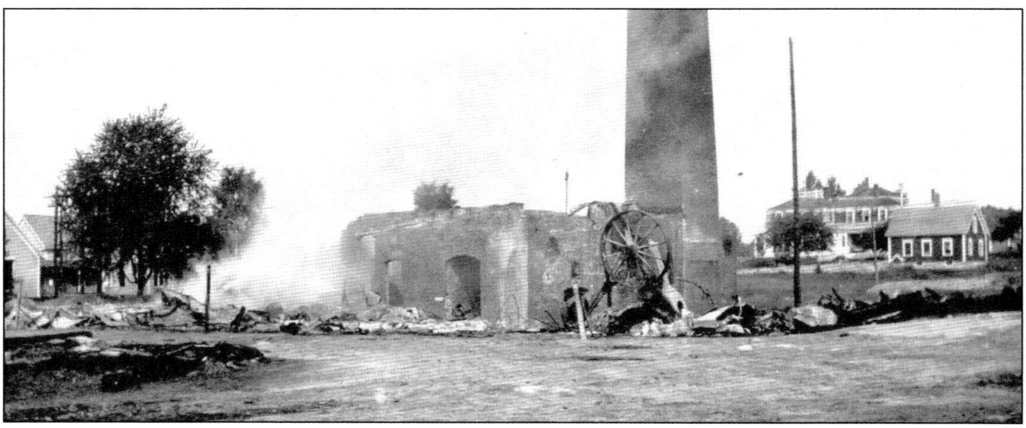

THE ANNIS GRAIN AND LUMBER COMPANY AFTER THE DEVASTATING FIRE OF 1921. Ten buildings were destroyed in this fire on July 7, 1921, which is believed to have started in the building housing the planer. Only the brick structures survived. A railroad passenger car temporarily replaced the Boston & Maine station. The untouched home of one of the founders of the Londonderry Historical Society, Jessie Beckley, still sits on the knoll. The immediate area was rebuilt but on a much smaller scale.

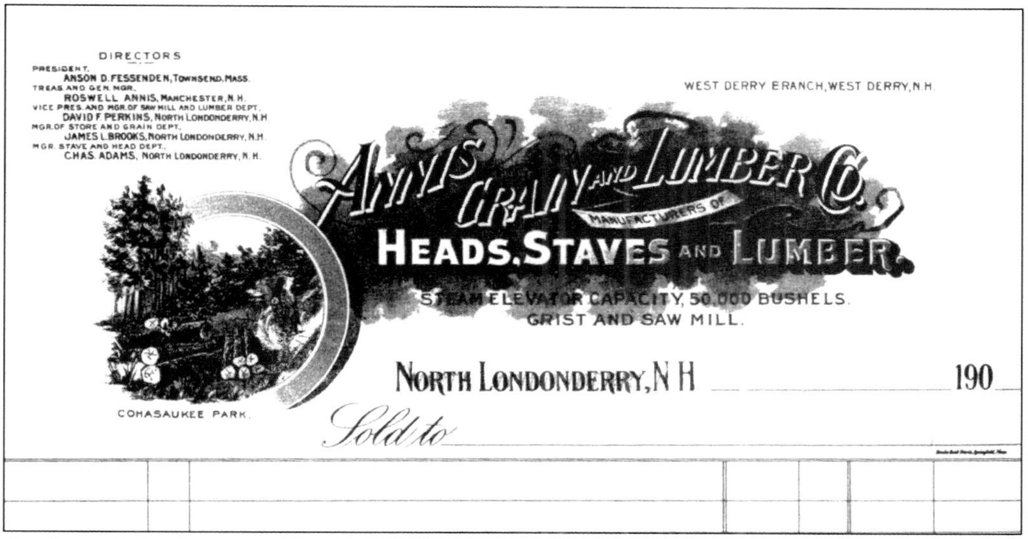


**AN ANNIS MILL INVOICE.** This fancy billing receipt from the Annis Grain and Lumber Company makes a clear and attractive statement for buyers. The list of directors includes some of the leading businessmen in the village in the early 20th century, who were responsible for making and selling useful products. Heads and staves are wooden keg and barrel parts. Cohasaukee Park may refer to the woodlands in the Cohas watershed, some of which is now located within the airport.

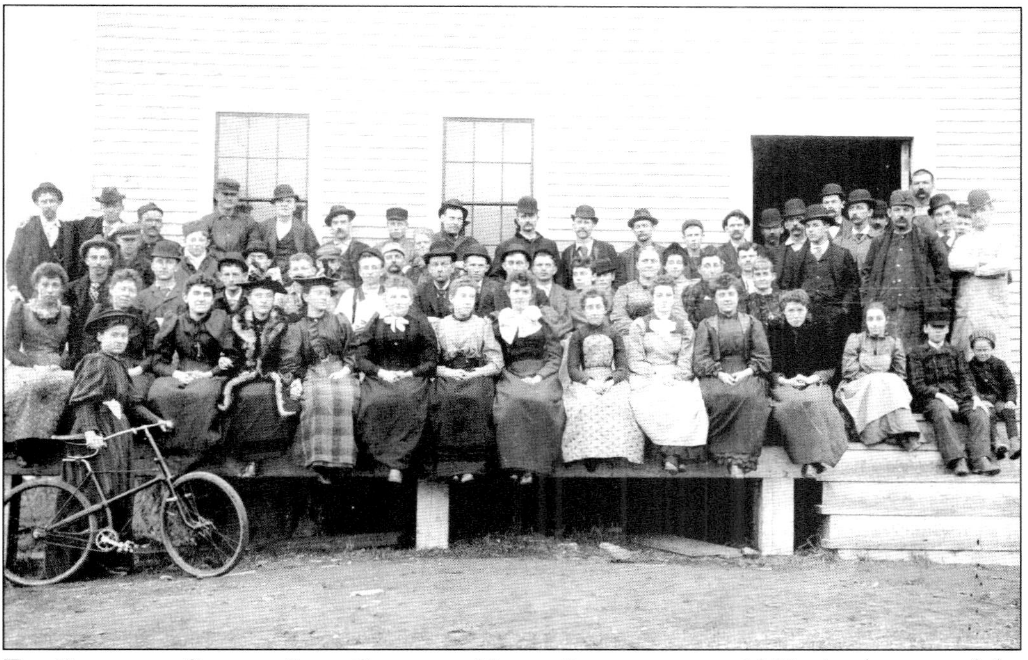

**THE ELLIS AND CONNOR SHOE COMPANY, NORTH LONDONDERRY, 1893.** At the turn of the century, the Merrill Cider Mill was in this building near the railroad tracks. Earlier, the building housed the pictured shoe company. Later, in the early 20th century, it contained a label factory well beyond World War II. On what appears to be a loading dock are 20 women, 40 men, and a child, all of whom are connected in some way with shoe production.

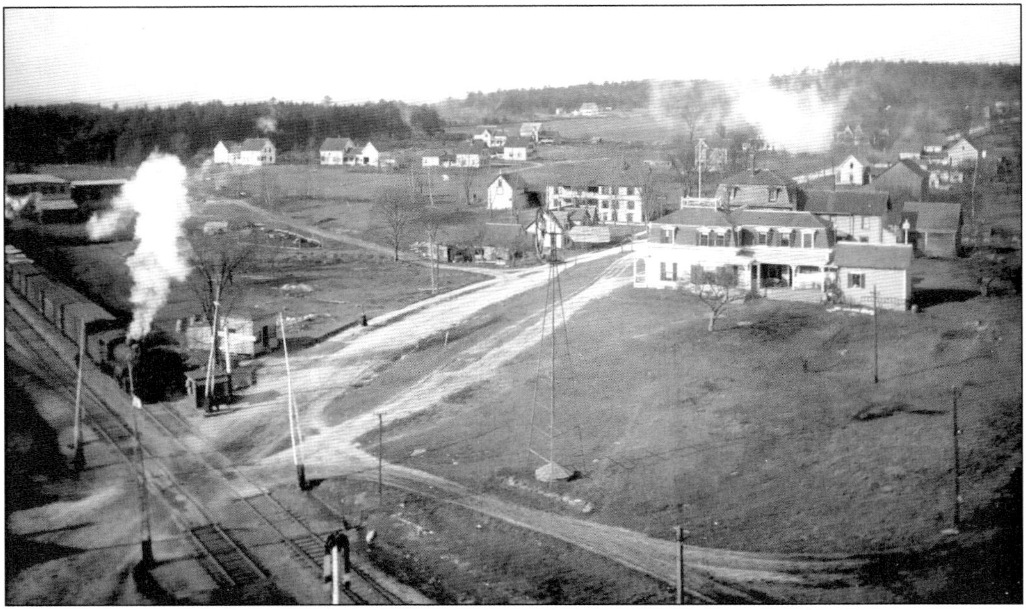

**LONDONDERRY, LOOKING NORTH FROM THE DEPOT, THE EARLY 1900S.** The Boston & Maine freight train waits at the Mammoth Road crossing, then the industrial and business hub of town. Spur tracks show additional freight-yard areas. The cluster of three late-Victorian houses near the windmill, all of which are still standing, formed part of the community that blossomed here. Merrill's cider mill can be seen to the left of the locomotive's steam plume.

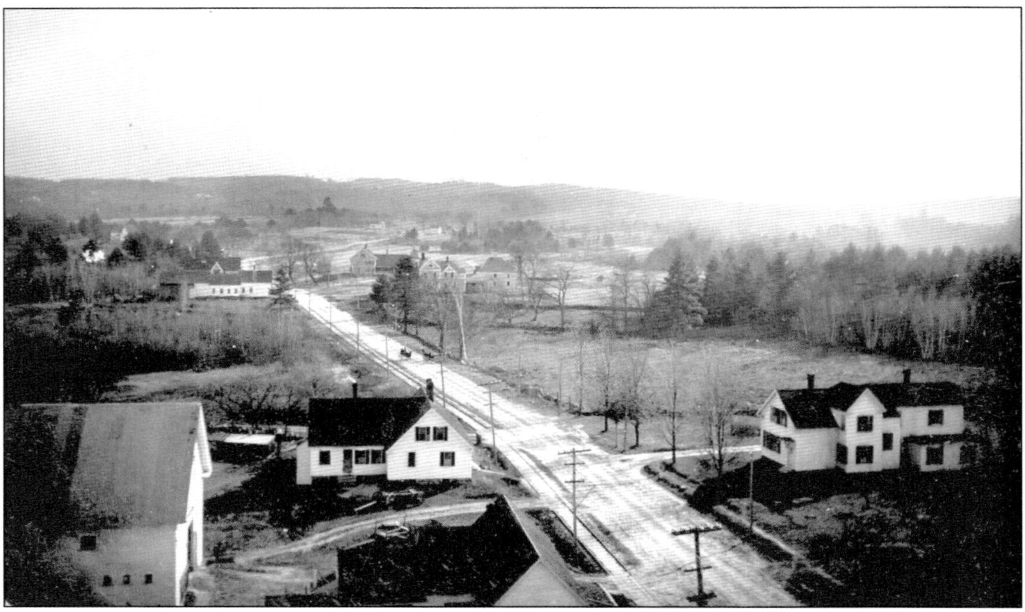

**NORTH LONDONDERRY, LOOKING SOUTH FROM THE DEPOT ALONG MAMMOTH ROAD.** From 1850 to the 1970s, the business center of town was at the Annis mills, where this photograph was taken. Mammoth Road met the railroad here, and for 19 years it carried the trolley, whose tracks run parallel to the evenly spaced row of electric poles carrying power to the cars that ran between Derry and Manchester. The nearby houses are still residences.

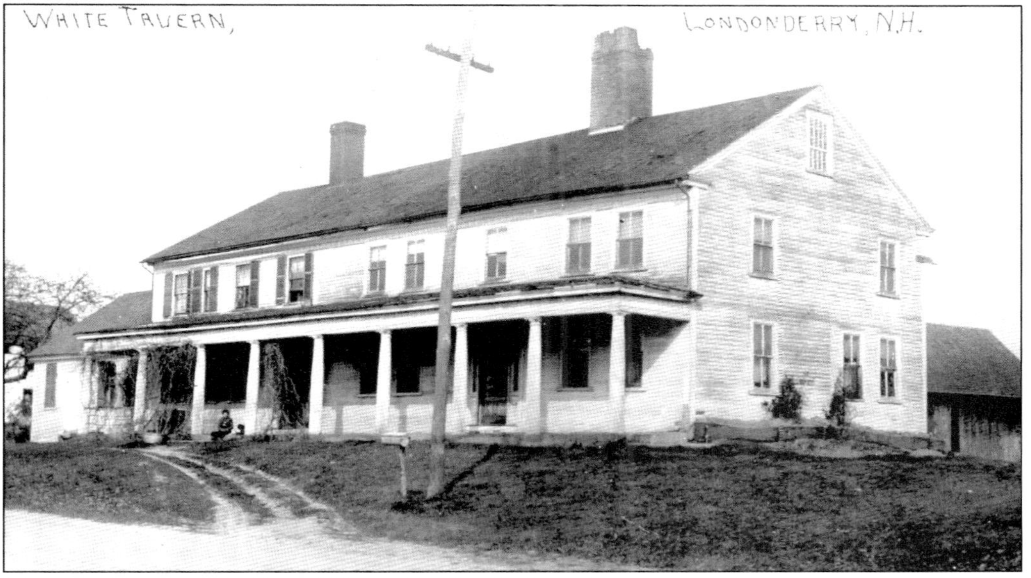


**WHITE'S TAVERN.** Reuben White (1785–1856) built and ran this stagecoach tavern on Mammoth Road. Daniel Webster stopped here, as did Presidents Jackson, Polk, and Pierce. After the Civil War, when the original innkeeper had died and Londonderry had regular rail access to the rest of New Hampshire and beyond, the building became two homes and, thus, as far as we know, the first Londonderry condo. It now houses three families.

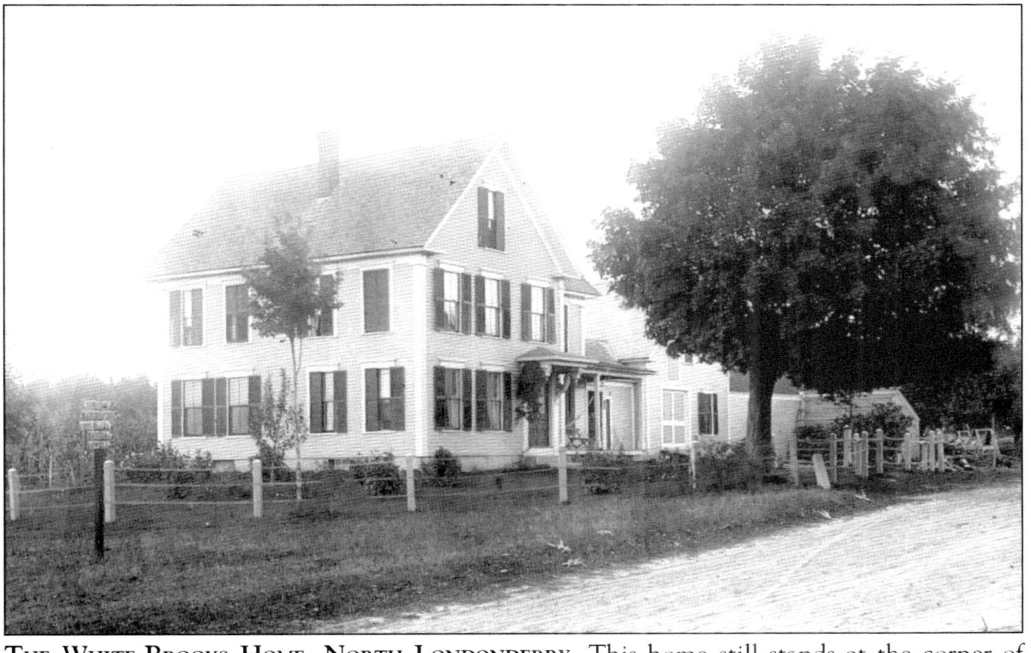

**THE WHITE-BROOKS HOME, NORTH LONDONDERRY.** This home still stands at the corner of Mammoth Road and Grenier Field Road (formerly Goffe's Falls Road) located diagonally across the intersection from White's Tavern. It was owned by Reuben White's third son, Henry White, father of Mrs. Bessie (White) Brooks, who for many years into the 20th century was a teacher in the Londonderry and Derry schools.

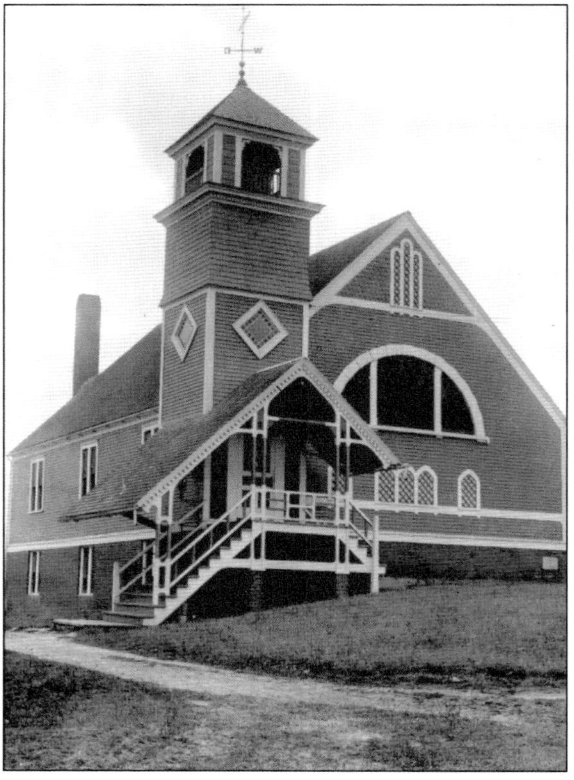

**The Baptist Church, North Londonderry.** In 1895, New Hampshire Convention Baptists raised this building in the village as their second church to meet the needs of a shifting population centering around the depot. Their first meetinghouse went up in 1829, 30 years after the congregation was formally organized in 1799 in Londonderry. The congregation then moved into its third and current building on Mammoth Road in 1976.

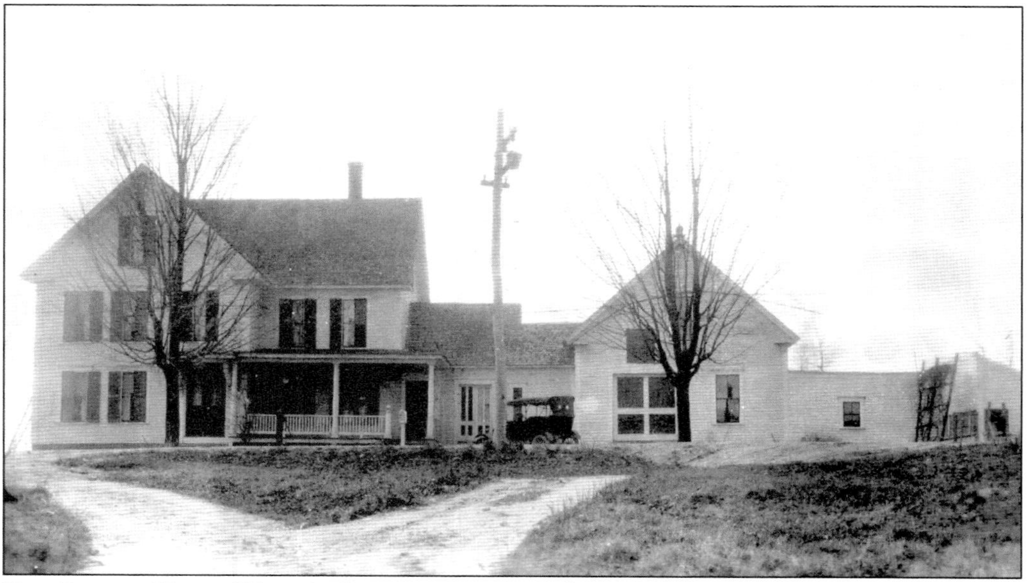

**The Brooks Home, White's Corner, c. 1925.** The Brooks home, seen previously on page 17, had changed by the time this photograph was taken 15 or 20 years later. A power pole with a transformer now stands out front along Mammoth Road, and the Model T Ford looks much like the one sitting by the Annis store in the photograph at the bottom of page 19. It may have belonged to the photographer who was making postcards.

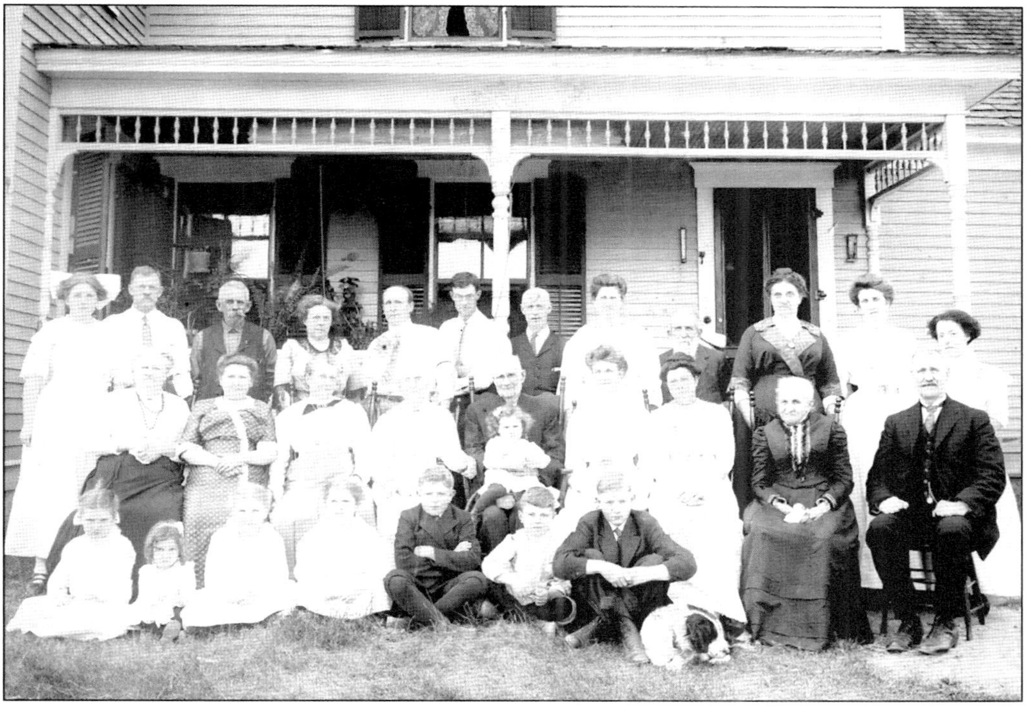

**A Brooks Family Reunion, 1910.** Edward W. Brooks, a carpenter, built this house in the village in 1898. The older gentleman holding the little girl may well be the builder himself, seated with his family in front of the house with his name. It still stands where it was built, on the northwest corner of Grenier Field and Mammoth Roads.

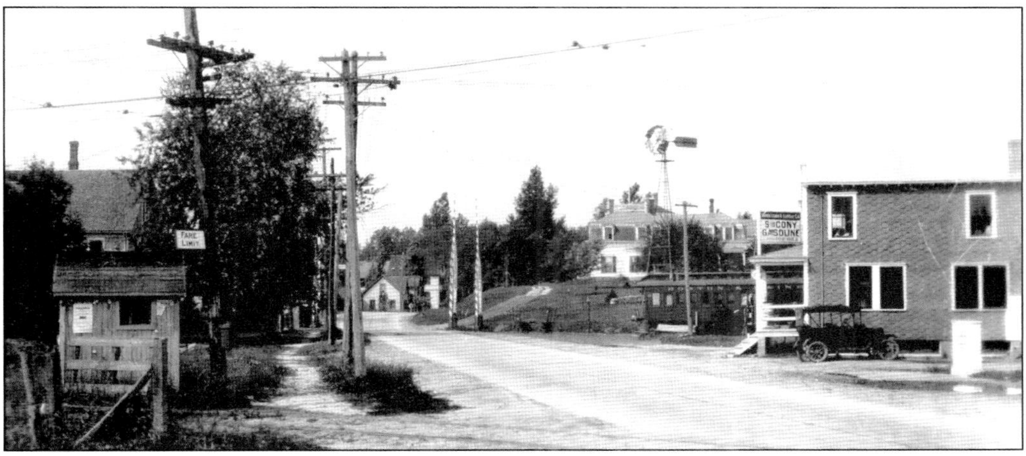


**The Depot and Mill Area, North Londonderry, c. 1925.** Modern Londonderry begins here. Much has happened since 1882. The impressive Annis mill and the attached train station, along with eight nearby buildings, had burned to the ground in 1921. An old passenger car has become the temporary station. The rebuilt Annis Grain and Lumber Company, much reduced in size but still housing businesses, sells Socony gasoline. The Model T Ford and the newly paved, concrete Route 28 (built in 1920–1921) are about to bury the trolley. Power poles carry electric and phone lines through the village beyond the trolley tracks, which turn west here. The windmill is pumping water for the house on the hill.

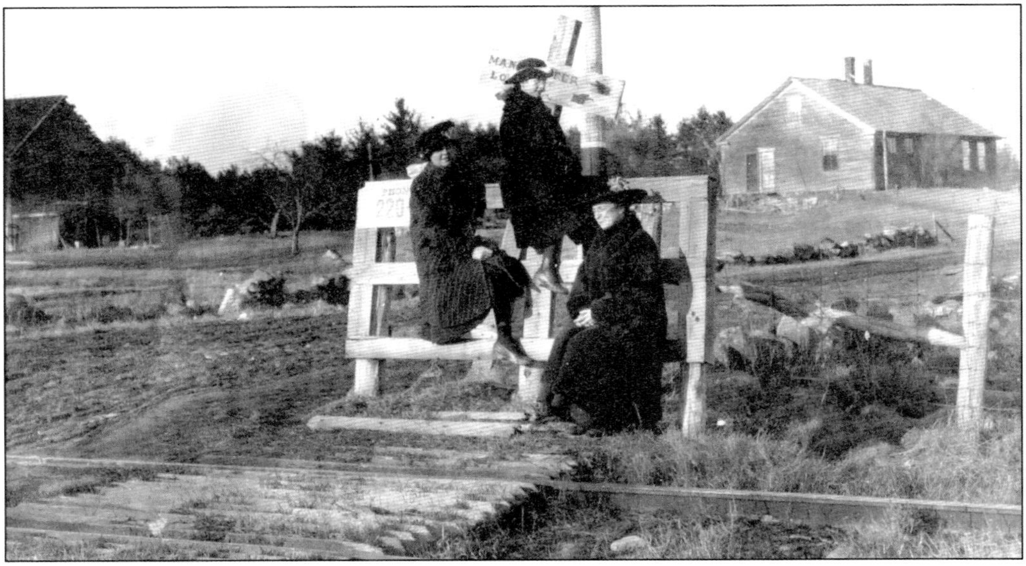

**Waiting for an Electric Car at Smith's Corner, North Londonderry.** Between 1907 and 1926, a trolley made scheduled stops at the corner of Smith Lane and Mammoth Road near the Smith-Strino home. In this early photograph, three women, identified only as Ruth Barker, Helen, and Hope, decorated the cattle guard and signboards. Cattle could not cross the barrier planks placed on edge between the rails. Today, a busy gas station and convenience store on Route 28 is located where the barn stood. The house, which has been modernized, still survives.

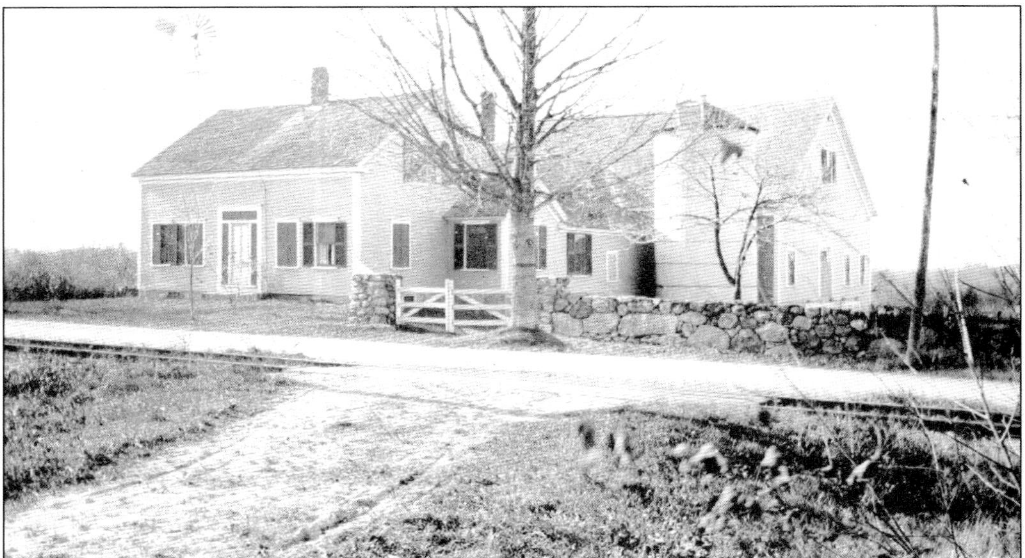

**The Ray-Kent Farm, 1908.** John E. Ray operated a wholesale cattle and meat business and sold milk from this farm home for many years. He served the Annis Grain and Lumber Company as manager and the town as selectman and auditor as late as 1954. Smith Lane intersected Mammoth Road and the trolley line here. A silo and windmill helped to mark this as a well-maintained, up-to-date farm. A retirement community now occupies the site.

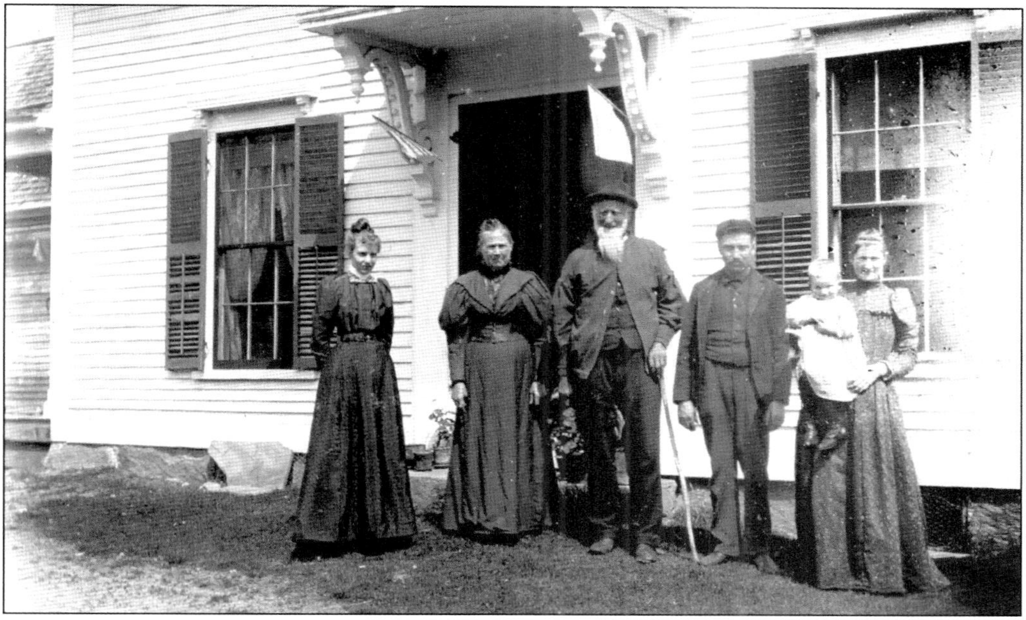

**THE MERRILL FAMILY, NORTH LONDONDERRY, C. 1895.** This photograph of a group of Merrills seems typical of most family photographs of the day. It shows that at least three generations lived together in the same house, including baby Walter. The photograph speaks clearly of how Londonderry and American culture have changed in 110 years. It is interesting to note that only two of the five adults in the photograph could vote at the time.

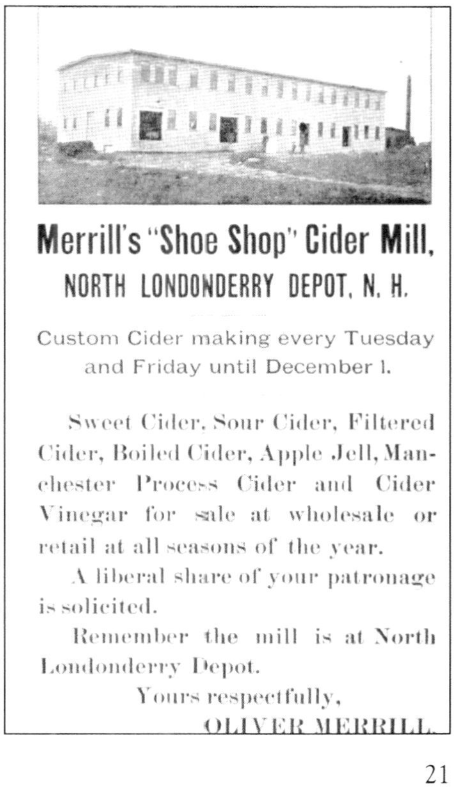


**MERRILL'S SHOE SHOP AND CIDER MILL.** While most surviving apple orchards are in the southern end of town, the Merrill family in the village has a long, successful agricultural history. Oliver Merrill took over the shoe shop building by the tracks and produced cider there *c.* the end of the 19th century and into the early 20th century. The Merrill farm is still a family business. The Merrills have a history of Four-H achievement and community involvement.

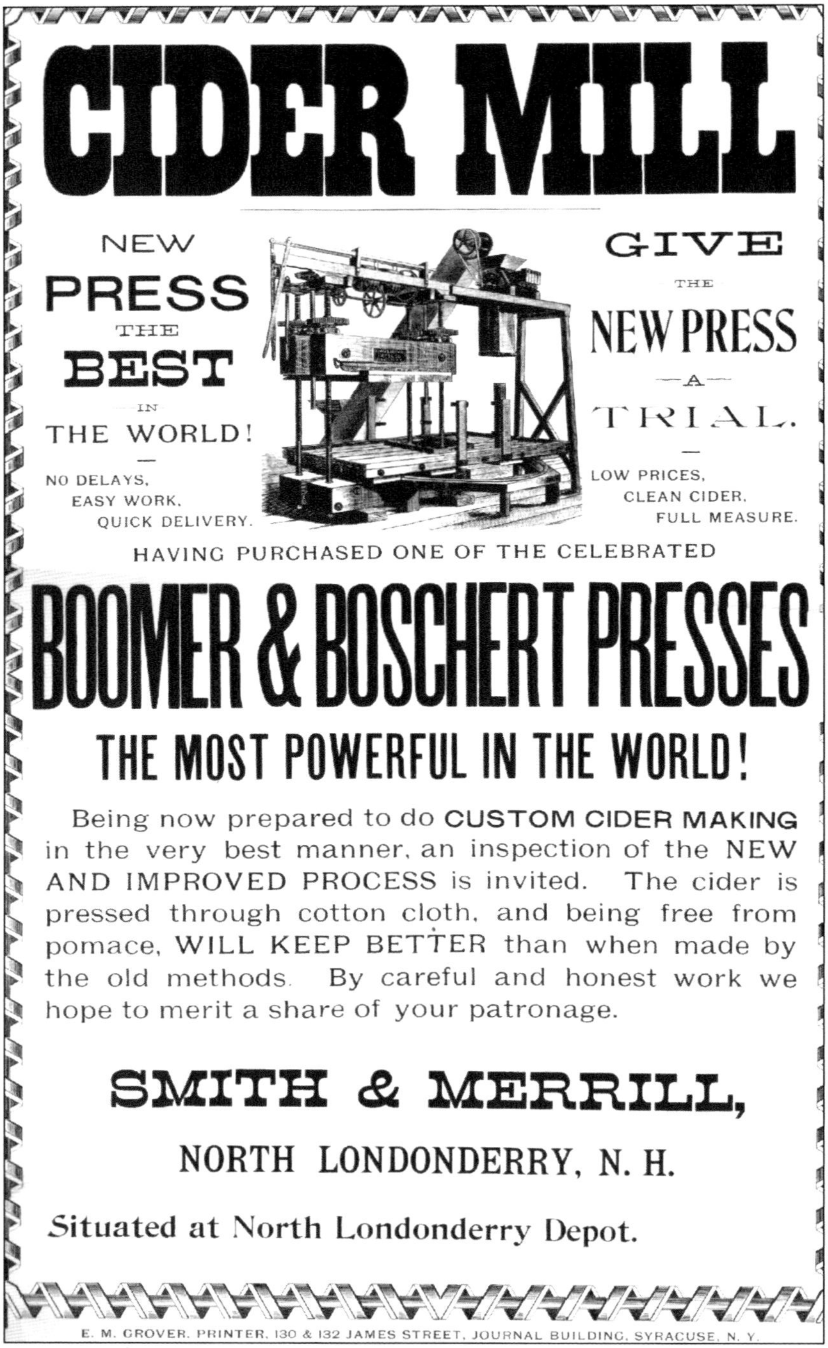


**The Smith and Merrill Cider Mill, c. 1900.** For four generations, the depot area could boast of train service; stores; grain and lumber production; agricultural, social, and veterans organizations; and other services. This advertisement is an example of innovation and good business practice putting its best face forward in the village at that time. The many varieties of apple cider, both sweet and hard, were an important staple in the New England diet.

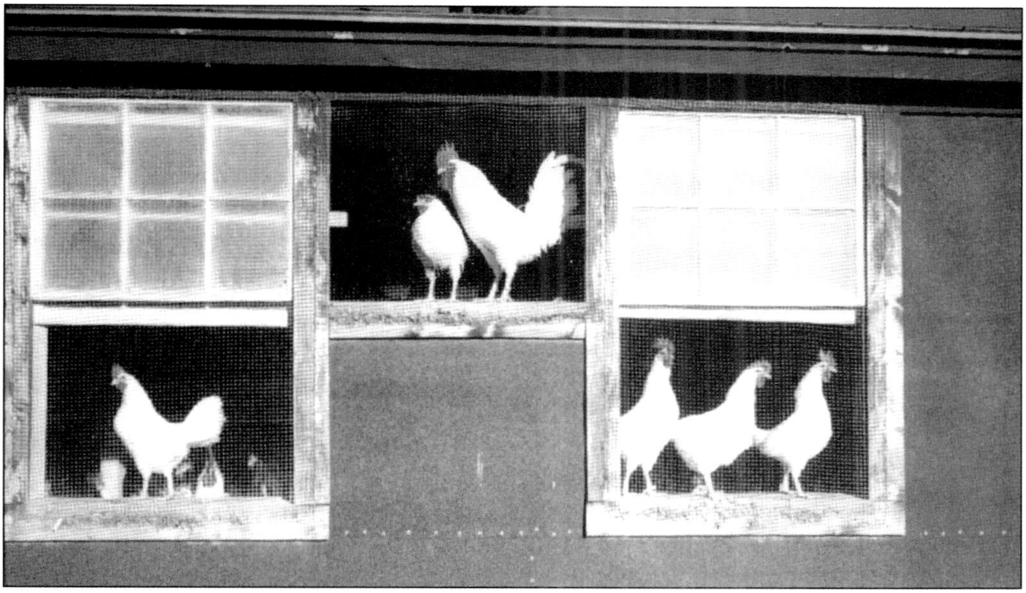

**Oliver Merrill and Son's Poultry Farm.** Like much of northern New England, New Hampshire went through several agricultural periods starting in the 19th century. Londonderry was no exception. At different periods, the town was home to the sheep and wool industry, dairy and poultry farms, and apple orchards. Londonderry had its chickens, as this north Londonderry photograph shows. A few poultry barns, or henhouses, still exist. They coexisted with apple orchards in the 20th century. The Merrills supplied white eggs for vaccine production and medical research.

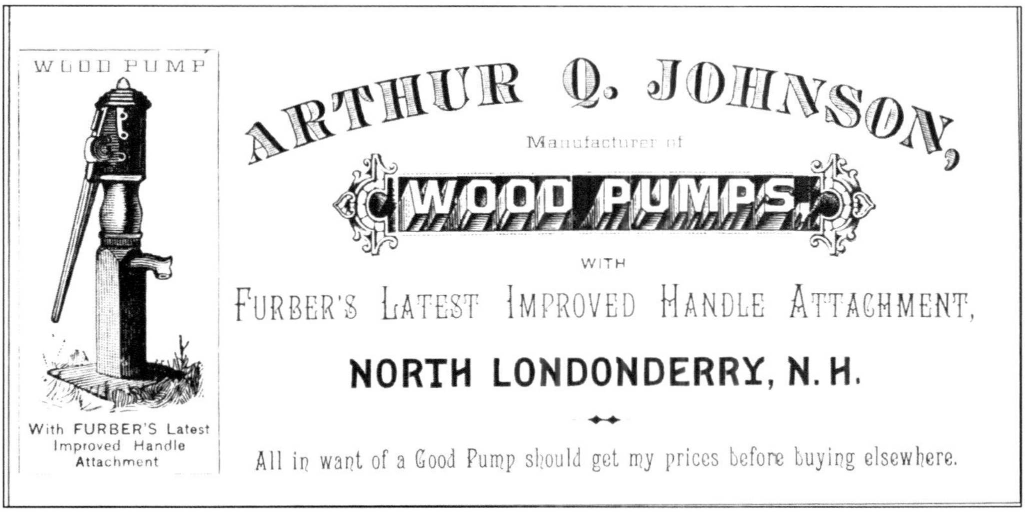


**A Furber Pump Advertisement, North Londonderry.** Even today, most Londonderry residents get their water from private wells. It is probably safe to say that a century and a half ago, all residents depended on well water. Without electricity, pumps had to be operated either by windmill or by hand. In 1857 a man named Furber, who lived in the village, invented the pump seen in this advertisement. Later, Arthur Q. Johnson manufactured and sold them there c. the turn of the century. They were made of tree trunks and included 16-foot lengths of wood bored with augers by horsepower to fit the depth of the dug well.

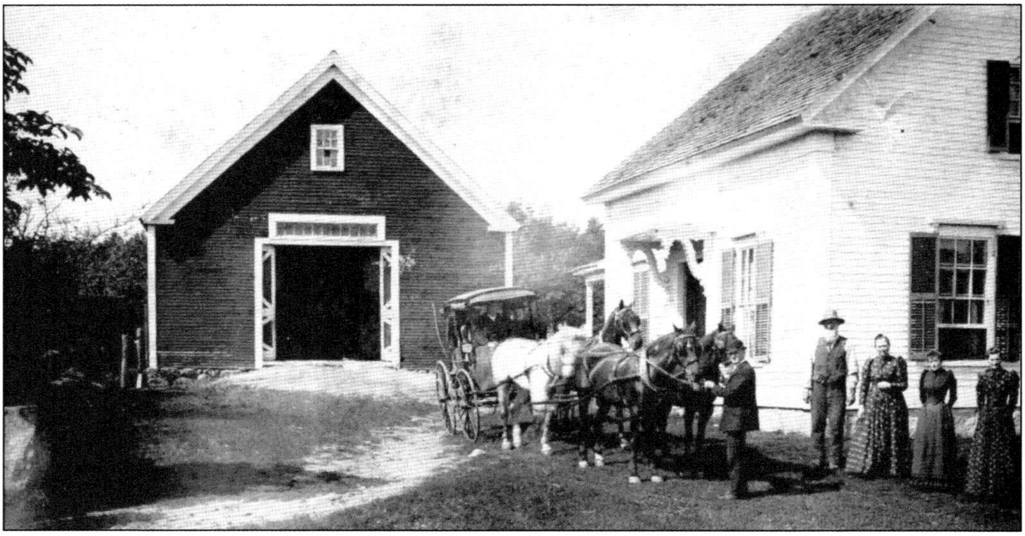

**The Merrill Farm, North Londonderry, c. 1885.** This family farm on Mammoth Road is still the home of the 21st century Merrills, descendants of the family posing in this photograph. Although the house has changed its face some and there are no more four-horse hitches standing in the dooryard, this scene today looks much the same. The modern Merrills are still farming and producing many of the same crops as their forebears.

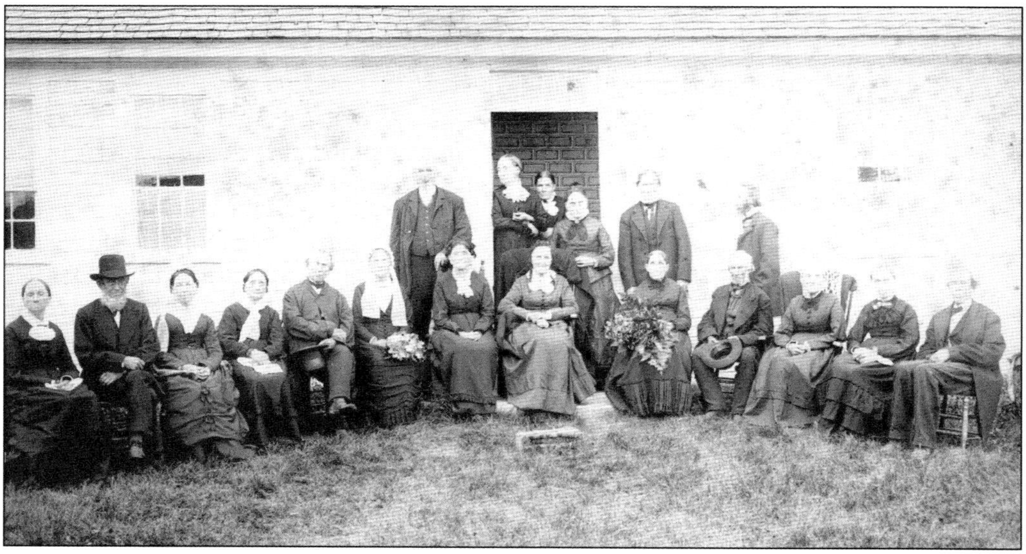

**The Morrison Family.** Compared to a photograph of a later Morrison family gathering (see page 25), this group photograph, perhaps taken a generation earlier, shows fewer, more somber adults and no children. They seem much more reserved. Even the clothing styles seem relatively happier and more relaxed in the later photograph. The two photographs seem to reflect a status change in the family.

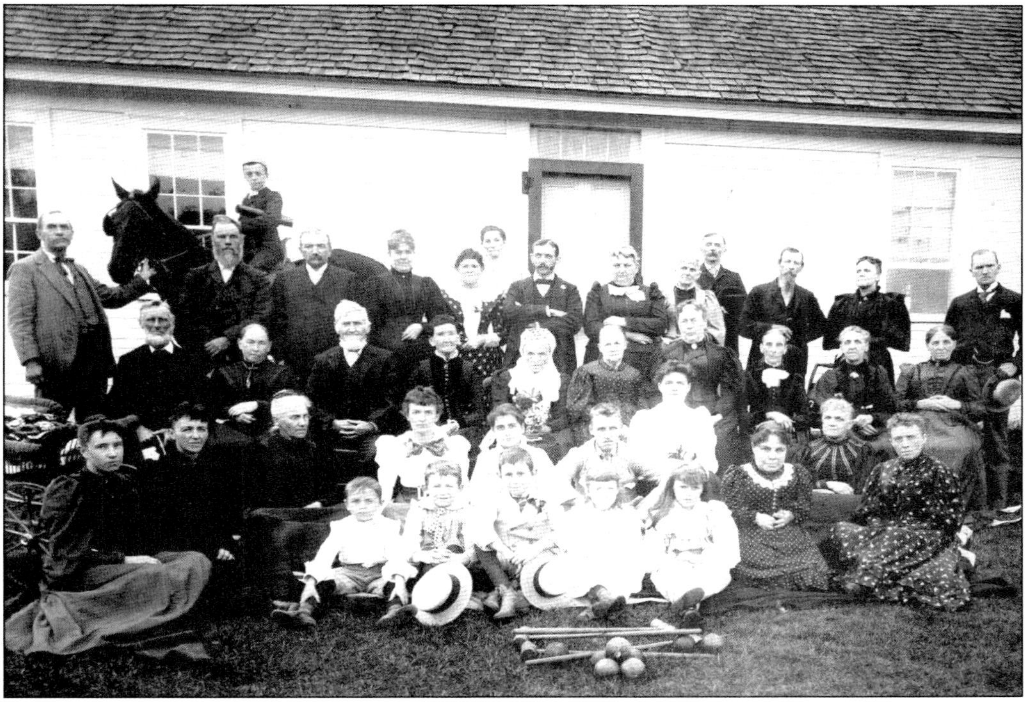

**A Gathering at the Morrison House, 1894.** Posing in front of the Morrison house when it still sat at the corner of Rockingham and Clark Roads are 39 members of the Morrison family. The house is now the museum of the Londonderry Historical Society, located on Pillsbury Road near the town common. The last owners of the house, the Welches, donated it to the historical society, and it was moved in 1990 to its new location on land donated by Andrew Mack Sr.

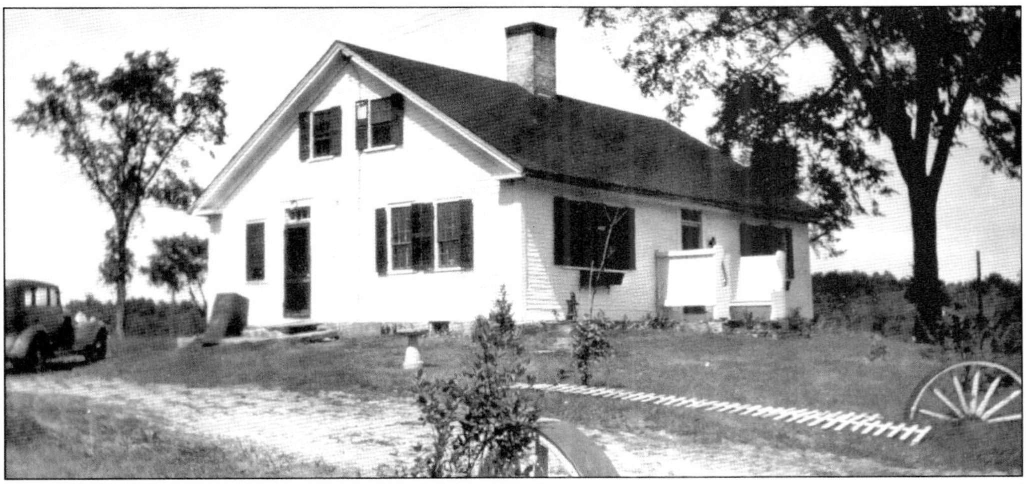

**The Morrison House, 1948.** Over the years, the Morrison house served as a dwelling and eventually as a summer home and homecoming place for generations of Morrisons. In time, the house passed out of the hands of the Morrisons, but the family name stuck. The house changed too. Here, only the chimney reveals its 18th-century antiquity.

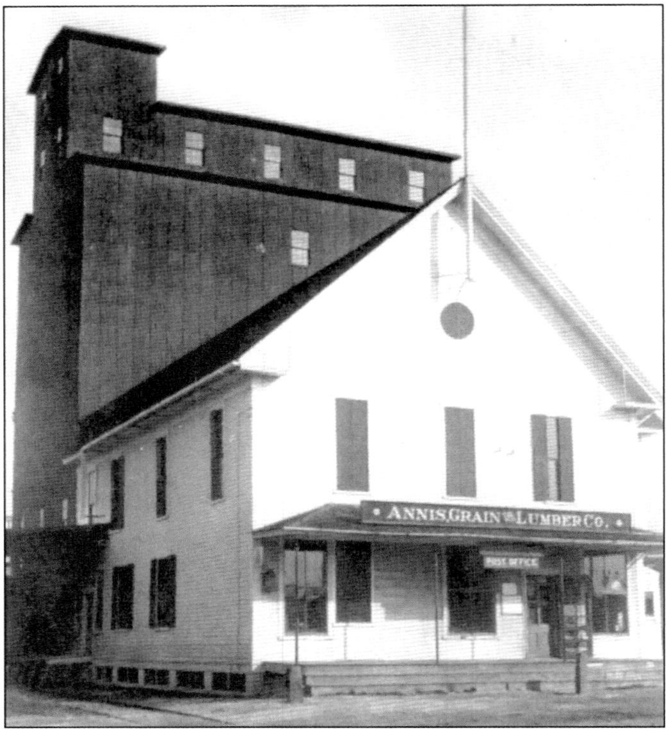


**THE ANNIS GRAIN AND LUMBER COMPANY.** In addition to serving as the Londonderry offices of the Annis mill and as a general store, the white building adjoining the railroad station also housed the post office and hardware store. Mail came on special railroad cars. The second story had multiple uses; it housed community dances, the veteran's hall, and a Congregational church, among other things. The building's destruction by fire in 1921 was a town tragedy.

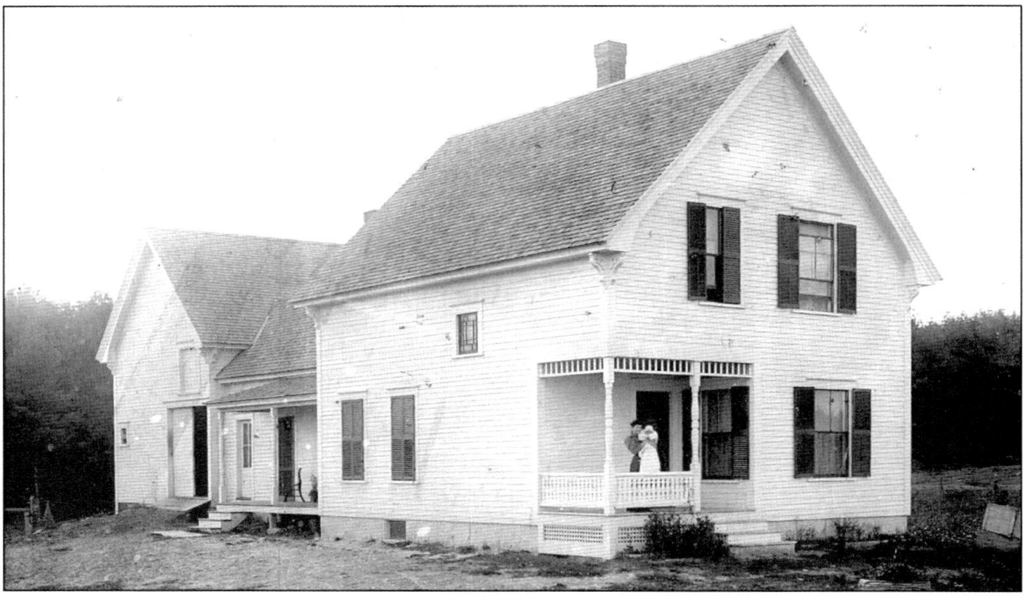

**THE ANNIS GRAIN AND LUMBER COMPANY HOUSE, NORTH LONDONDERRY, 1895.** Just before the turn of the century, a number of houses were built for the Annis Grain and Lumber Company and its workers in the village. Many, if not most, still stand on a little group of four streets named Buckthorn, Coin, Loan, and Foxglove, which connect to Mammoth Road. The streets are just west of the fire station. This one was built at the corner of Foxglove and Loan Streets.

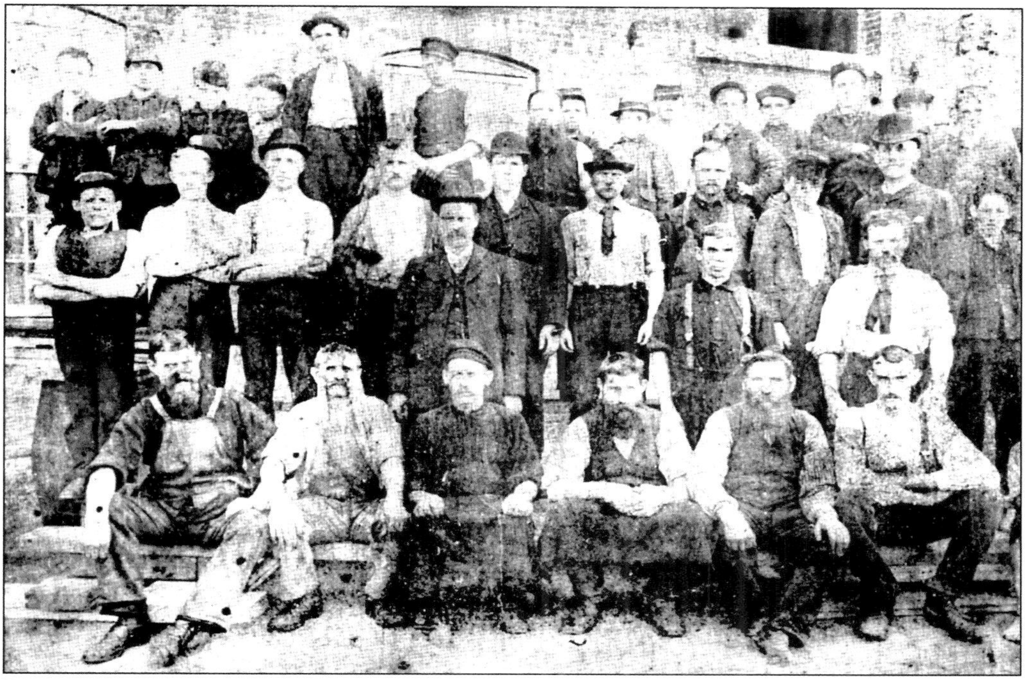

**WORKERS AT THE SHOE FACTORY.** There is little evidence today that the intersection of Auburn and Rockingham Roads was once a town business center, identified on old maps as Wilson's Crossing. Located there were a Boston & Maine Railroad station named Wilson's, various businesses served by the railroad, and the post office. This photograph was used in a 1922 presentation about the town's future given by Scott Earle Haseltine, great-grandson of Reuben White, one year after the destruction of the Annis Grain and Lumber Company plant. This factory may have been at Wilson's Crossing.

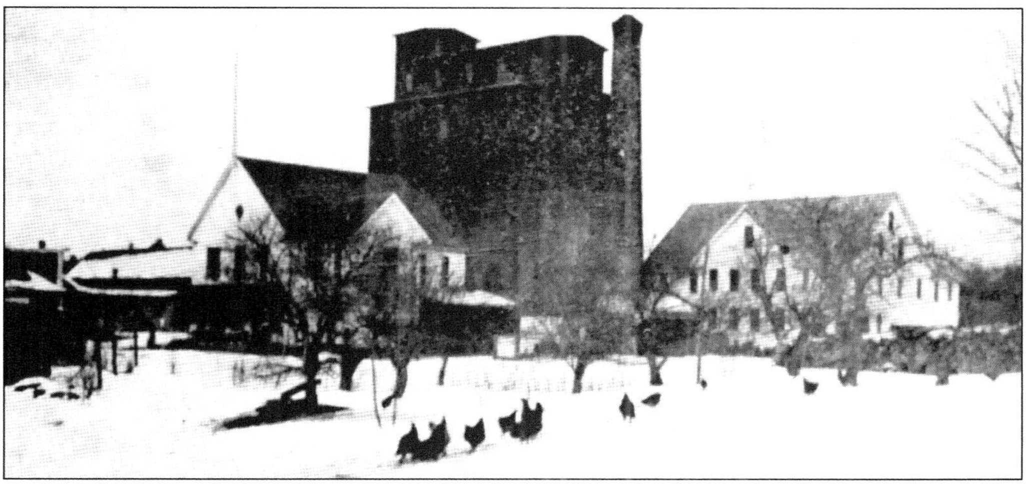

**THE ANNIS MILL AND STORE, 1907.** A neighboring farm to the southeast provides the setting for north Londonderry's commercial center. It also illustrates the juxtaposition of the modern businesses of the time with the traditional subsistence farming that has characterized the town for most of its history. Some of the town's major sources of income have been apples, poultry, and, at the mill, grain, lumber, and wood products.

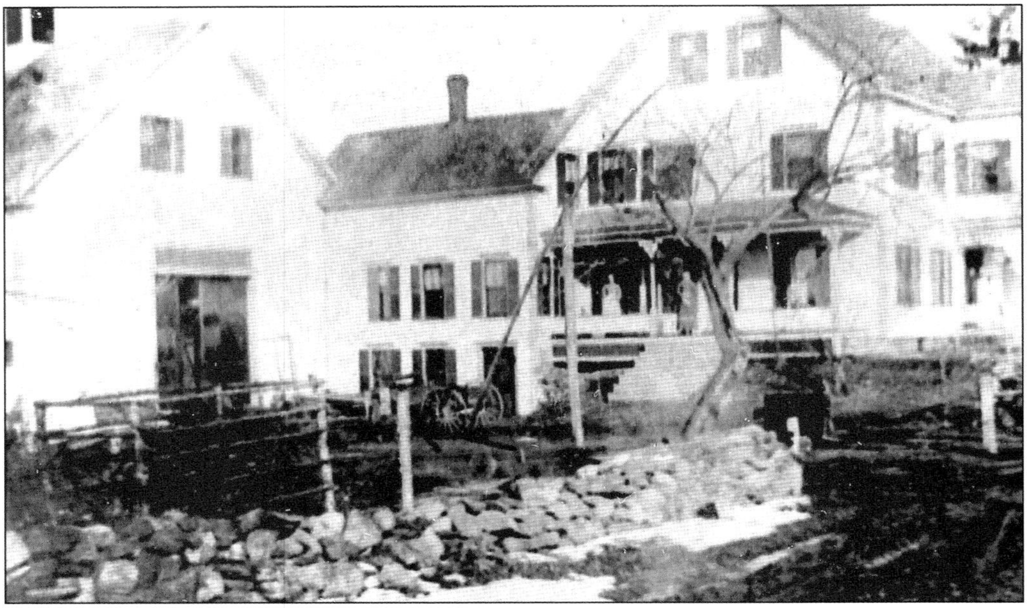

**THE ECHO FARM, ROCKINGHAM ROAD, C. 1900.** This handsome, grand house and its farm buildings were built in 1893 not far from today's intersection of Auburn and Rockingham Roads, then called Wilson's Crossing. The extensive farm estate was the home of the Blodgett-Evans family. In the front yard, with the milk wagon behind it, is a huge well sweep, a good two stories tall, for bringing up well water. All of these buildings burned in 1916.

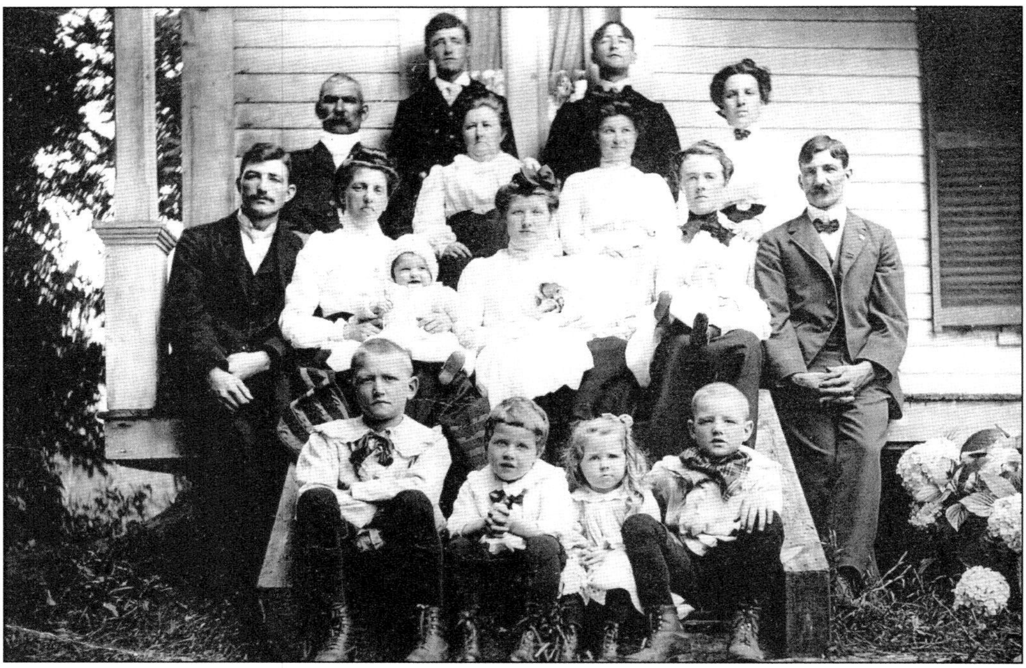

**THE NOYES FAMILY, 1899.** This photograph of the Noyes family illustrates a typical family scene a century ago. They are outdoors, where natural light made taking pictures much simpler than trying to work inside. There are at least three generations in this handsome family group.

**FLORA STEWART, 1867.** "Old Flora" Stewart came to live in Londonderry on Rockingham Road in 1810, when she was 60. She was said to have been freed from slavery by the Windham man who bought her. Gov. Fredrick Smyth invited her to his home in Manchester in 1867 and had her photographed in a studio. She was a faithful member of the Methodist Church and was loved by those who knew her. She died in 1868 at age 118 and is buried in Valley Cemetery.

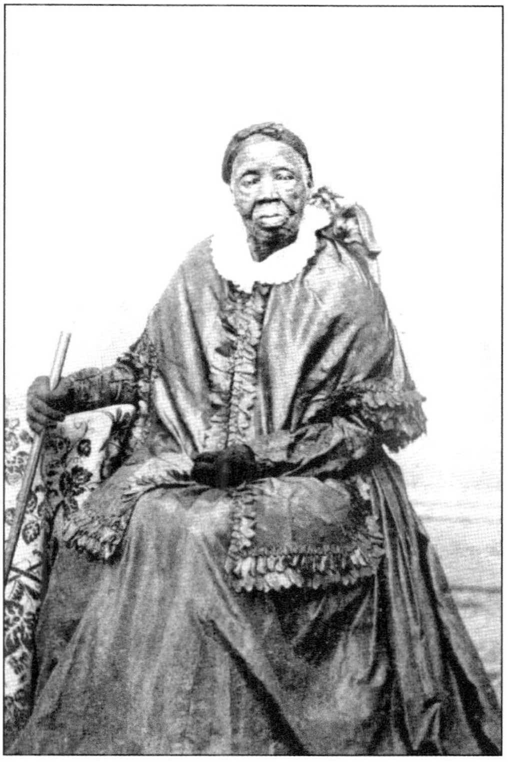

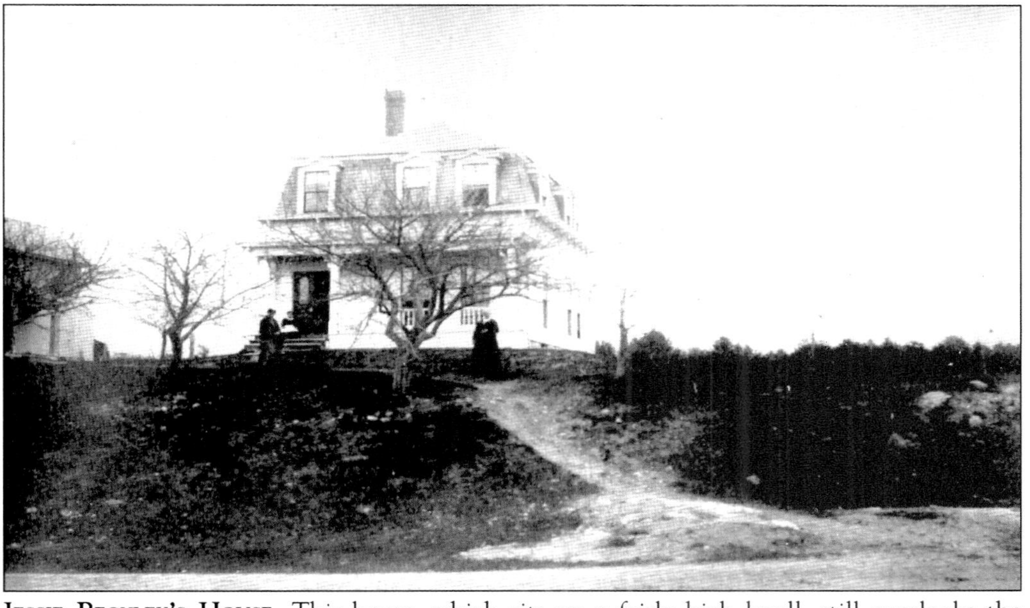

**JESSIE BECKLEY'S HOUSE.** This house, which sits on a fairly high knoll, still overlooks the buildings next to the railroad tracks at the location of the depot and the Annis Grain and Lumber Company. It was the home of Jessie Beckley, town historian, for 48 years, until her death in 1991. If it could talk, it would have some hair-raising tales to tell of at least four major fires and one boiler explosion in the mill area in a 60-year period.

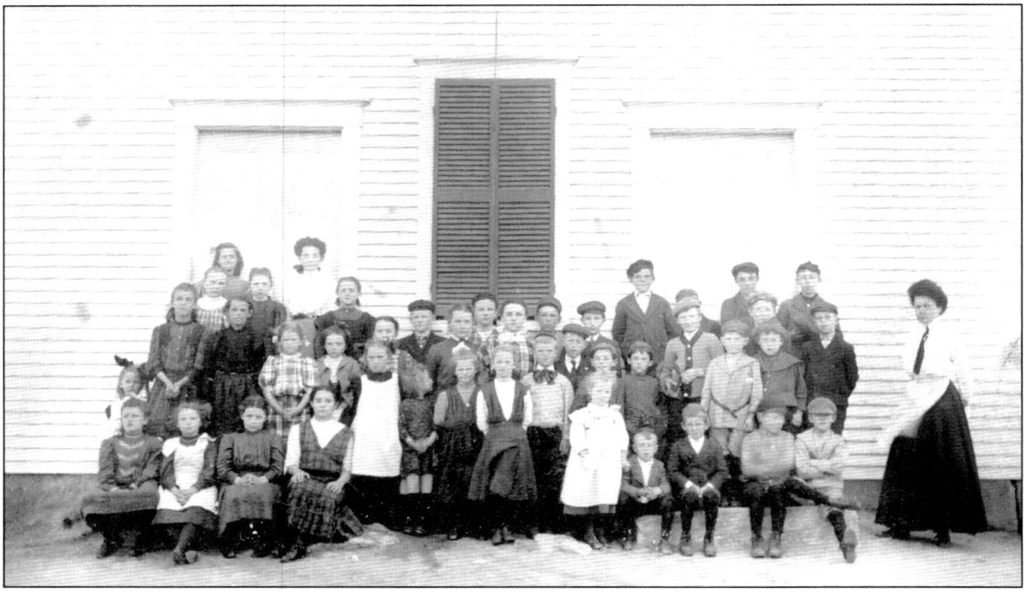

**YOUNG FACES OF LONDONDERRY, C. 1900.** School House No. 7 still stands, now a private residence on Grenier Field Road (originally Goffe's Falls Road). The building, located near White's Tavern, served the eight grades of grammar school scholars (elementary and middle school students) who lived in north Londonderry. The 22 girls entered and exited the school through the left door, the 20 boys through the right. The school probably had one teacher.

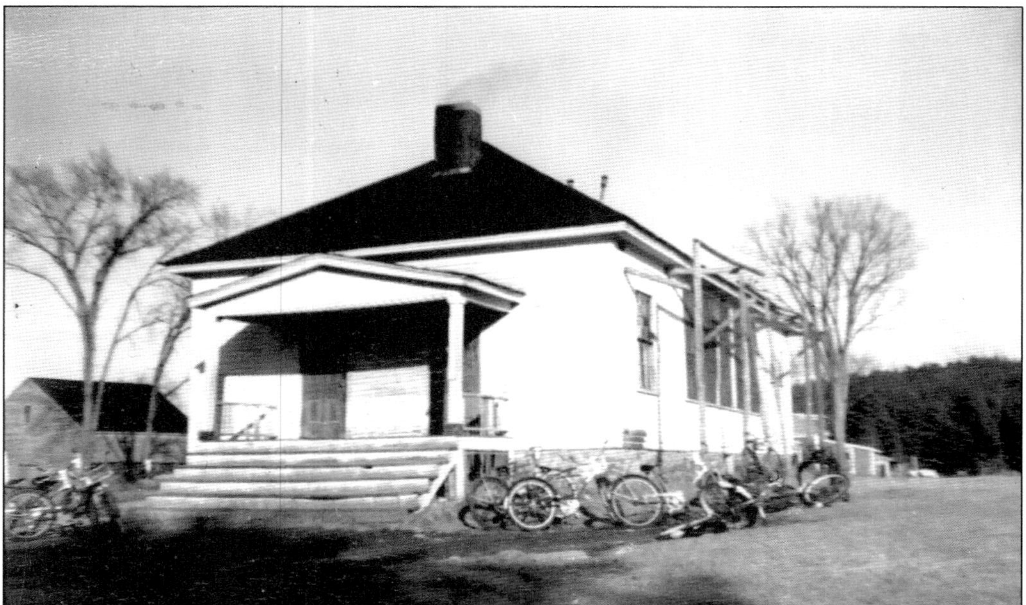

**THE MORRISON JUNIOR HIGH SCHOOL.** In 1921, the town decided to merge two grammar schools into one. In 1922, the town built the Morrison Junior High School for grades six through eight at Morrison's Corner near Rockingham and Noyes Road. It cost $4,000 furnished and became the first junior high. The bicycles seem to place the photograph in the 1950s or 1960s. Today the building is a rental home.

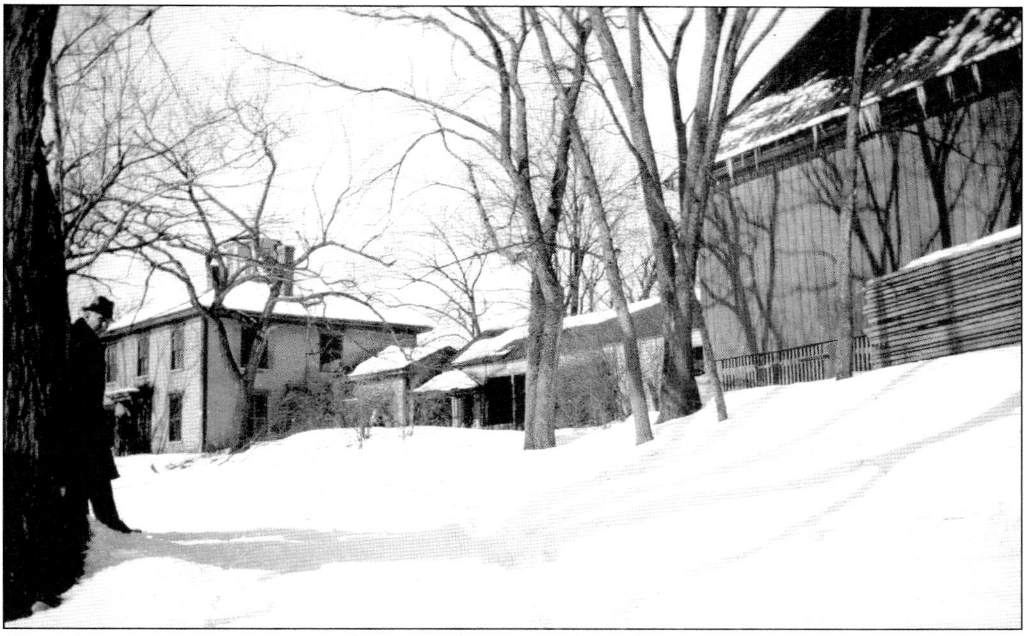

**THE HARVEY HOUSE, 1935.** The coastal region of northern New England is noted for its connected farm homes. This farm, built by Ephraim W. Harvey on Goffe's Falls Road just after the Civil War, has some of the same characteristics of the earlier farm buildings. A walk from the house to the barn or outhouse could be made without going out in the snow, an advantage in a New Hampshire winter. The farm has been bulldozed into a barren hill.

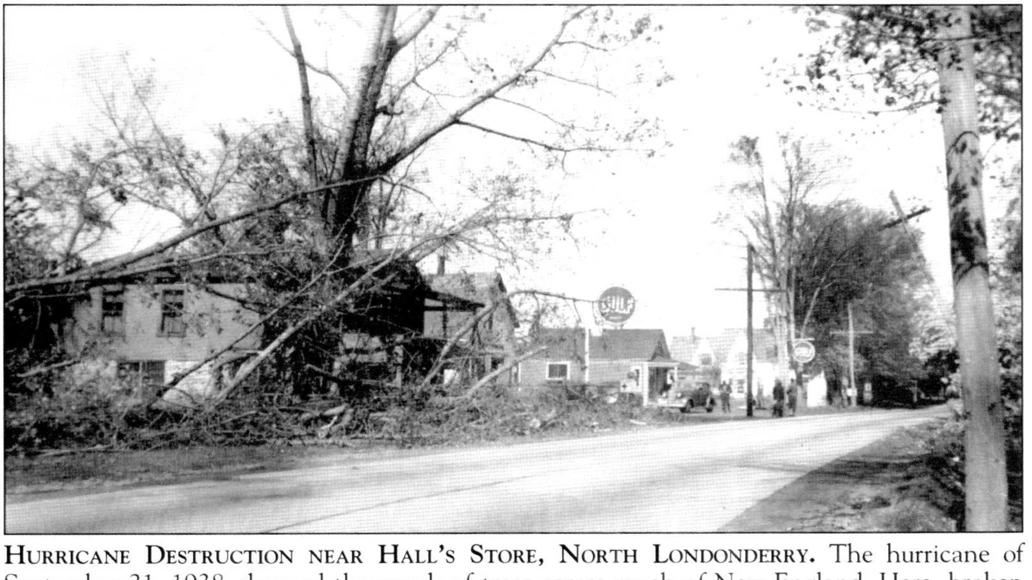



**HURRICANE DESTRUCTION NEAR HALL'S STORE, NORTH LONDONDERRY.** The hurricane of September 21, 1938, downed thousands of trees across much of New England. Here, broken trees, tilted power poles, and sagging power lines are the focus of some survivors. There was similar damage throughout the town. Farm buildings and homes lost roofs. The orchards suffered heavily in this major disaster. The cleanup took years in some places.

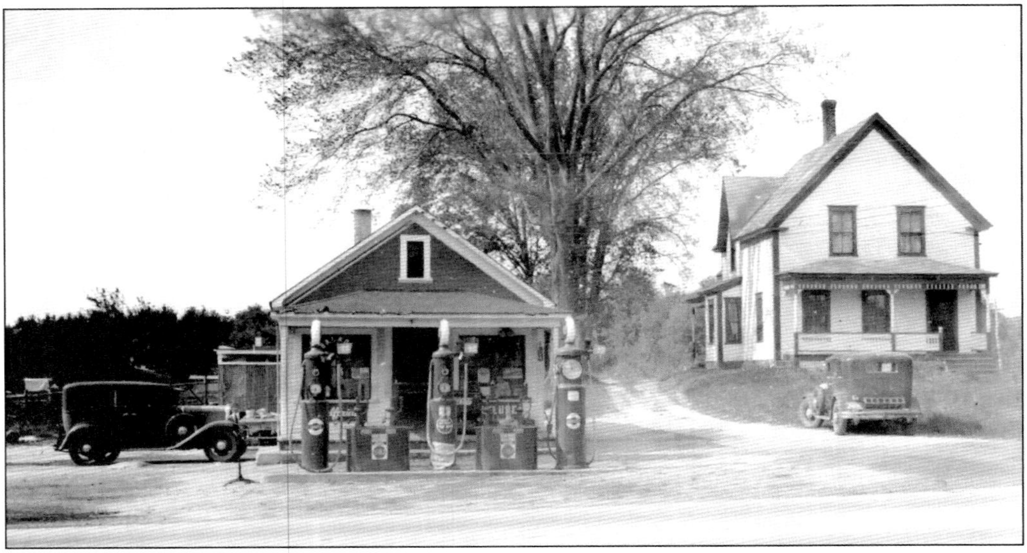

**The Old Hall's Store with the Ernest Smith House c. 1935.** The old Hall's Store, seen here in the early years of the automobile, has also become a service station. The early-1930s cars are fairly new, and the pumps are also typical of the period. In the background by the Smith house, adding grace to the photograph, is a grove of American elms, which, sadly, have been decimated by disease in the years since. The house, however, survives.

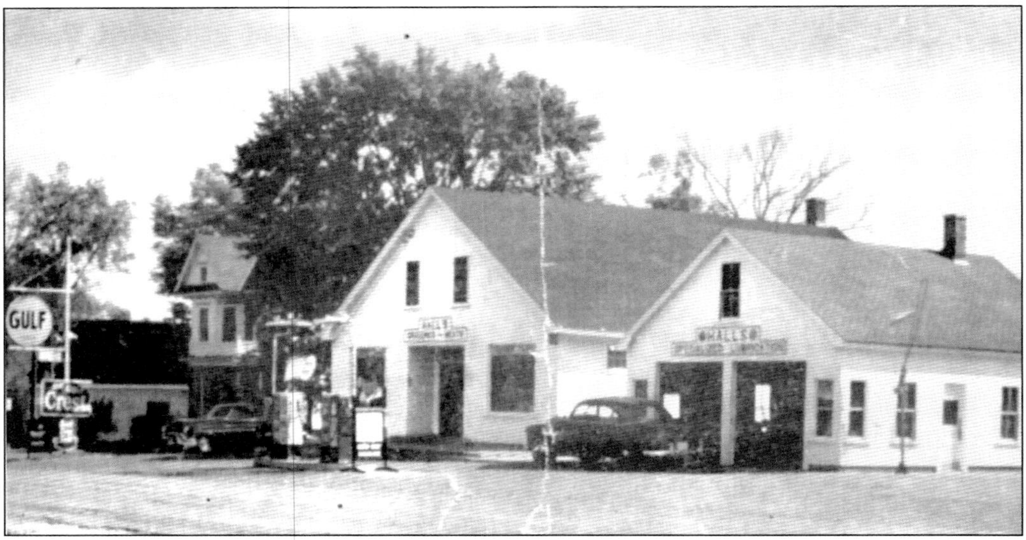


**Hall's Store and Garage in the Village.** Dating this postcard in the late 1940s is fairly easy. The parked cars are one of the giveaways, at least for people who lived at the time. There appears to be a "Chevy" by the garage and an "Olds" by the store, both of which are late-1940s models. Gulf sells for 29¢ a gallon. A sign on the interior wall of the garage reads "Five gallons for a dollar."

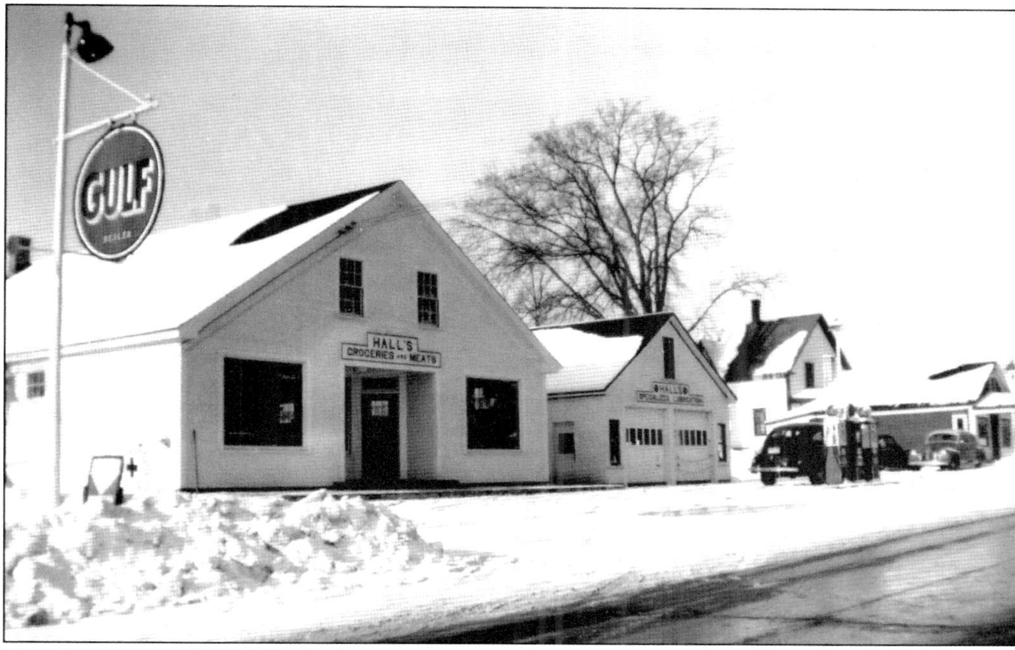


**THE NEW AND OLD HALL'S STORES C. 1947.** The three stores in this World War II–era photograph are still in use. The small house on the right is the oldest, having been the first Hall's Store. It later became Hayward's Shoe Store when the Halls built the larger building on the left. In those days before supermarkets, Hall's Store sold groceries and meats. Next to it is Hall's Garage, which also served as a gas station. They were part of the Hall's Store business. The cars are from c. 1940.

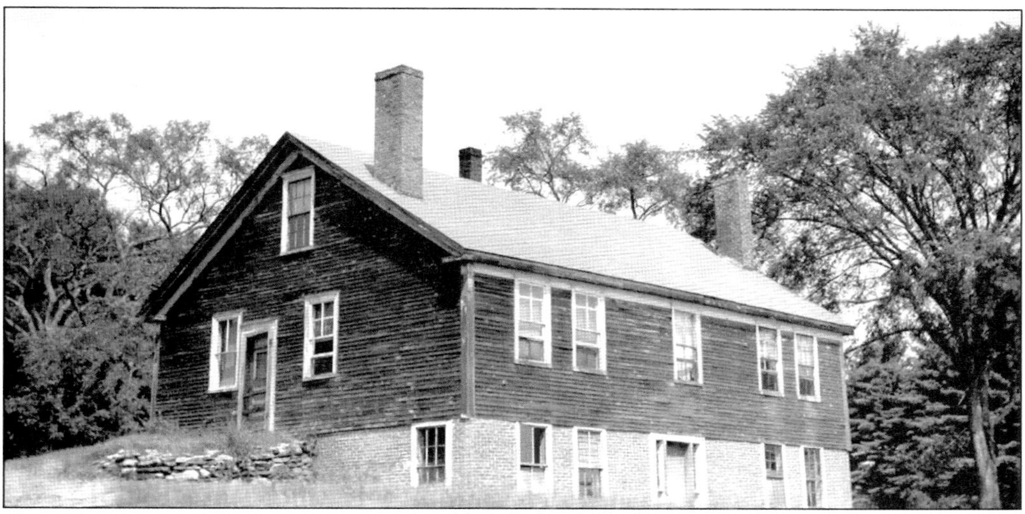

**THE LINNEHAN HOUSE, 1966.** Fire was the end of the line for many Londonderry houses, especially before modern motorized fire equipment became commonplace. Ironically, in 1966, after sitting vacant for a number of years and then being acquired by the town, the fire department destroyed the Linnehan family house in a controlled burn. North Elementary School now occupies the space on Sandown Road. The photograph shows the rear of the house as it looked before demolition.

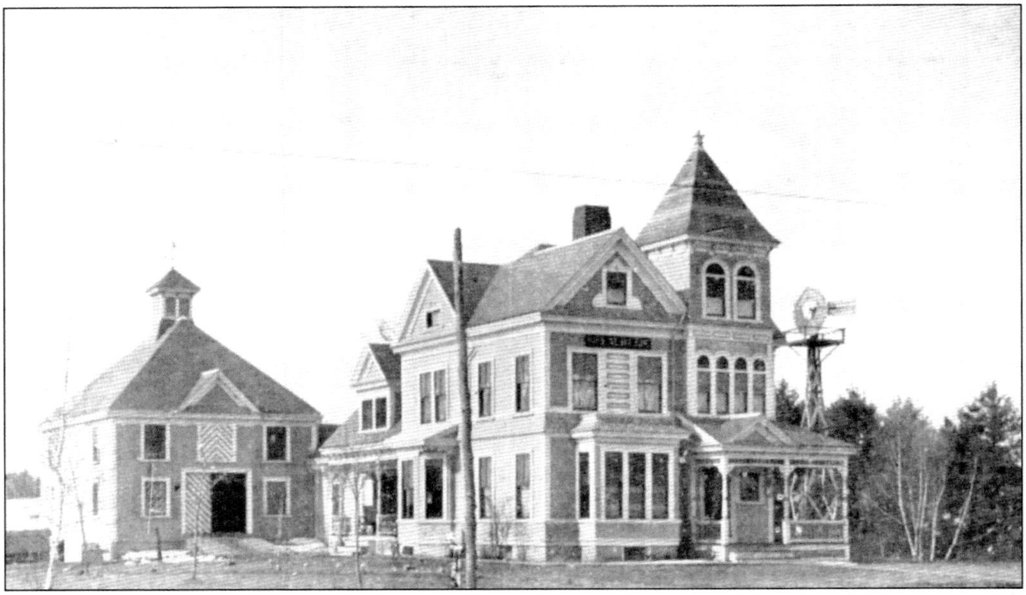

**THE LAURELS, NORTH LONDONDERRY, IN THE TROLLEY ERA.** This landmark on Mammoth Road, now painted in Victorian shades of pink, was for a time called the Laurels. It was owned and operated as a boardinghouse by Jack Pearson when the trolley served the village. In the late 19th century, this house belonged to Civil War veteran and whaling captain George S. Garvin. In this scene stands a windmill that once pumped water to this outstanding example of Victorian architecture.

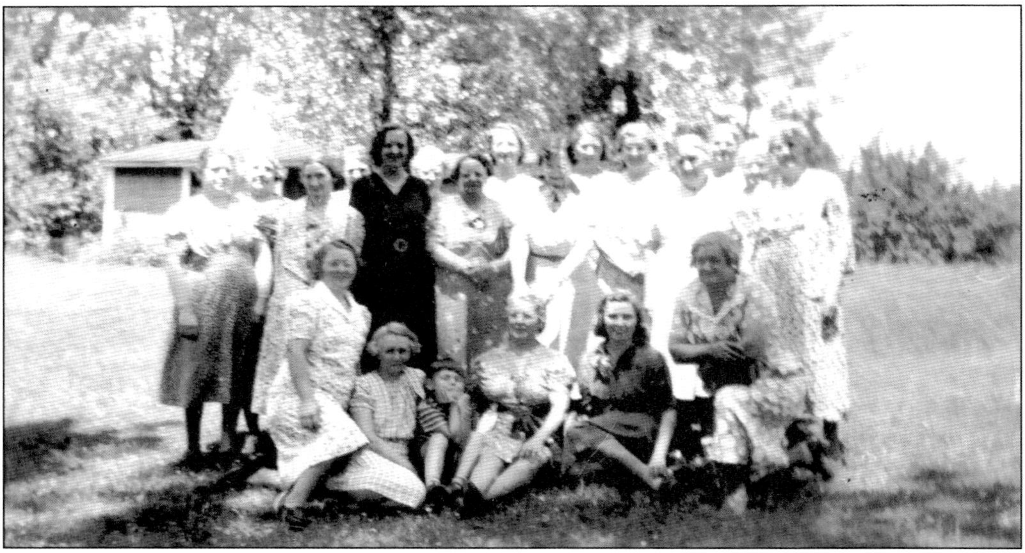

**THE NEIGHBORHOOD CLUB AT A BEAVER LAKE OUTING, 1939.** This group is thought to have become the Naborly Group in 1943 at the suggestion of a Rockingham County extension agent. Members met at the Mayflower Grange in the village to hone their homemaking skills, serve the Red Cross during World War II, and bring food baskets to the sick, shut-ins, and the elderly. Ethel Webster Chatterton, grandmother of Marilyn Ham, stands fifth from the right in the back row.

# *Two*

# GRENIER FIELD

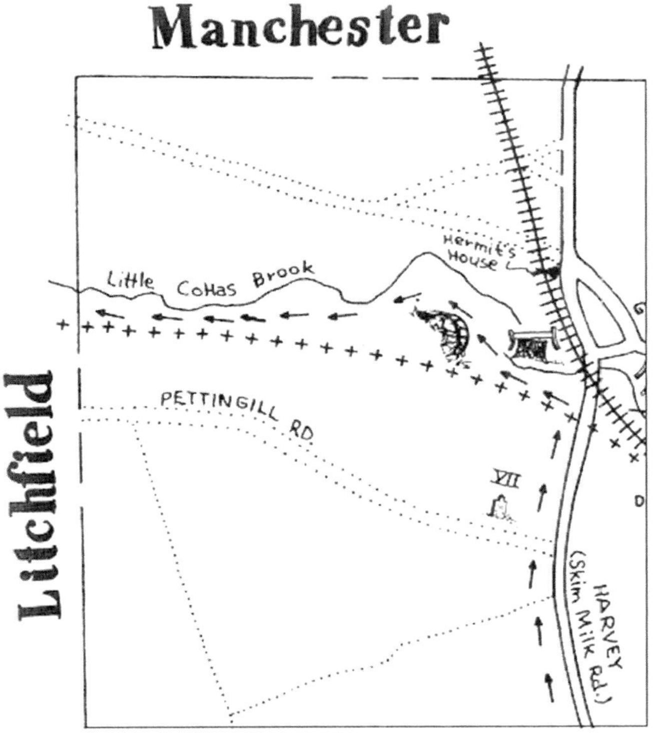


**NORTHWEST.** This area of Londonderry known as Grenier Field now contains the Manchester Airport.

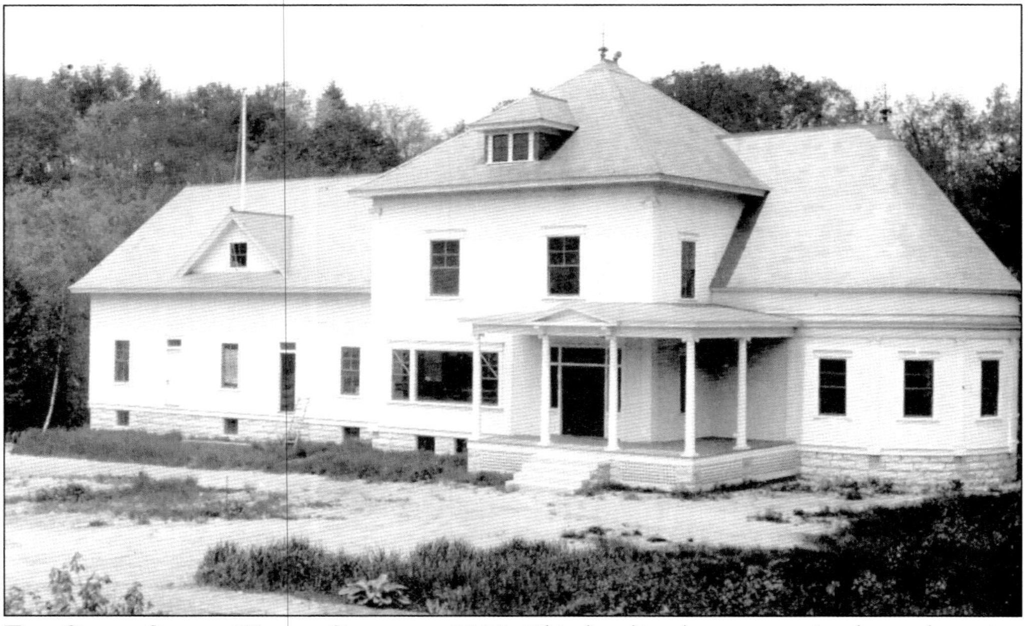

**The Cohas Spring Water Company, 1909.** This bottling house contained a carbonating room, a refrigerating plant, and a packing room. The company's motto was "Pre-eminence In Purity. Which no other Reached." The buildings burned in the 1920s, and the remnants may still be found by Little Cohas Brook, south of the Manchester Airport Perimeter Road.

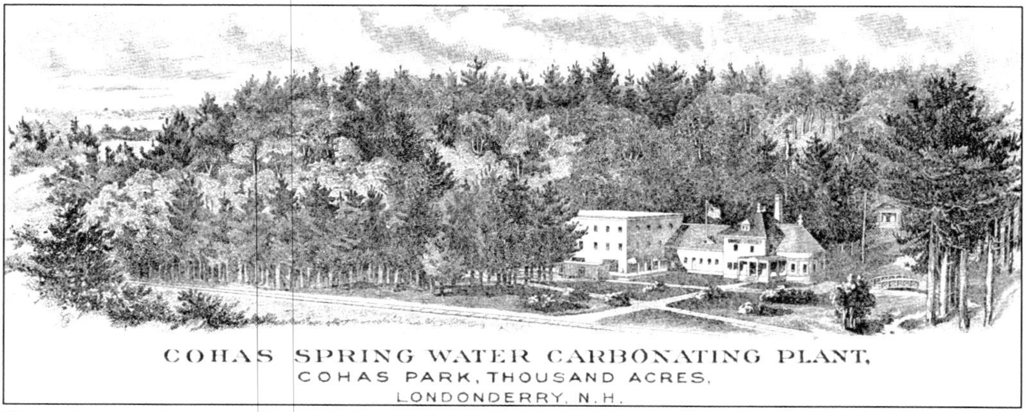

COHAS SPRING WATER CARBONATING PLANT,
COHAS PARK, THOUSAND ACRES,
LONDONDERRY, N.H.

**The Cohas Spring Water Company.** This photograph shows the bottling plant, the springhouse, a wooden bridge over Little Cohas Brook, and the Manchester & Derry Electric Trolley tracks, all nestled in 1,000 acres of beautiful woods. Roswell Annis, a business genius of 19th-century Londonderry, conceived this enterprise. The area is significant enough to be listed in the site files of the New Hampshire Division of Historical Resources, Archeology Division.

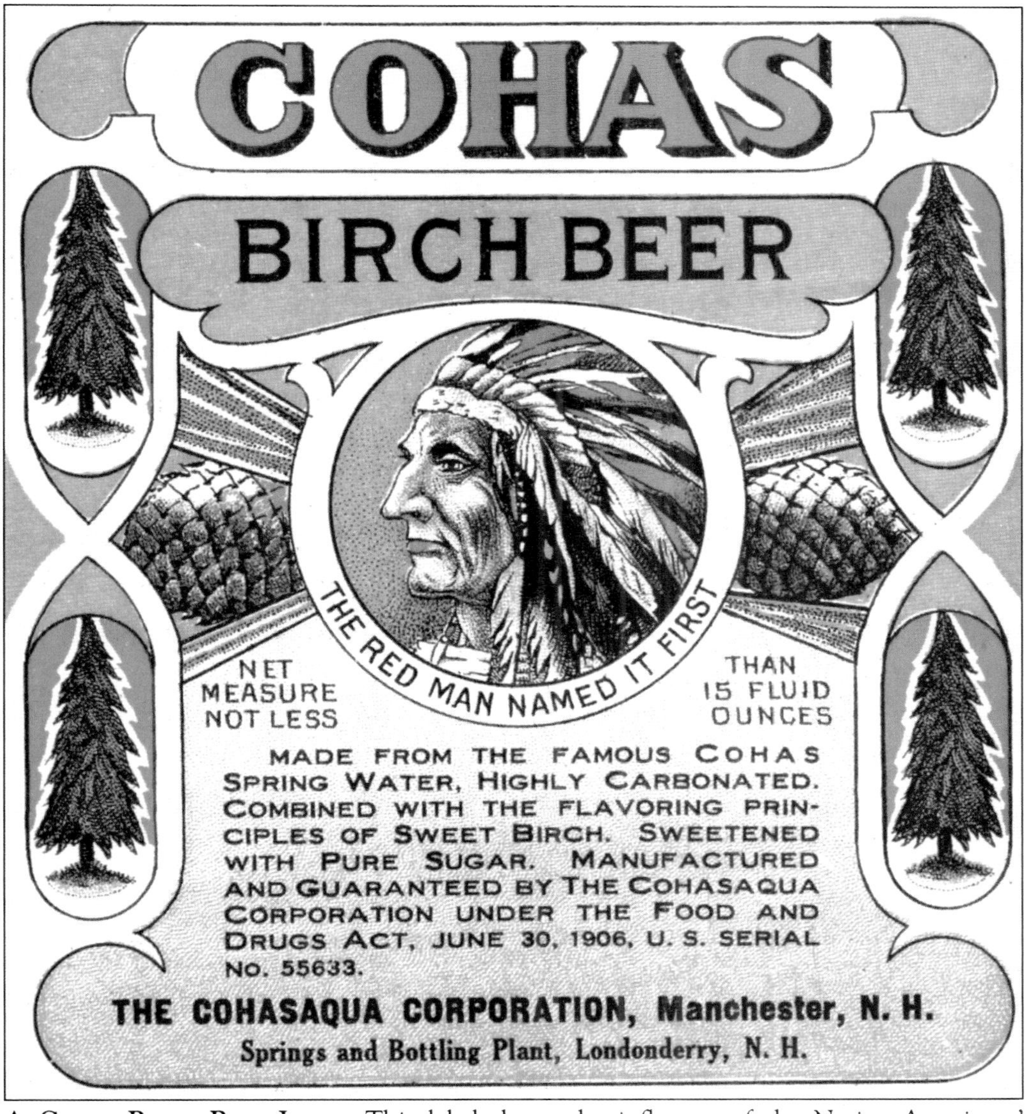


**A Cohas Birch Beer Label.** This label shows the influence of the Native Americans' discovery of Cohas Springs in deep pinewoods. The name Cohas means "pine." Flavors of birch beer and ginger ale, as well as still and carbonated water, were bottled at the bottling plant in Londonderry. Shards of broken glass can still be found near the ruins of the plant.

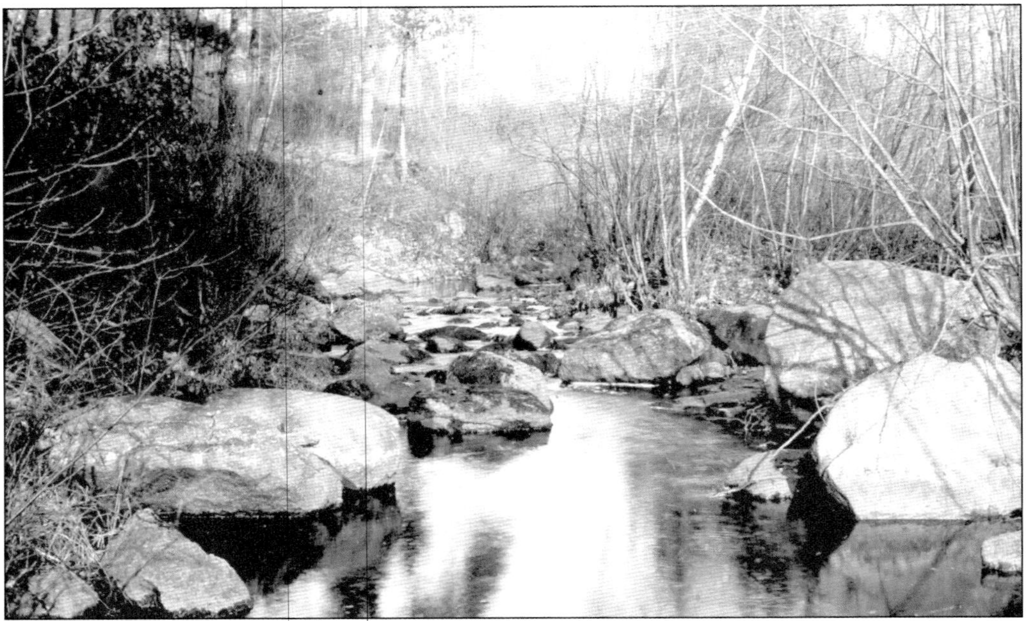

**LITTLE COHAS BROOK.** Native Americans camped along the shores of the Little Cohas Brook. It gathers momentum from wetlands and runs from east to west along the north edge of Londonderry. Its energy powered gristmills and sawmills and provided fishing, recreation, and tranquility to inhabitants of the area as it gurgled and rushed toward the Merrimack River. Slaves from the south seeking freedom followed the brook from the river. A section of the brook is now tunneled under the airport's south runway.

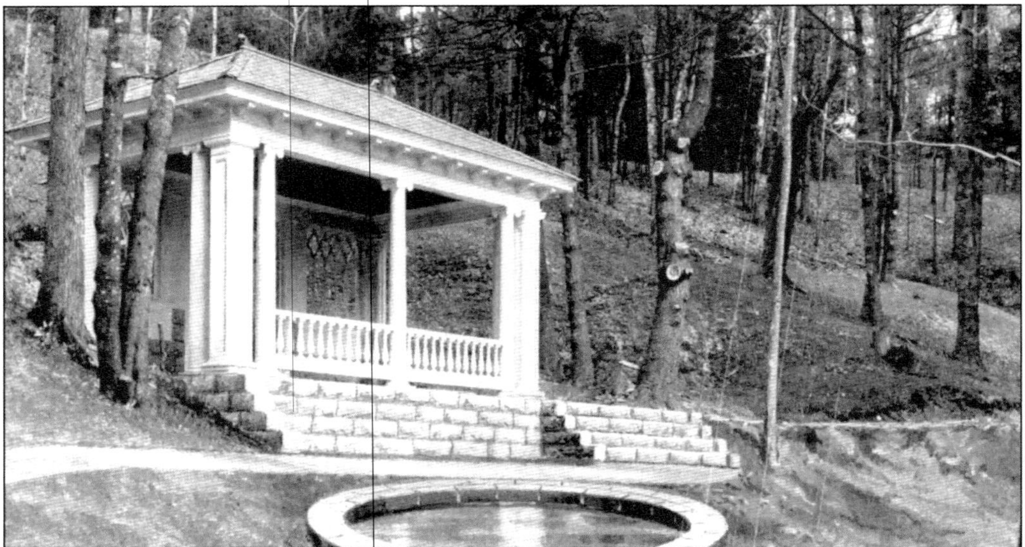

**THE COHAS SPRINGHOUSE.** This attractively designed springhouse, located near the bottling plant, was kept under lock and key to protect the purity of the spring water coming out of the rocky hillsides. The water flowed by gravity through pipes to the plant. In 1908, the state board of health commended the Cohas Spring Company for its pure water. The springs south of the airport continue to flow; however, they are not as pure as they were in earlier days.

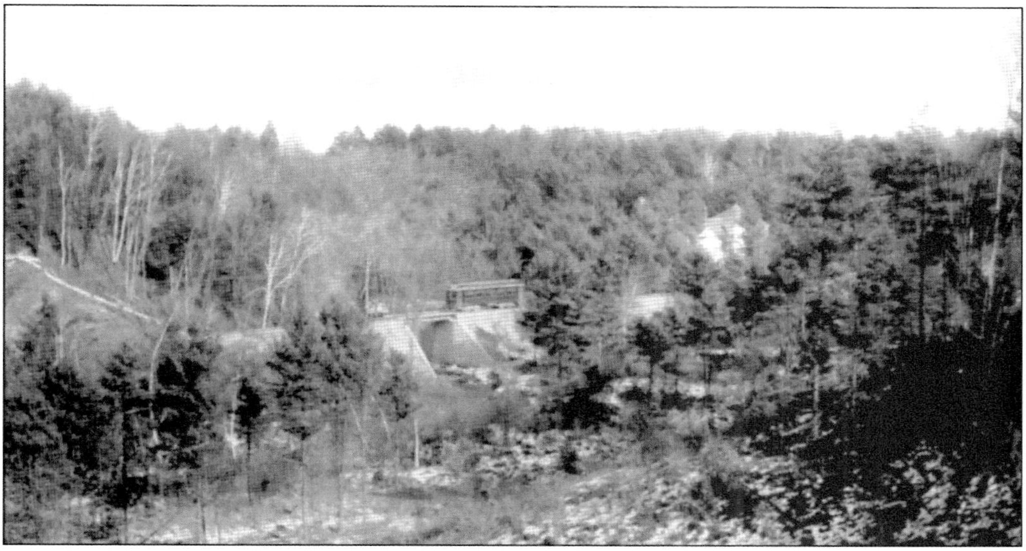

**THE COHAS SPRING TROLLEY STOP, 1926.** People descended at this last trolley stop to visit the picturesque Victorian health spa, with gazebos and a springhouse (just right of center, by the electric trolley). Stylishly dressed ladies and gentlemen came by horse-drawn carriages to take the sparkling waters and enjoy the sylvan setting. Many navigated the 134 steps to the spring. People still enjoy a leisurely walk along this former trolley line south of the airport in Londonderry.

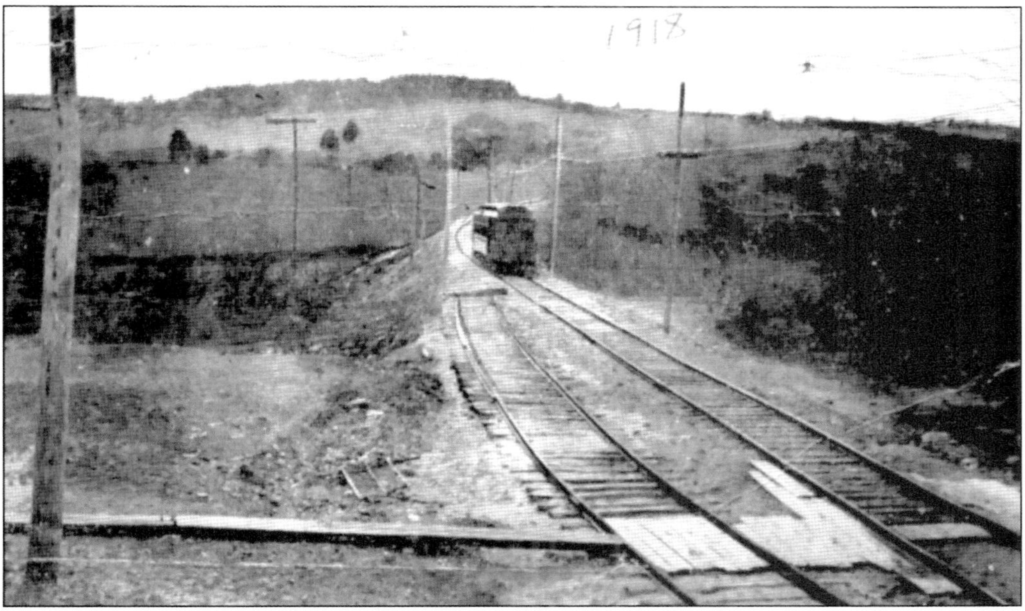


**THE ELECTRIC TROLLEY, 1907–1926.** In this photograph, the electric trolley has passed by the Londonderry North Depot area and Plummer's Crossing on Skim Milk Road (now Harvey Road) on its way to the next stop, Cohas Junction. The trolley line wound its way from Derry through Londonderry to Manchester. A one-way trip lasted 50 minutes and covered eight miles. The fare was 15¢. Part of this area is now the south runway of the Manchester Airport.

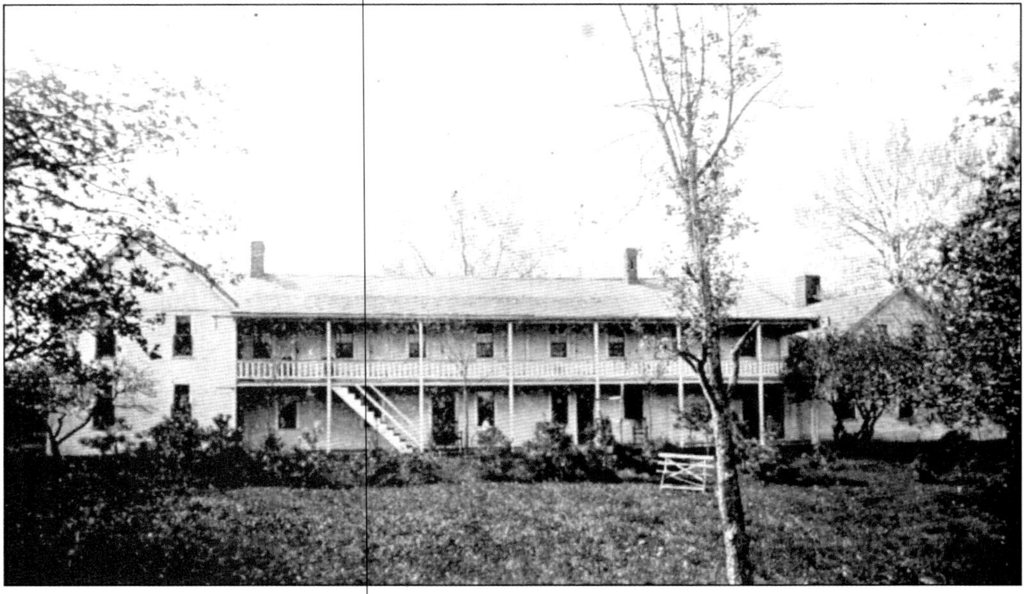

**Wildwood Farm c. 1850.** Located on Skim Milk Road (now Harvey Road), Wildwood was an experimental cattle farm that allowed Dr. Bennett to study diseases caused by milk. Paint from skim milk was also made here. In 1869, the Perrys bought the farm and turned parts of it into a summer retreat that could accommodate 40 guests. In 1902, the price was $1 per day or $6 per week. In the winter, local folks had fun in the dance hall.

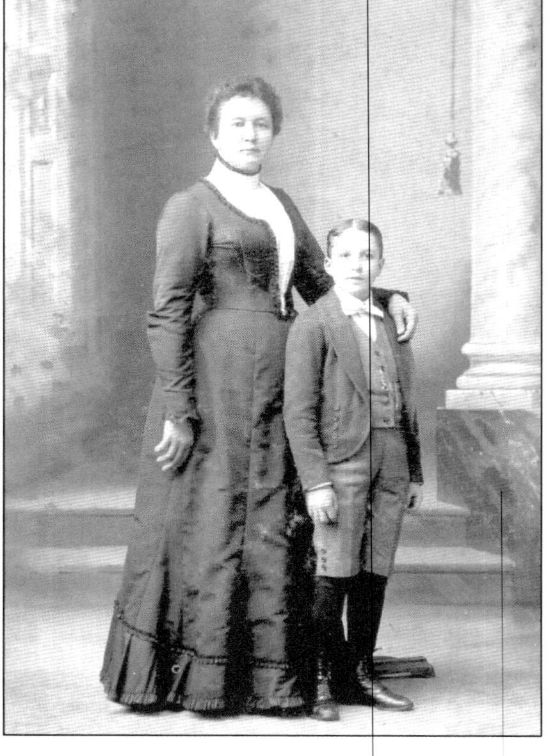

**Mrs. Peter Perry and Son Bernard.** A woman of great stature, Mrs. Perry was known to heft 100-pound sacks of grain. She ran Wildwood Farm on Skim Milk Road (now Harvey Road) and hosted summer boarders. The Perrys later moved to Londonderry Village and bought Captain Garvin's Victorian residence on Old Mammoth Road, naming it the Laurels. Again, Mrs. Perry ran the farm, was cook and housekeeper, and welcomed boarders. The house is still a Victorian showpiece.

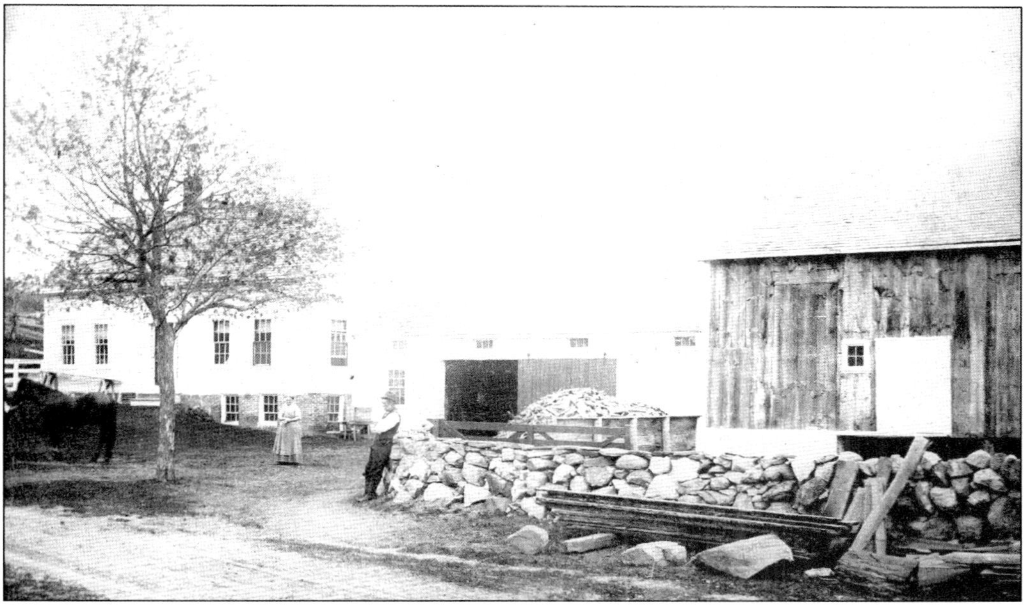

**THE BOYCE-SMITH FARM, 1889.** Nelson Smith bought this home, located on Skim Milk Road (now Harvey Road), from the Boyce family in 1935. It became the home of his son Ernest and his wife, Ruth, who lived there until 1942, when the U.S. Air Force base (Grenier Field, now Manchester Airport) was built across the road. The U.S. government bought the land and tore the buildings down.

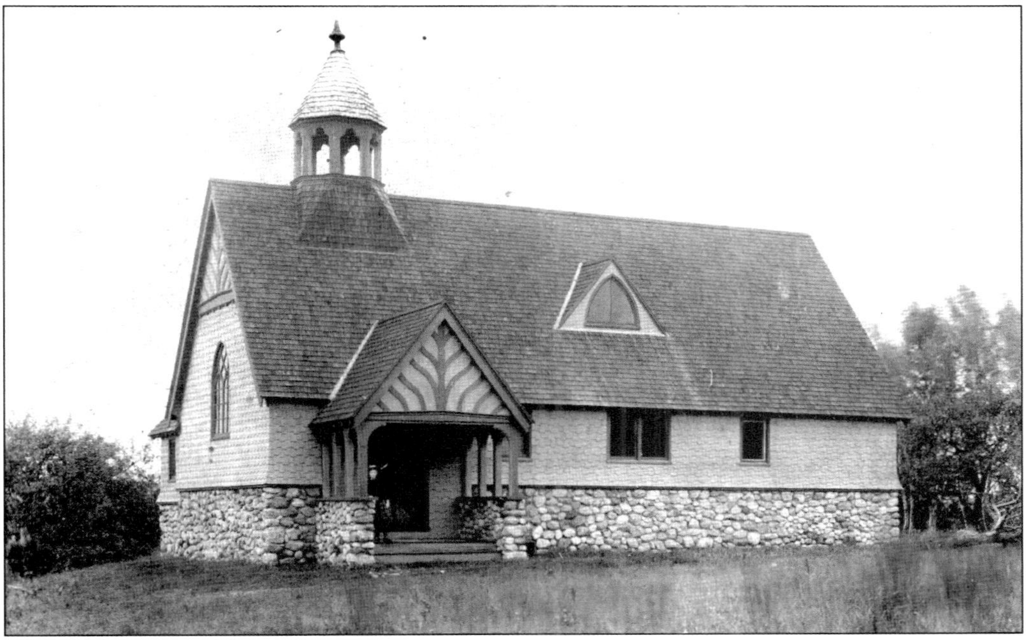

**BETHANY CHAPEL C. 1900.** The chapel was built in the early 1900s on the bank of Great Cohas Brook near the Merrimack River, north of the Manchester Airport. It was a haven for World War II servicemen and women stationed at Grenier Field. Now completely refurbished, it is fondly dubbed a "respite by the runway." It remains an active church to this day.

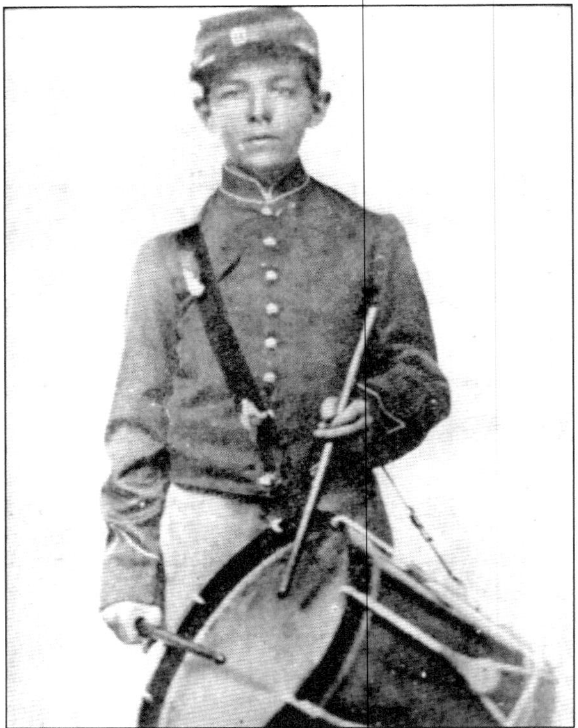

**A CIVIL WAR DRUMMER BOY.** On July 19, 1861, at the age of 14, James M. Lurvey enlisted in Company A of the 40th Massachusetts Volunteers. The drum was cut to fit his youthful frame. James was assigned to the medical division but, being too small to carry the wounded, he was ordered to work in the amputation tents with the surgeons.

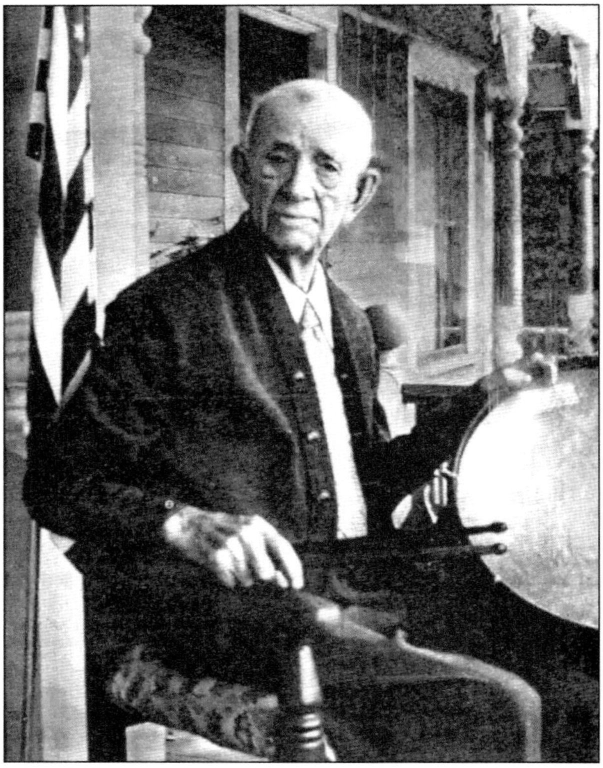

**JAMES M. LURVEY.** The Civil War "Drummer Boy" is shown on the porch of his home in 1949, at 102 years of age. Lurvey, the last known Civil War veteran in New Hampshire, was buried with honors in Londonderry in 1950.

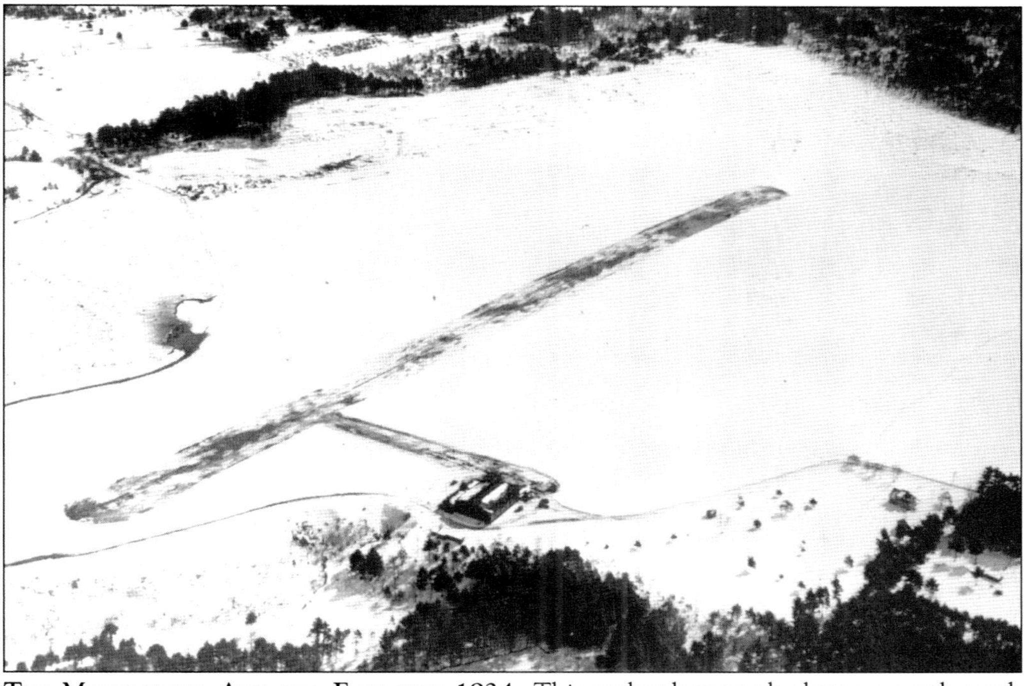

**The Manchester Airport, February 1934.** This early photograph shows a north-south runway. The south end is in Londonderry (at the upper right side of photograph). The early brick hanger at the north end is in Manchester. In 1940, the airport became Grenier Field Air Force Base, and in 1959, the name changed back to Manchester Airport. In 2004, the first airport terminal became a historical aviation museum.

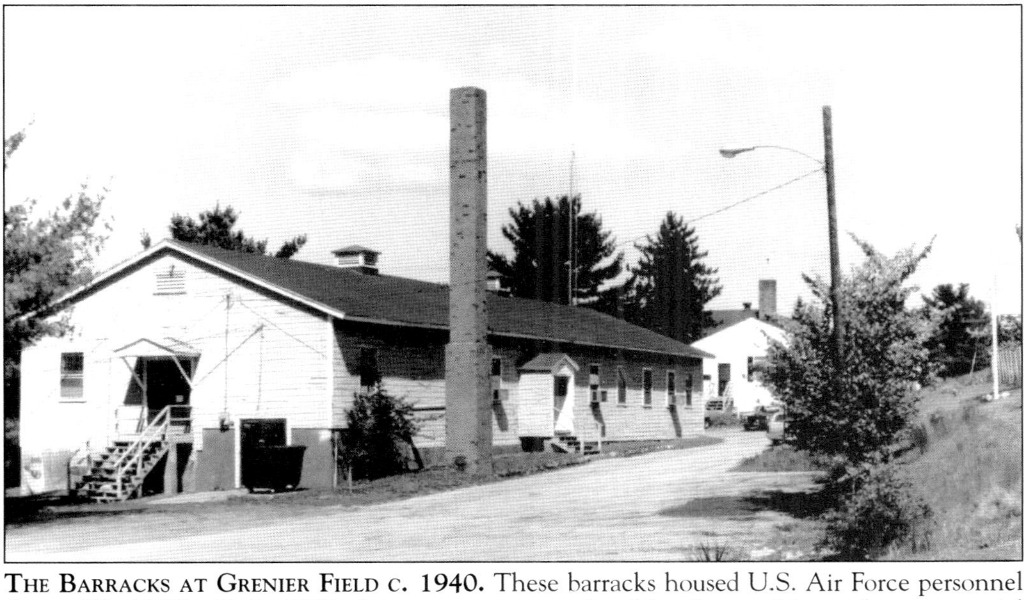

**The Barracks at Grenier Field c. 1940.** These barracks housed U.S. Air Force personnel during World War II. In 1957, the area was returned to Manchester Airport for commercial and public use. In the 1970s, the barracks housed some Londonderry town offices and the police station.

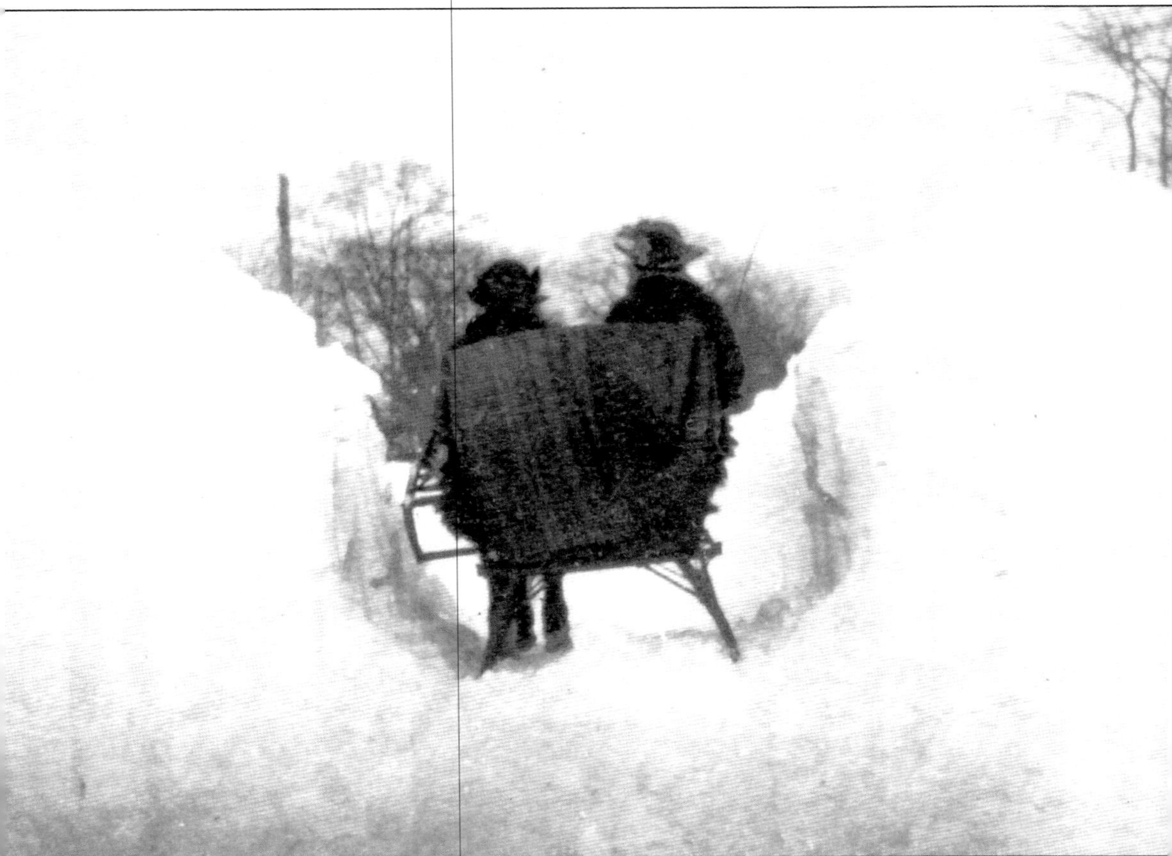

**A One-Horse Open Sleigh c. 1920.** Jessie Webster Beckley and Pearl Reid Parmenter head home on snowbound north Mammoth Road. Teams of horses pulled large rollers to pack the snow. When it was too deep, hand shoveling was necessary. People could walk on the highest drifts and touch the telephone wires. Roads were not cleared by plow until 1926.

# *Three*

# Wilson's Crossing

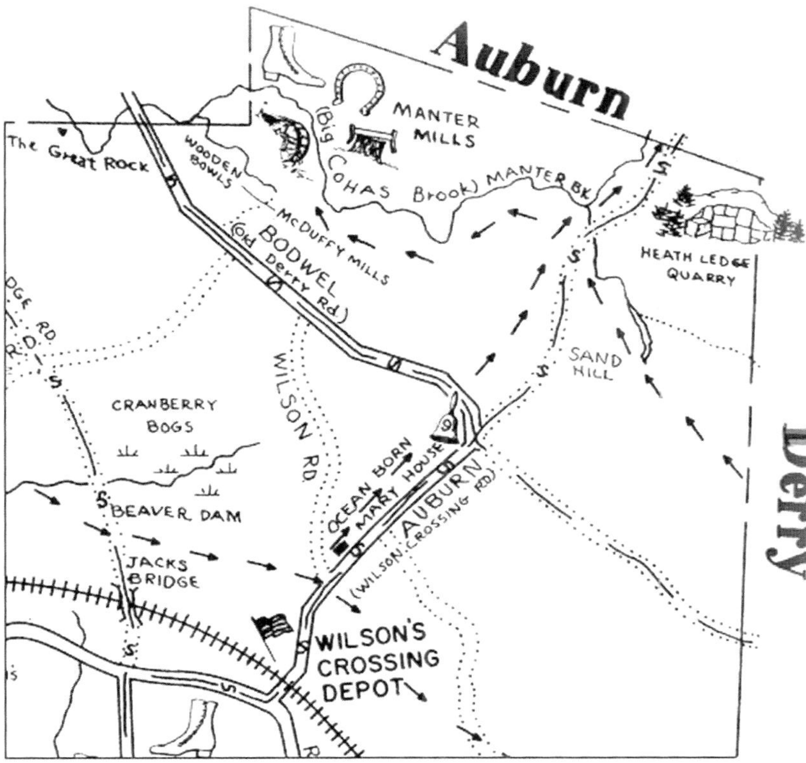


**Northeast.** This area of Londonderry was once known as Wilson's Crossing. Schoolhouse No. 9 was located at the intersection of Auburn and Bodwell Roads.

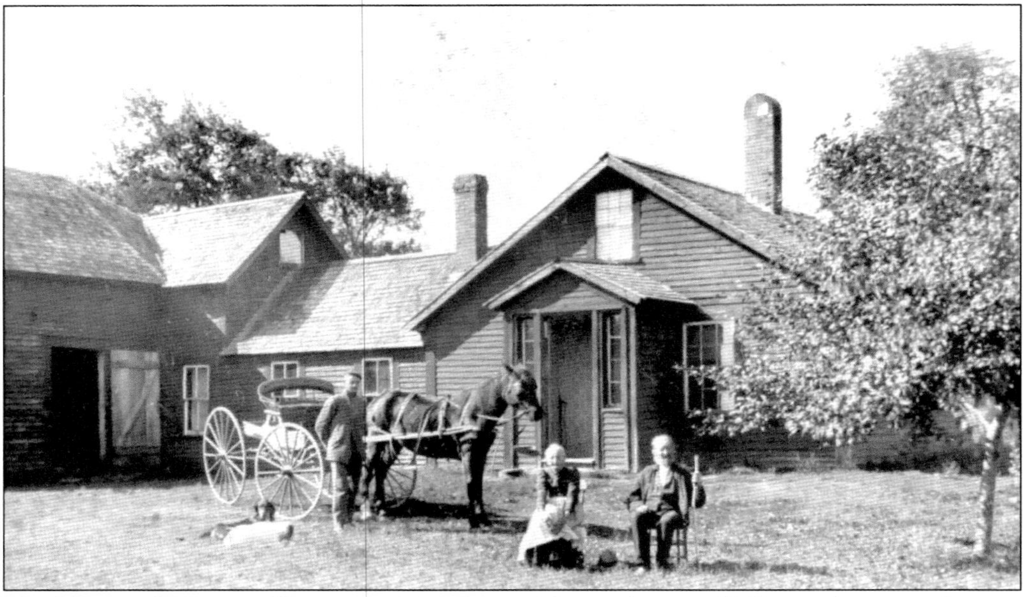

**The Manter-Pelletier House c. 1899.** George Manter, born in 1769, was the original owner of Manter Mills. Holdings of the Manter family numbered "hundreds of acres and was a grant from the King," (*Early Londonderry*, vol. IV). In 1930, Ethel Pelletier acquired the home. She added a porch to the house and a shed to the original barn. This farm on Old Derry Road was razed to make room for new development.

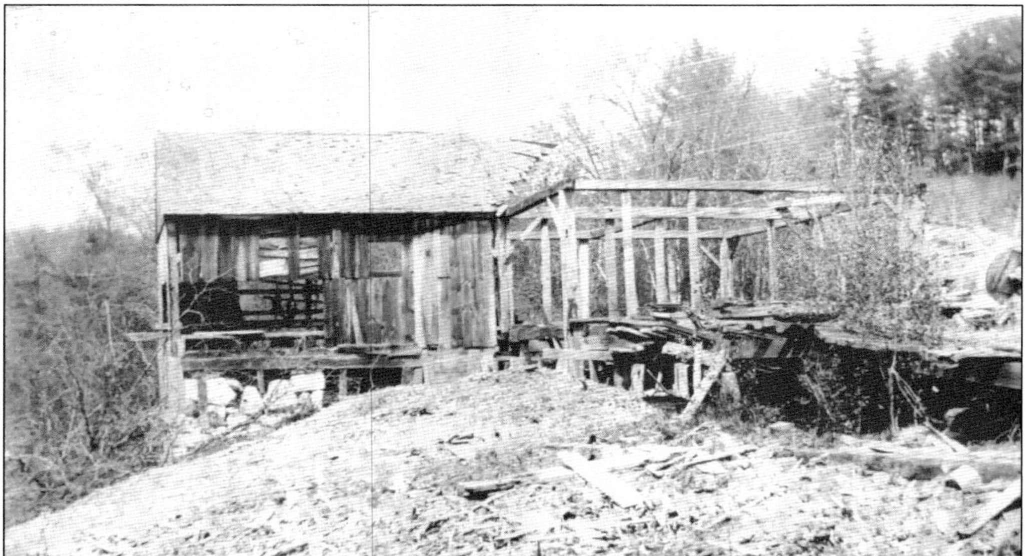

**The Manter Sawmill.** This 1898 photograph shows one of George Manter's three mills after it had closed. The mills and sluiceways were once noisy with sounds of grinding millstones, buzzing saws, and rushing water. This former center of industrial importance stands along Big Cohas Brook off Manter Road near the Manchester line. The ruins of these mills and sluiceways have been documented in the site files of the New Hampshire Division of Historical Resources, Archeology Division. This beautiful area is much changed by housing developments.

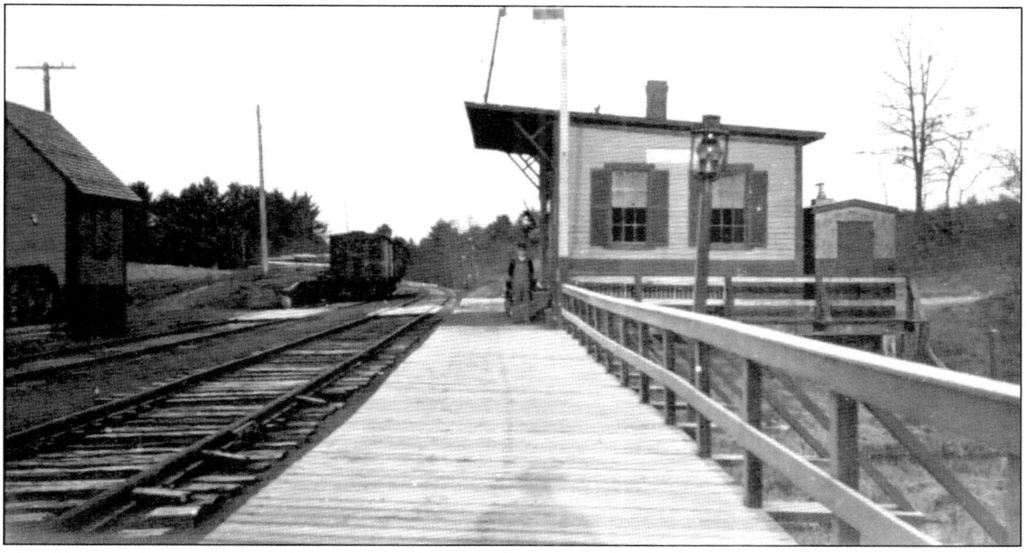

**The Wilson's Crossing Depot.** In 1874, the depot beside the Boston & Maine Railroad tracks housed the Wilson post office, serviced passengers, and handled freight. Crushed white quartz rock was shipped from here to Boston. The depot building, originally located near the present intersection of Rockingham and Auburn Roads, stood until the 1970s in its second location by the rail crossing in the village.

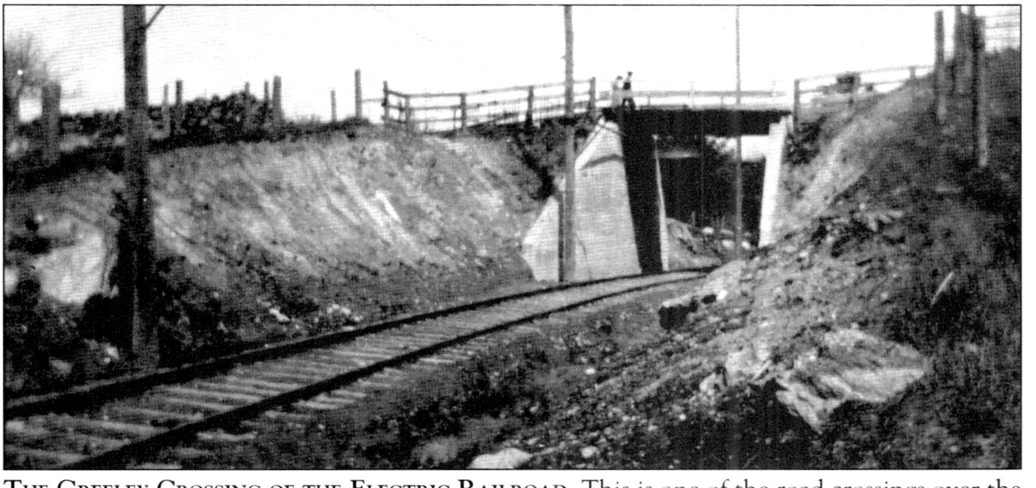

**The Greeley Crossing of the Electric Railroad.** This is one of the road crossings over the trolley line. We have been unable to identify which road this was, but it is likely to have been either Pillsbury Road or Hardy Road.

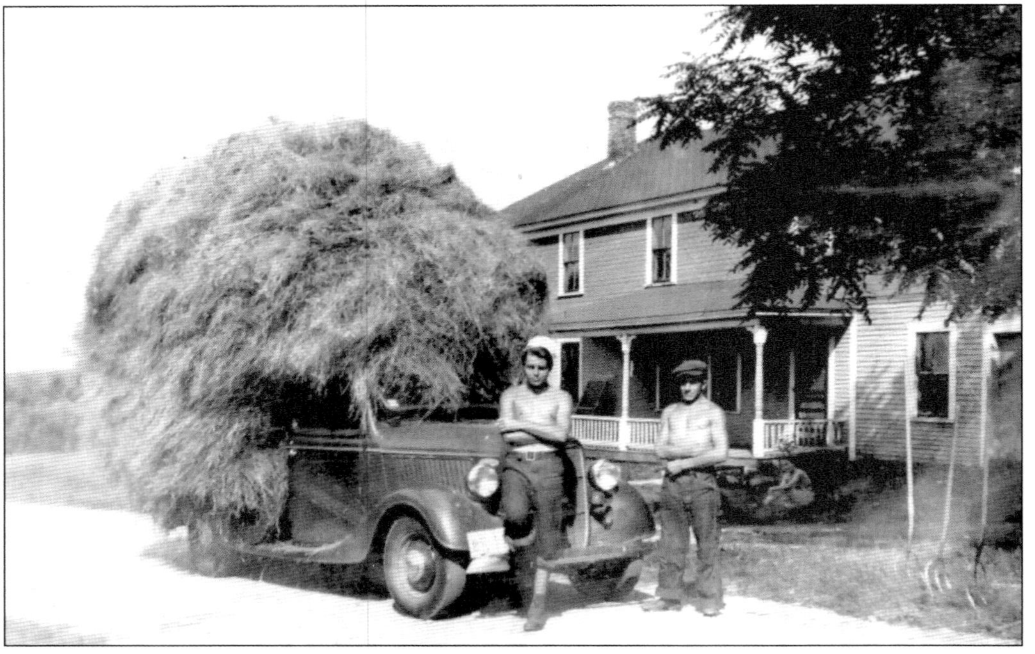

**Bringing in the Hay.** This 1937 photograph shows two hired hands coming from the hayfield with their load parked in front of Samuel Manter's home, later the Hall residence. This home still stands today on Old Derry Road. The original gristmill stone from Manter Mills is a step at the back door.

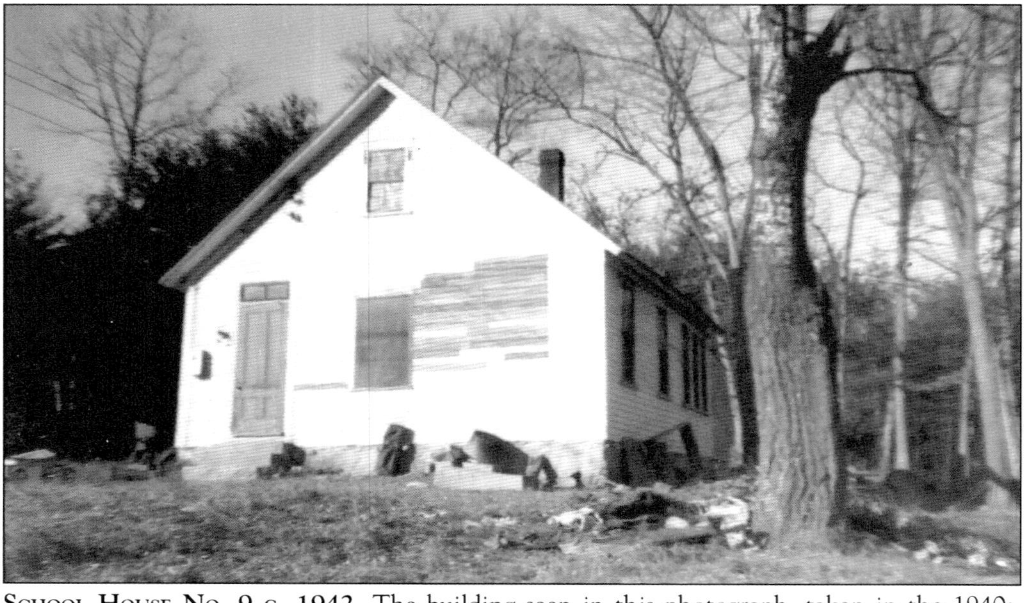

**School House No. 9 c. 1942.** The building seen in this photograph, taken in the 1940s, is the second schoolhouse to be built on the corner of Auburn and Bodwell Roads in north Londonderry. Once, this school was dismissed due to horrific forest fires in the area. Students hoped the school would burn! In 1907, a teacher boarding with a family received $200 to teach 30 weeks a year. This schoolhouse was bought and remodeled into a home.

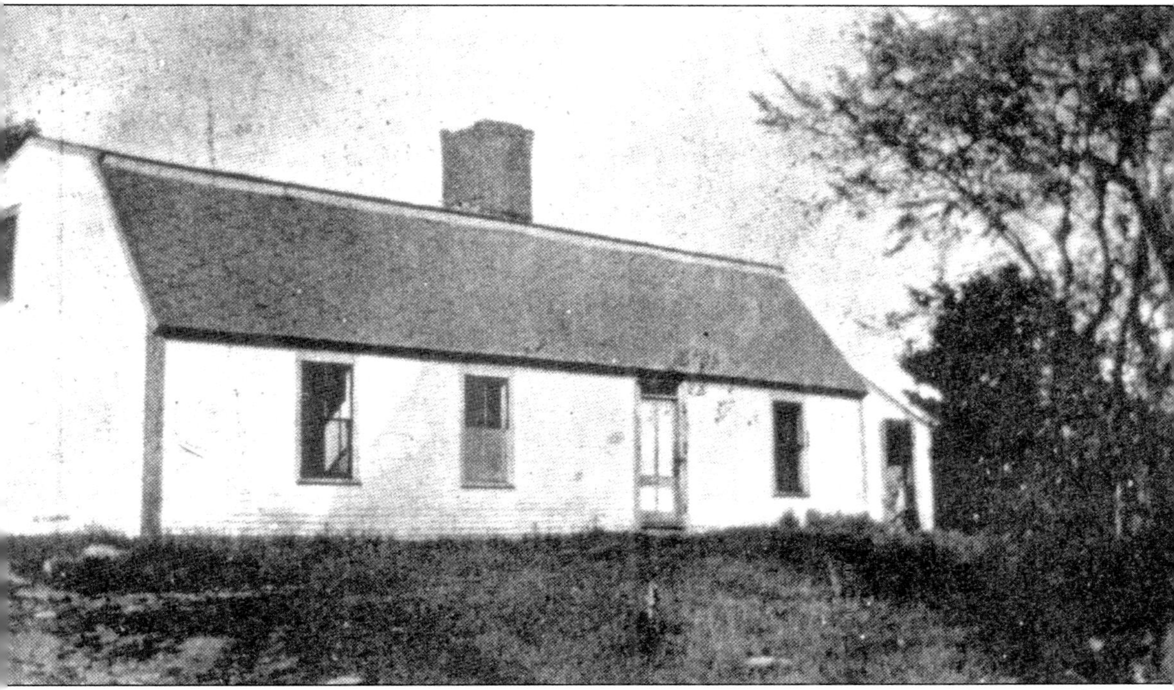

**OCEAN-BORN MARY'S HOUSE.** This house was named for Mary Wilson, daughter of James and Elizabeth Wilson. Mary was born on a sailing ship and named by a pirate captain during the emigration of the Scottish families from Londonderry, Ireland, in 1720. The family lived in this house at the corner of Wilson and Auburn Roads. It was built before 1730 of hand-hewn timbers cut at the site. In 1930, the house was dismantled piece by piece. Each piece was numbered and taken to Little Compton, Rhode Island, where the house was reassembled and is now known as "Sea-Born Mary's House."

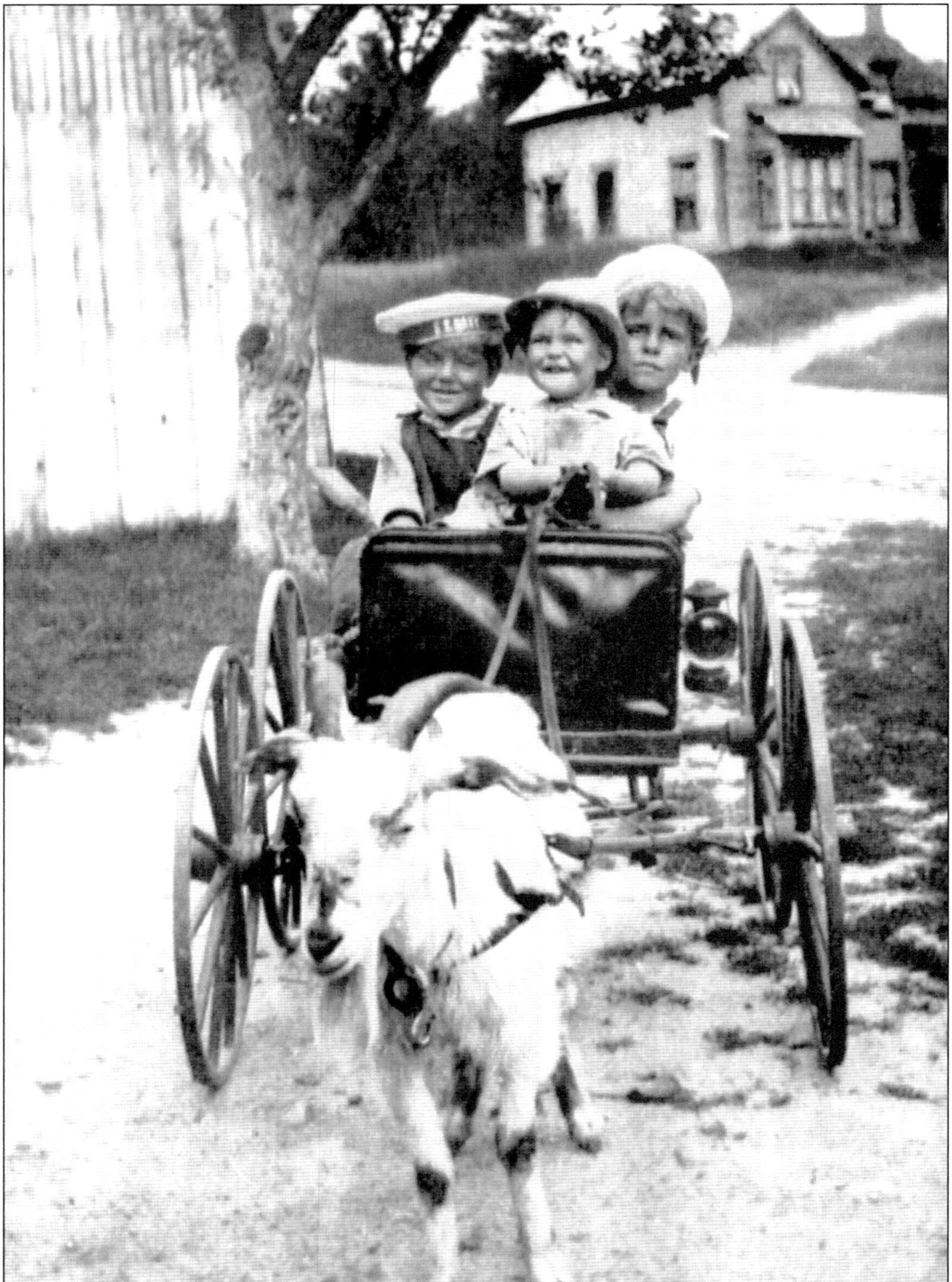

**The Moody Children in a Goat Cart.** Warren, Arnold, and Wallace Moody are seen here with smiles on their faces as they harnessed their pet goat and drove along Auburn Road. The Moody farm is in the background.

*Four*

# THE TOWN COMMON

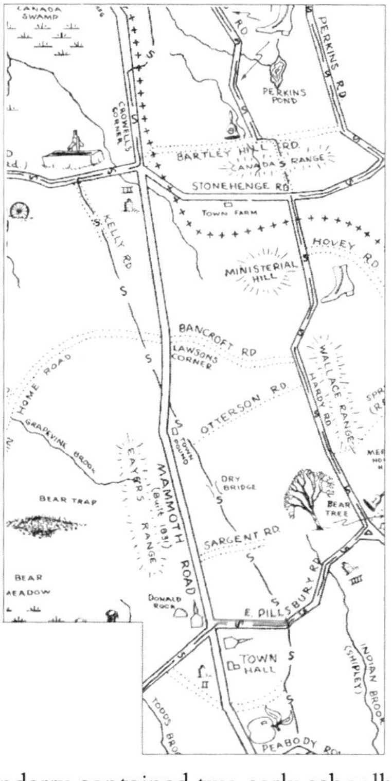


**CENTRAL.** This area of Londonderry contained two early schoolhouses: Schoolhouse No. 1, at the corner of Pillsbury and Hardy Roads, and Schoolhouse No. 8, at the intersection of Bartley Hill and Noyes Road.

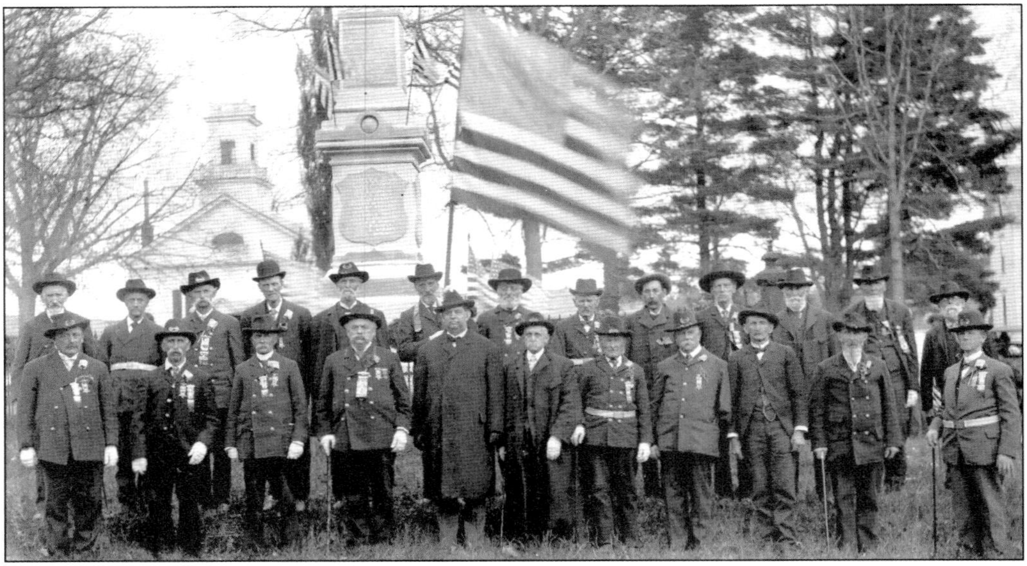

**CIVIL WAR VETERANS ON THE TOWN COMMON, 1890.** This is the Wesley B. Knight Post No. 41. John E. Webster is second from the right in the front row. He served in the 1st Calvary Regiment of New Hampshire and was at the battles of Opequan and Cedar Creek. His regiment led a charge on the enemy and captured 1,500 prisoners. Col. William Pillsbury is seen seventh from the right in the front row. He served in Company I of the 4th New Hampshire Regiment until an accident forced him to return home. After recovering, he enlisted 30 more men to fight for the Union and returned to the war in Company H of the 4th Regiment.

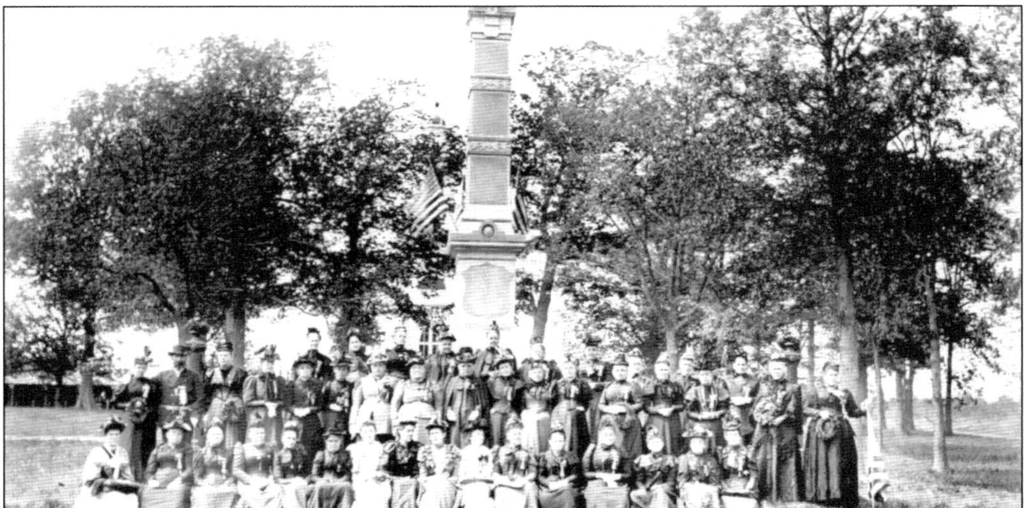

**THE DEDICATION OF THE CIVIL WAR MONUMENT, 1893.** This photograph is of the Wesley B. Knight Women's Relief Corps of Londonderry and Derry Depot, auxiliary to Wesley B. Knight Post No. 41, Grand Army of the Republic, instituted on February 7, 1889, by Kate M. Thayer. Wesley B. Knight may have been the first citizen of Londonderry to enlist in the Civil War. He died while a prisoner in South Carolina. The group was created in memory of Wesley Knight to raise and distribute money for the relief of needy and distressed Civil War soldiers and their families.

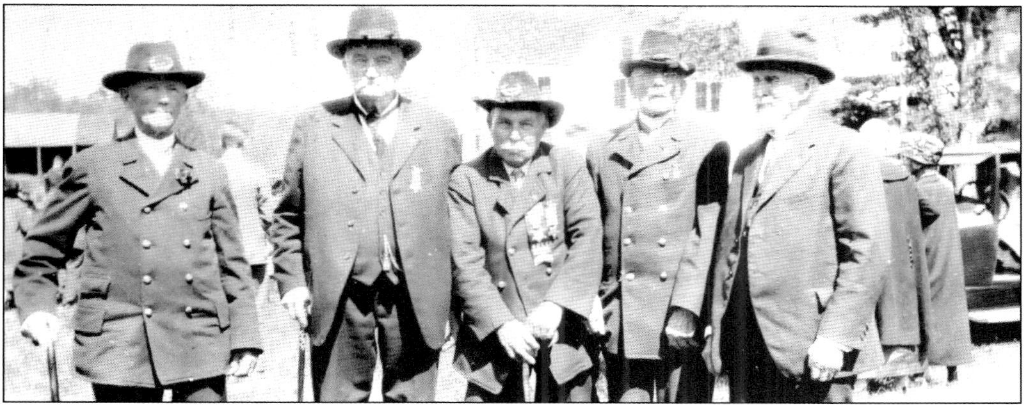

**CIVIL WAR VETERANS ON THE TOWN COMMON C. 1920.** From left to right are Granville F. Plummer, James Byard, G. F. Hamblet, L. H. Pillsbury, and Dea. Joseph L. Day. Granville F. Plummer of the 18th New Hampshire Regiment was involved in protecting Fort Stedman and participated in the Appomattox campaign march. He also assisted in the assault on Petersburg and served guard duty in Washington, D. C., during the trial of Abraham Lincoln's assassins. James Byard probably fought with a Maine regiment. Very little is known of the next soldier, G. F. Hamblet. L. H. Pillsbury fought with the 9th New Hampshire Regiment in battles at Antietam, Fredericksburg, Vicksburg, and Cold Harbor. Dea. Joseph L. Day served with the 18th Massachusetts Regiment for four years and later moved to Londonderry. He became one of the longest living Londonderry veterans of the Civil War and received a 100th birthday greeting from Calvin Coolidge.

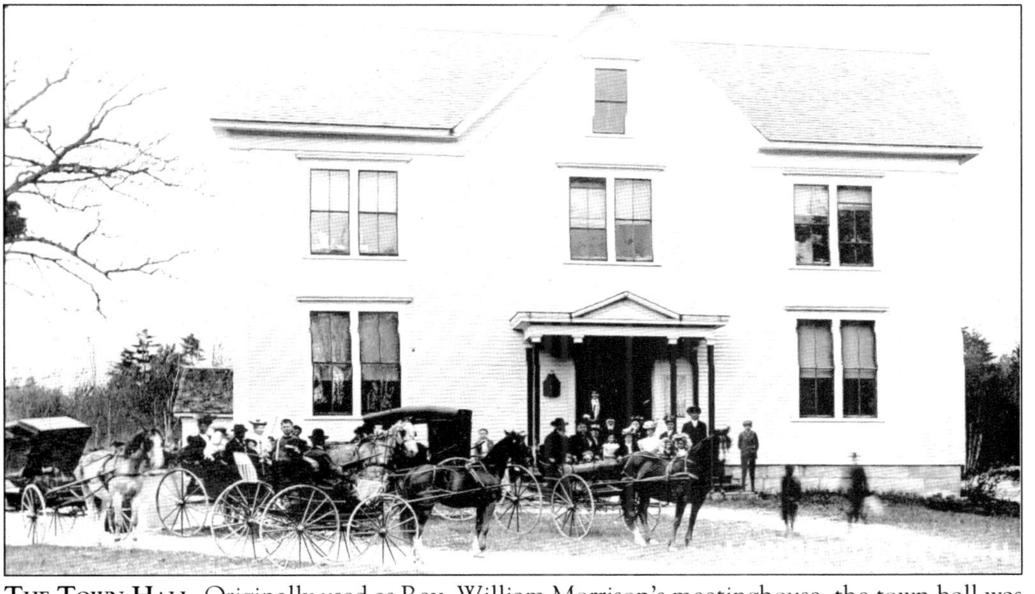

**THE TOWN HALL.** Originally used as Rev. William Morrison's meetinghouse, the town hall was located near James Wallace's tobacco yard by the Valley Cemetery at the corner of Pillsbury and Hardy Roads. It was moved to Mammoth Road after the Presbyterian church was built in 1837. Over time, the building was enlarged and hosted social functions, including parties, suppers, and town meetings. In 1929, funds were appropriated to add a garage to the rear of the building. In 1956, all town offices were located here, but by 1967, they were moved to Central School (now Matthew Thornton). The Lions Club has leased the building since 1972.

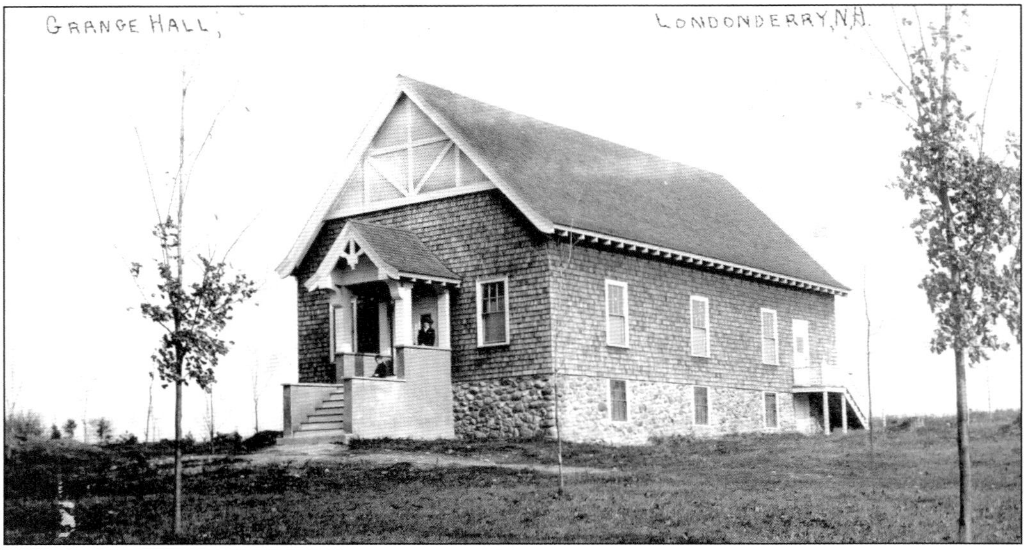


**LONDONDERRY GRANGE NO. 44 c. 1910.** Organized on January 18, 1875, Londonderry Grange No. 44 began with 24 members. Before this hall was built in 1909, meetings were held on the second floor of the old town hall (now the Lions Club). The Grange is a national nonprofit educational organization geared toward families. The ideals of the Grange include leadership, cooperation, community service, frugal living, improved agriculture, citizenship, and patriotism. It continues to serve the Londonderry community today.

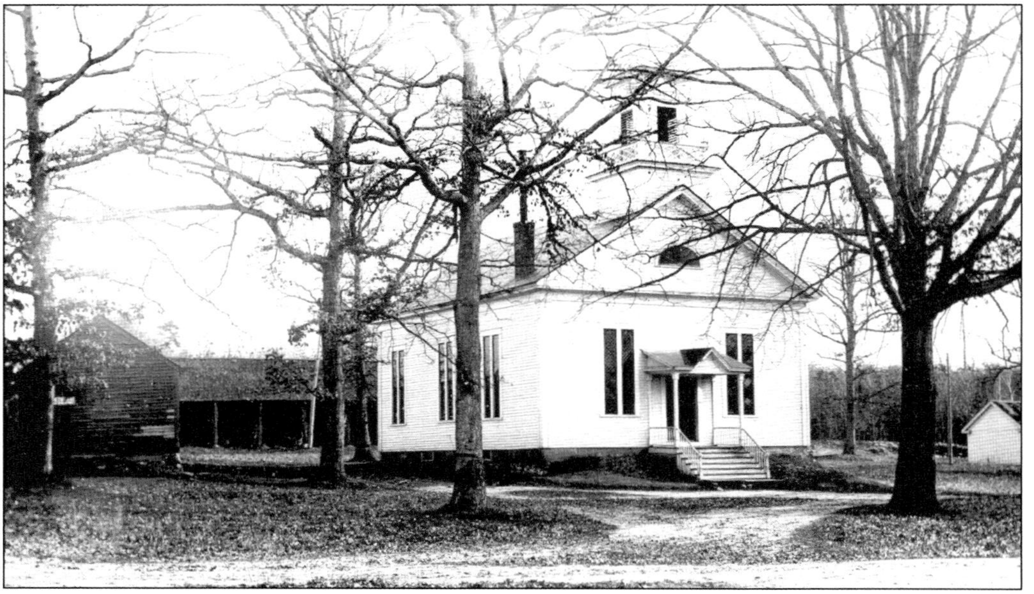

**THE METHODIST CHURCH c. 1912.** Prior to this structure being built, the Methodist Episcopal Society met at Jackson Hall (on High Range Road) and later at the old town hall (now located on Mammoth Road and used as the Lions Club). In 1855, $2000 was raised for the building of a meetinghouse, which was dedicated in 1856. Originally the building had two chimneys. Remodeling done in 1870 and 1892 included raising the building one to two feet, installation of a furnace, and the addition of a slate roof, vestry, and coatroom.

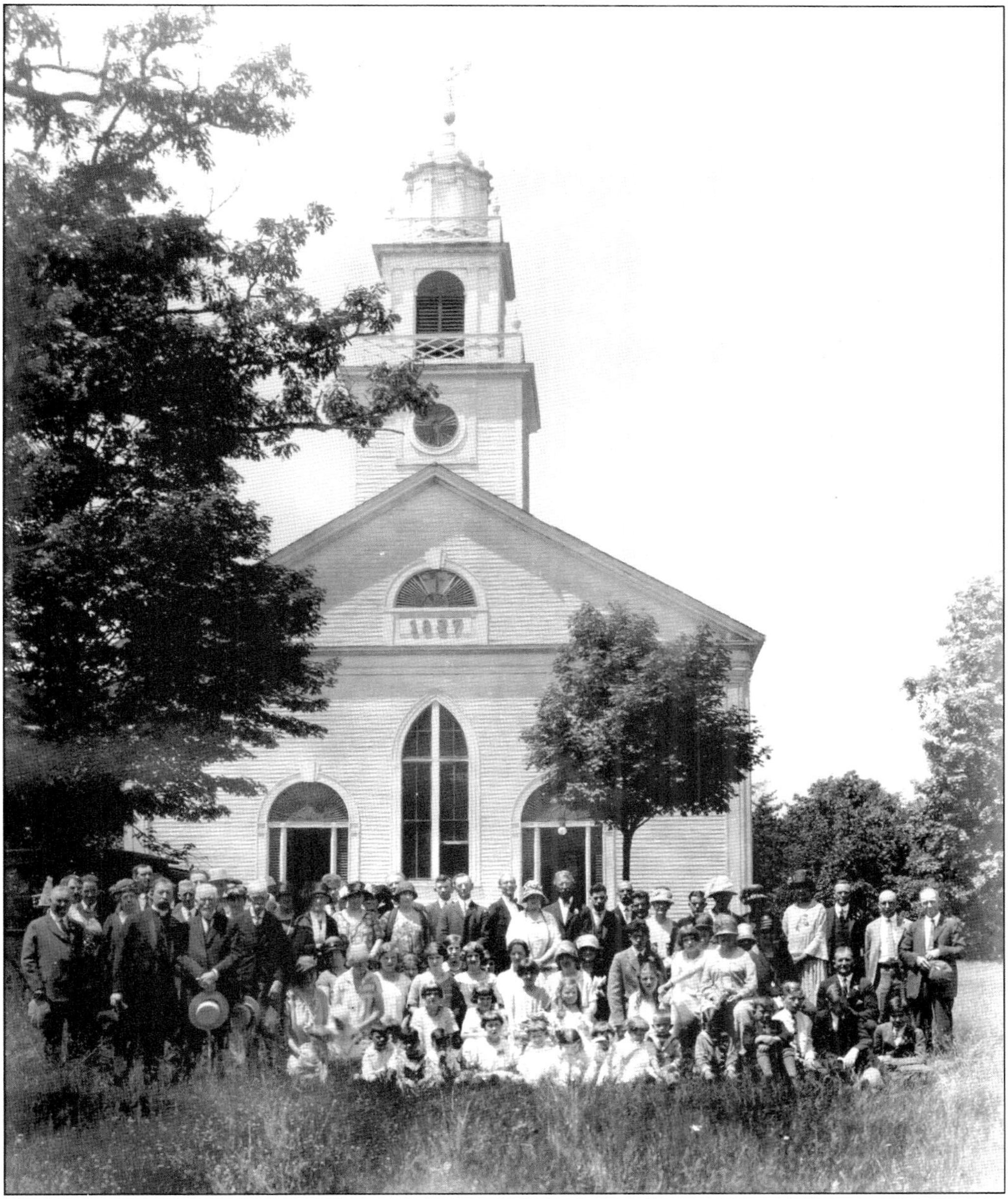

**An Old Home Day Celebration in front of the Presbyterian Church c. 1920.** Standing in front of the oldest Presbyterian church in New England are townspeople attending Old Home Day. The tradition of Old Home Day began in New Hampshire in 1897. It has traditionally been a time when former New Hampshire residents return to visit their old hometowns. Londonderry has faithfully continued the tradition since it was first proclaimed by Governor Rollins. Although this church was not built until 1837 (for a mere $4,000), the Presbyterian church in Londonderry began its services shortly after the arrival of the first citizens in 1719. Famous members of the Presbyterian church include Gen. George Reid, Mary Woodburn Reid, Gen. John Stark, Elizabeth "Molly" Page Stark, and the parents and grandparents of Horace Greeley.

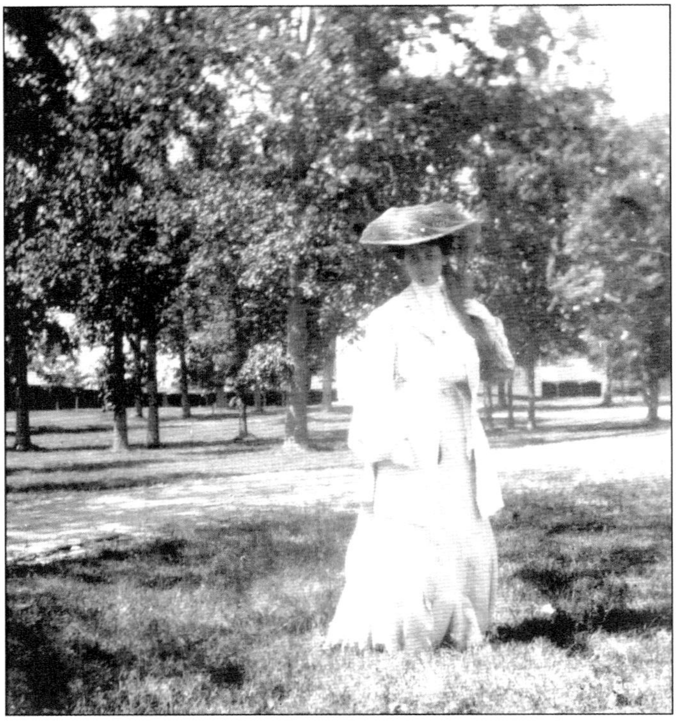

**THE TOWN COMMON, 1904.** Sara Lamborne is seen here on the Londonderry Town Common. This photograph was probably taken by her friend Reed Paige Clark II.

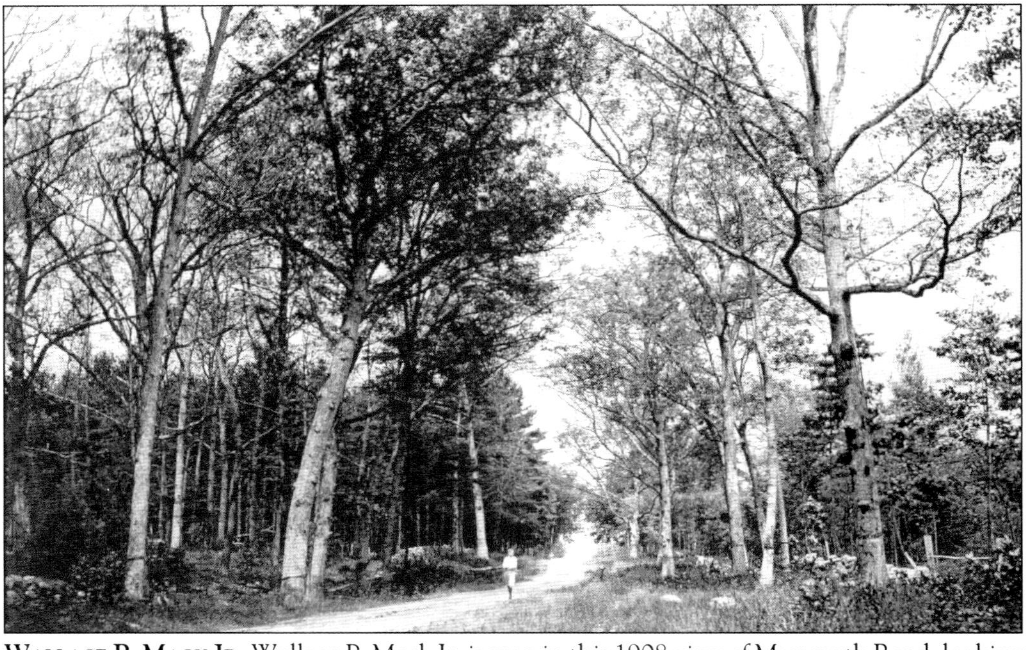

**WALLACE P. MACK JR.** Wallace P. Mack Jr. is seen in this 1908 view of Mammoth Road, looking north, in front of Glenwood Cemetery. Mammoth Road was once a term of derision used by opponents of its construction in the summer of 1831. It was a very wide and straight road for its time. It soon became a popular route between Boston and Concord, and in 1832, President Jackson and his cabinet traveled over this road on their way to Concord.

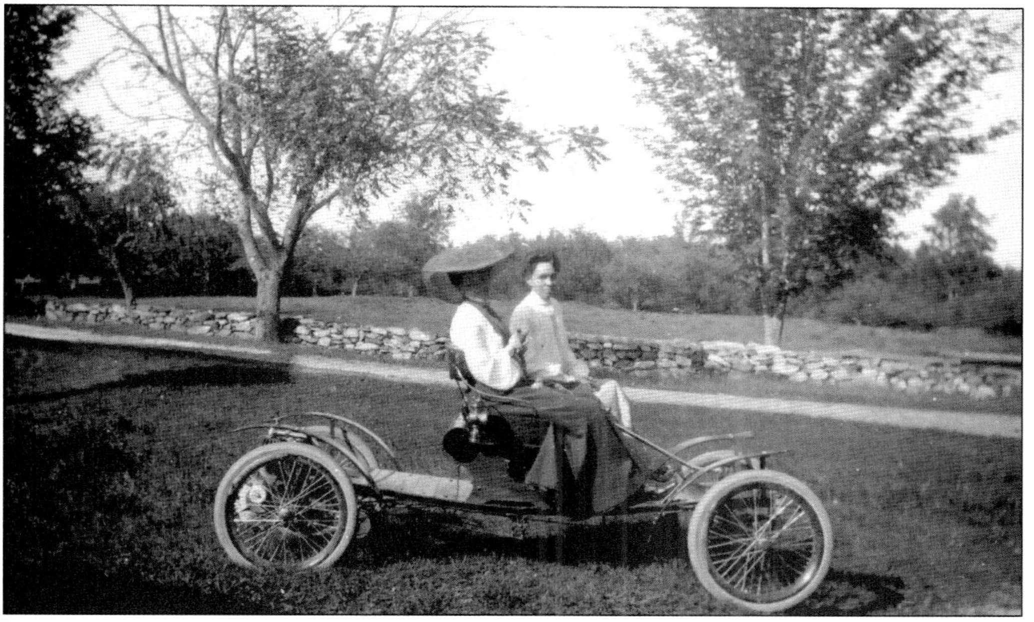

**LONDONDERRY'S FIRST AUTOMOBILE, 1904.** Anne and Sara Lamborne seem to enjoy riding in this early car, owned by Reed P. Clark of Stonehenge. It was built like a buckboard wagon and had a small gasoline motor under the seat.

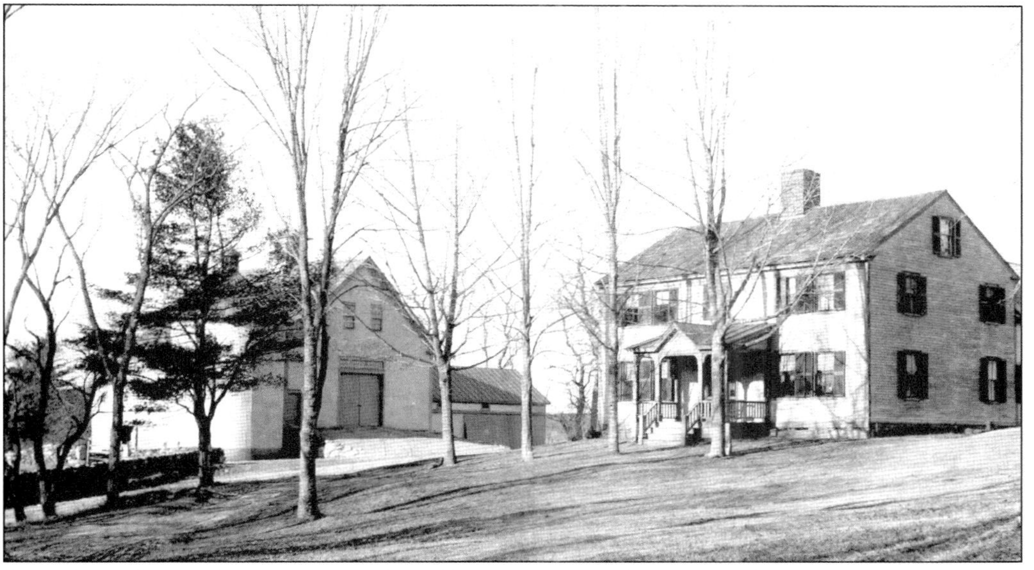

**THE MACK FAMILY HOMESTEAD, 1900.** This classic New Hampshire farmhouse, also known as "the Glenwoods," was built by Robert Mack. He was the grandson of John and Isabella Mack, who came to Nutfield in 1732 from Londonderry, Ireland. The family settled here and grew various crops, raised cattle, and entered the apple business. The home on Mammoth Road overlooks the Mack farm store and is surrounded by many acres of apple trees on the gently rolling hills of Moose Hill Orchards. Close by, a duck pond and a steep hill ideal for sledding attract visitors to the Mack homestead throughout the year. The Mack family still resides in its ancestral home.

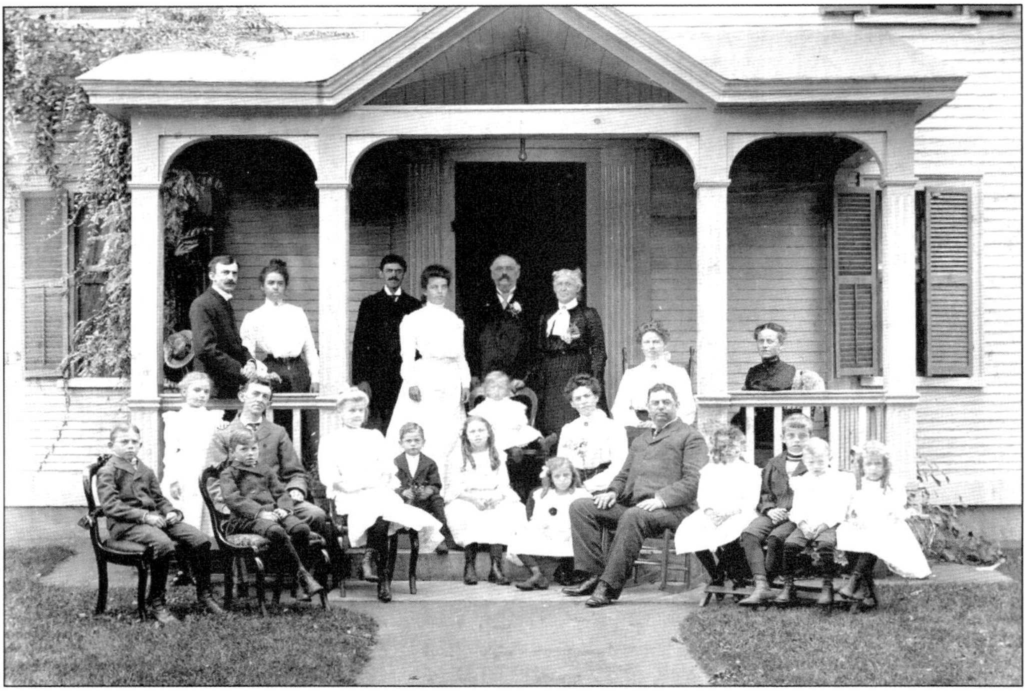

**The Mack and Pillsbury Families.** The Mack and Pillsbury families were united on February 24, 1892, when Wallace Preston Mack married Harriet Lavinia Pillsbury, the daughter of Col. William S. Pillsbury.

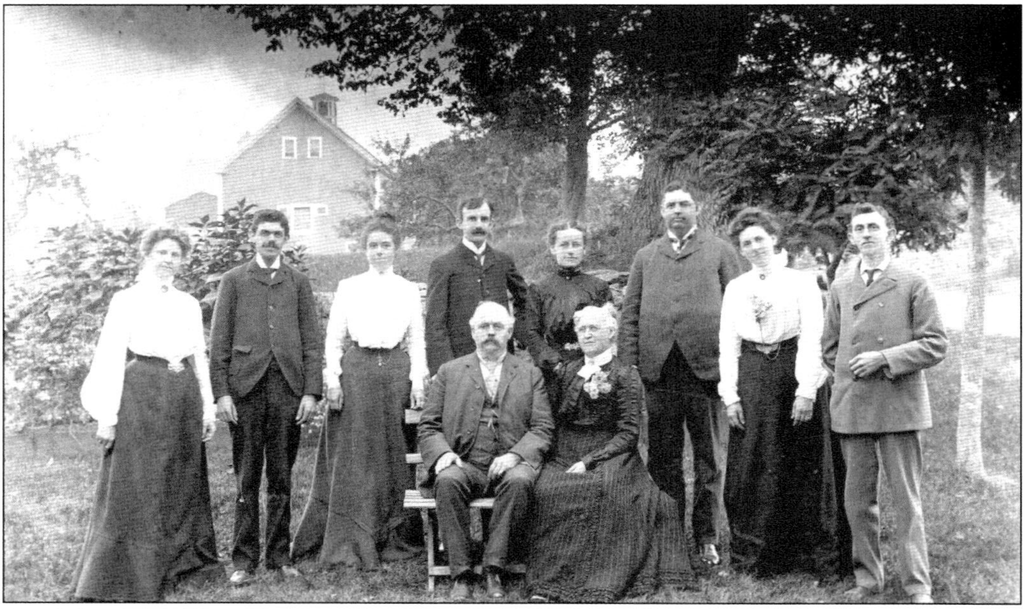

**The Mack and Pillsbury Families, August 23, 1902.** Pictured here are Harriet L. Mack, Wallace P. Mack Sr., Fannie A. Pillsbury, Charles H. L. Pillsbury, Annie W. Pillsbury, Rosecrans W. Pillsbury, Edith D. Pillsbury, Ulysses S. Grant Pillsbury (sitting in front row), Col. William S. Pillsbury, and Martha S. Pillsbury.

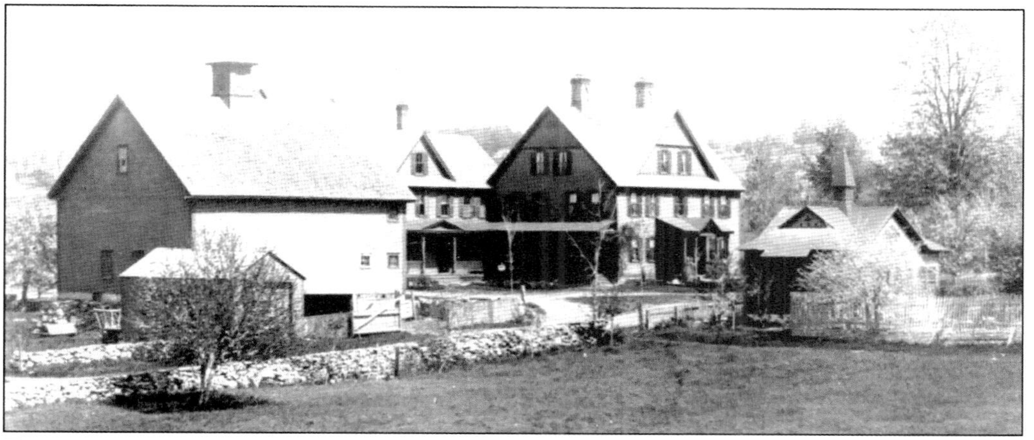

**THE PILLSBURY HOME.** This was the home of Col. William S. Pillsbury; it is still located on Pillsbury Road. Colonel Pillsbury, born March 16, 1833, began his career as a shoemaker at the age of 14. At age 20, he was a superintendent in a shoe factory. He eventually owned his own business in Londonderry and Derry Depot. Colonel Pillsbury was a dedicated Union soldier during the Civil War. After the war, he married Martha Silver Crowell on April 15, 1865. Colonel Pillsbury held numerous public offices at the state and local levels. He and Martha had four children: Rosecrans W., Charles H. L., Harriet L., and Ulysses S. Grant Pillsbury.

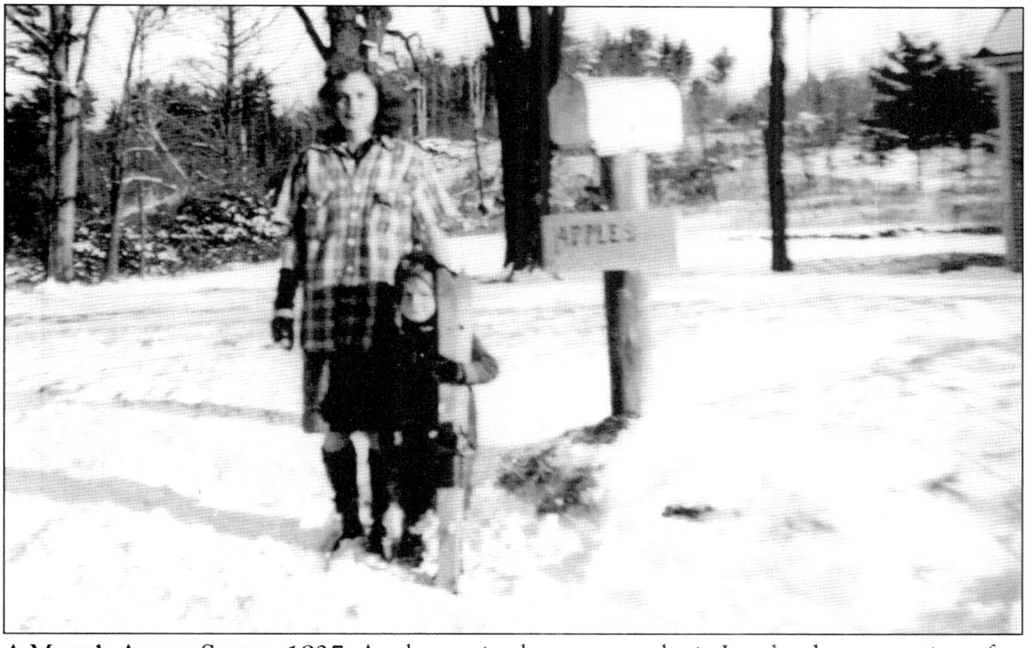


**A MACK'S APPLES SIGN C. 1937.** Apple growing became popular in Londonderry sometime after World War I with the increased demand for the Macintosh apple. Rosecrans Pillsbury planted the first Macintosh trees in Londonderry on the Pillsbury farm, which later became Woodmont Orchards. Mack's Farm (which later became Moose Hill Orchards) followed Pillsbury's example of growing apples, as did other farms, such as Elwood Orchards on Elwood Road, Sunnycrest Farm on High Range Road, Hussey Farm on south Mammoth Road, Whittemore Farm on north Mammoth Road, Nesmith Farm on Skim Milk Road, the Wesley Adams Orchard on Nashua Road, and the Cheney Orchard on Litchfield Road.

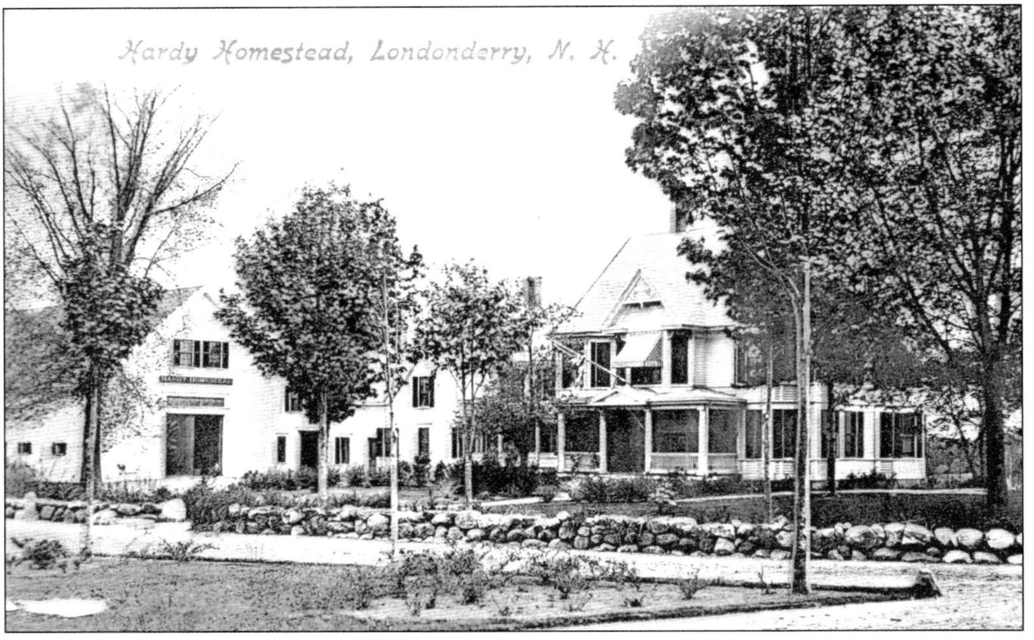


**THE HARDY HOMESTEAD C. 1910.** Aaron P. Hardy, the son of Daniel and Sarah Hardy, owned this beautiful home. An industrious man, Hardy learned to make shoes at a young age, and by 1836, at age 21, he had earned $400. He later used the money to buy land, and his holdings soon grew from 35 acres to 800 acres. Delia W. Brickett married Hardy and helped support the family by making braided hats at home, which she sold for 7¢ each. In addition to farming and shoe manufacturing, Aaron Hardy owned two retail stores: Hardy & Pillsbury and A. P. Hardy and Son.

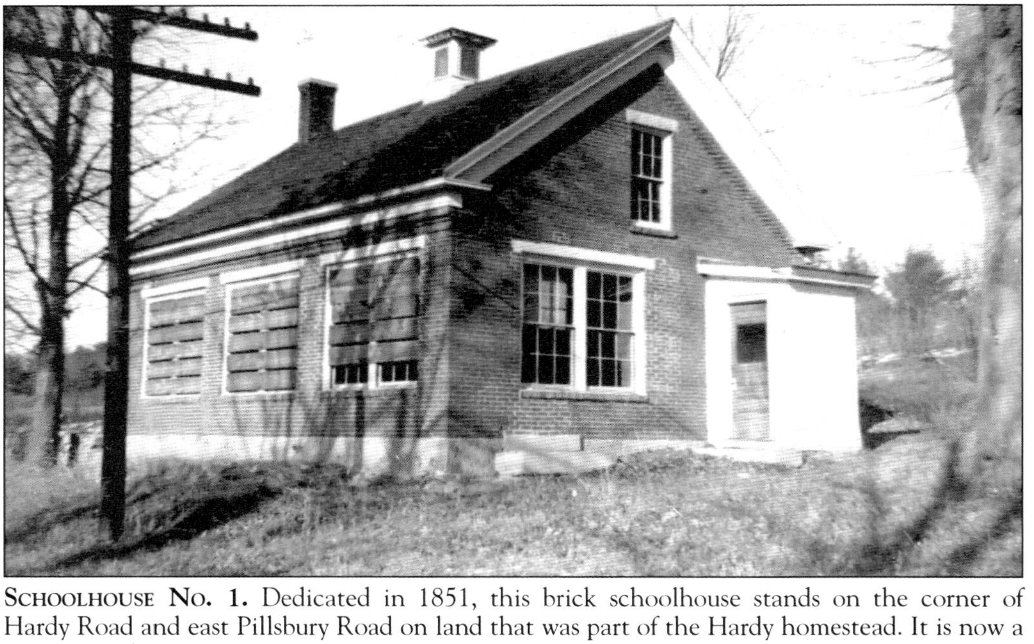

**SCHOOLHOUSE NO. 1.** Dedicated in 1851, this brick schoolhouse stands on the corner of Hardy Road and east Pillsbury Road on land that was part of the Hardy homestead. It is now a private residence.

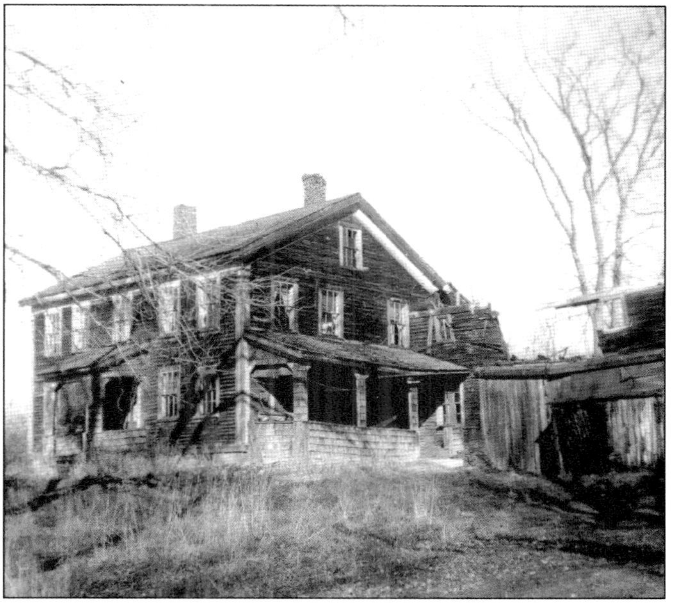

**The Hiram Cross House.** This home was located on Mammoth Road where Leach Library is today. Hiram N. Cross was born on March 3, 1876, and married Ernestine E. Nugent on June 14, 1909. It was estimated in 1962 that the home was 200 years old. It was beautifully landscaped with forsythia and lilacs. Civil War veteran Granville Plummer remembered attending "kissing parties" held in the front parlor.

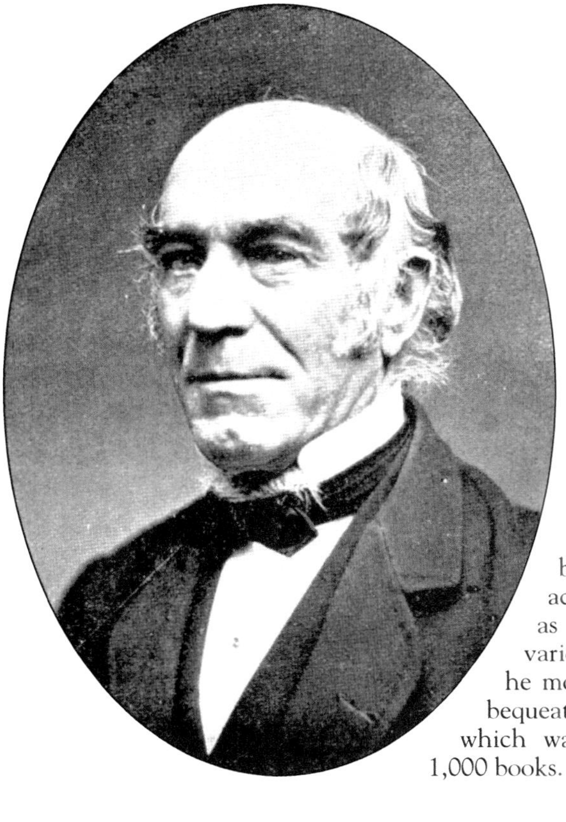

**David Rollins Leach.** Born in Londonderry on August 8, 1806, David Rollins Leach worked in the brick business and settled in Bedford and Hooksett. Eventually he bought land in Londonderry and went into the lumber business. He lived on Auburn Road across from Schoolhouse No. 9. He served as selectman and in the state legislature at various times from 1851 to 1865. Although he moved to Manchester in his later years, he bequeathed $3,000 to found the Leach Library, which was opened on February 25, 1880, with 1,000 books.

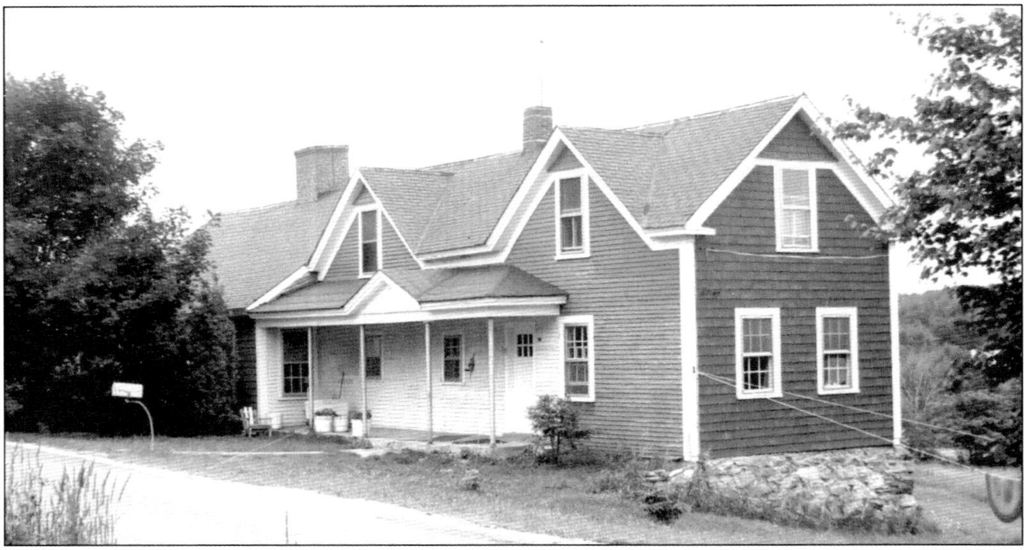

**THE BRESNAHAN-MACDONALD HOUSE (THE POOR HOUSE).** Early records show that Londonderry did not neglect its poor. In the early 19th century, destitute people were sold off to the lowest bidder at public auctions. The winning bidder would be under contract to provide room, board, and medical treatment for the pauper. Bidders were paid by the town at the end of the year for their service. Londonderry also cared for its poor by operating the poorhouse on Stonehenge Road from 1833 to 1877. Here, the destitute lived, worked, and maintained the building, growing their own food in order to reduce the town's cost of caring for them. Eventually the town poorhouses were abandoned and replaced with county poorhouses, as required by the state. In 1874, the Bresnahans bought the house and donated part of the property to connect Stonehenge Road to Mammoth Road. Elsie MacDonald was a later owner of the property.

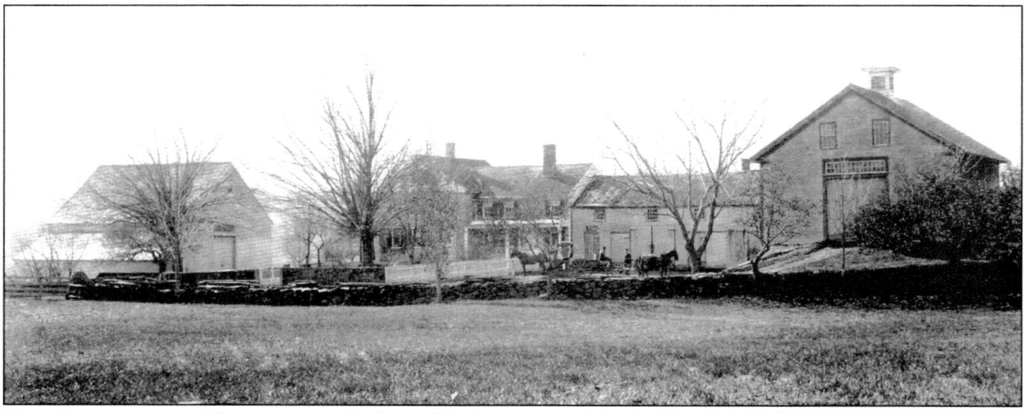

**THE STONEHENGE HOMESTEAD.** Robert Clark came to Nutfield in 1725 from Northern Ireland. His descendant Reed Paige Clark bought a farm owned by John Dickey in Londonderry in 1840. He built this stone house in 1844. Reed Paige Clark III, born August 27, 1929, had this to say about Stonehenge: "It is a typical New England farmhouse with all sheds and barns attached. The stones were taken from the surrounding grounds, and it was built with strictly utilitarian as opposed to luxury standards. Electricity was added in 1956, and the indoor bathroom was placed by my grandfather in 1915. The running water was pushed from the well by a forced-air system, which has been replaced with an electric pump."

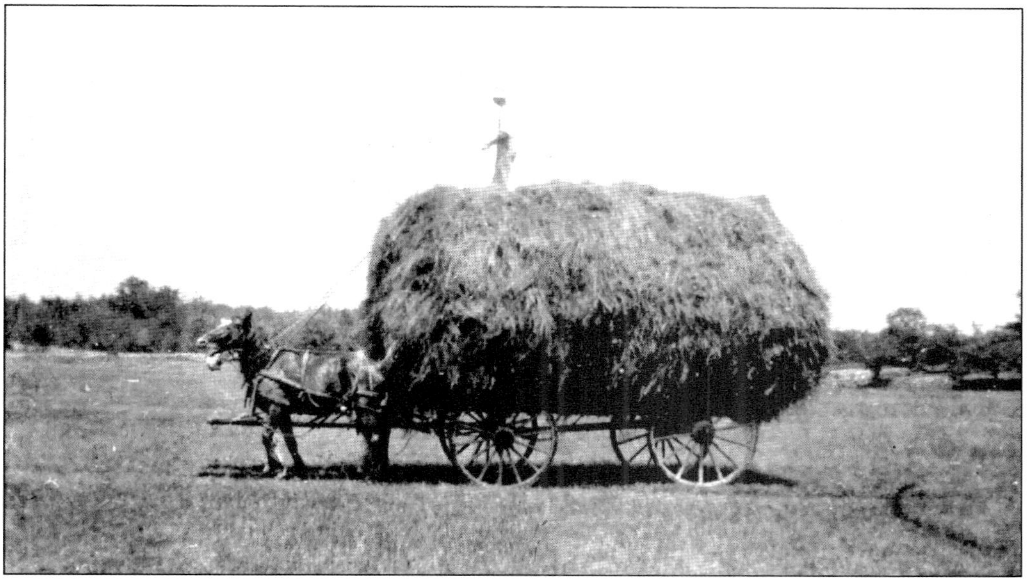

**HAYING AT STONEHENGE, 1897.** This team of horses is pulling a full hayrick, which is a large, wooden, basket-like wagon with a flat bottom and slats placed two to three feet apart on the sides. Hay was piled carefully into the rick to prevent tangling and to assist unloading at the barn. It was customary for people to make wishes when seeing a full hayrick pass by.

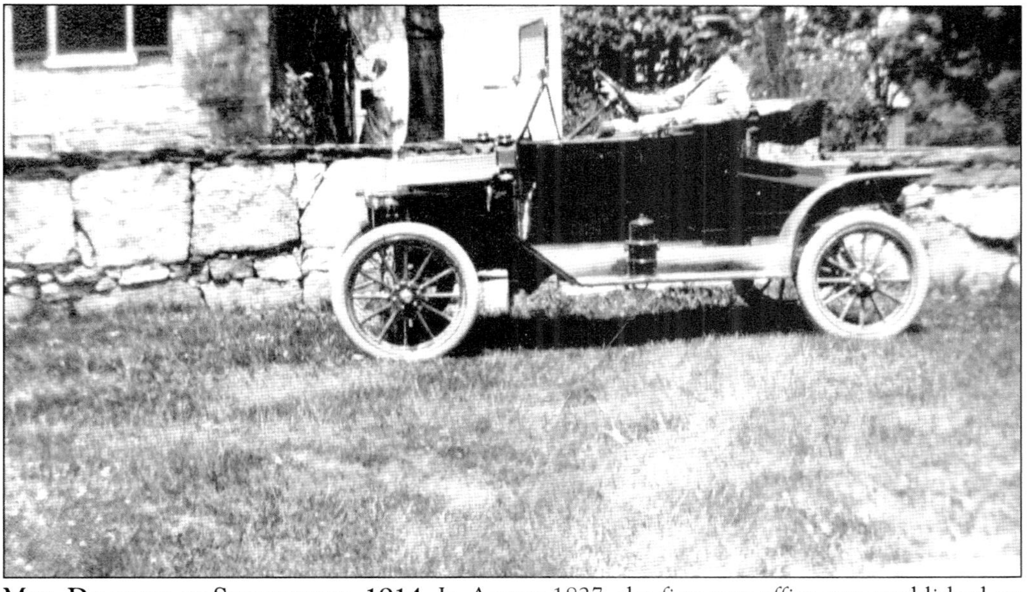

**MAIL DELIVERY AT STONEHENGE, 1914.** In August 1827, the first post office was established on High Range Road. The first postmaster was Ebenezer Whittier. During the following years, the post office moved often, and postmasters changed frequently, sometimes on a yearly basis. A post office was established in the north end of town on May 21, 1832, with Reuben White serving as postmaster. Many of the various sites of the post office were in stores and other public spaces, such as William Anderson's store, William Caldwell's store, and the hotel of Reuben White.

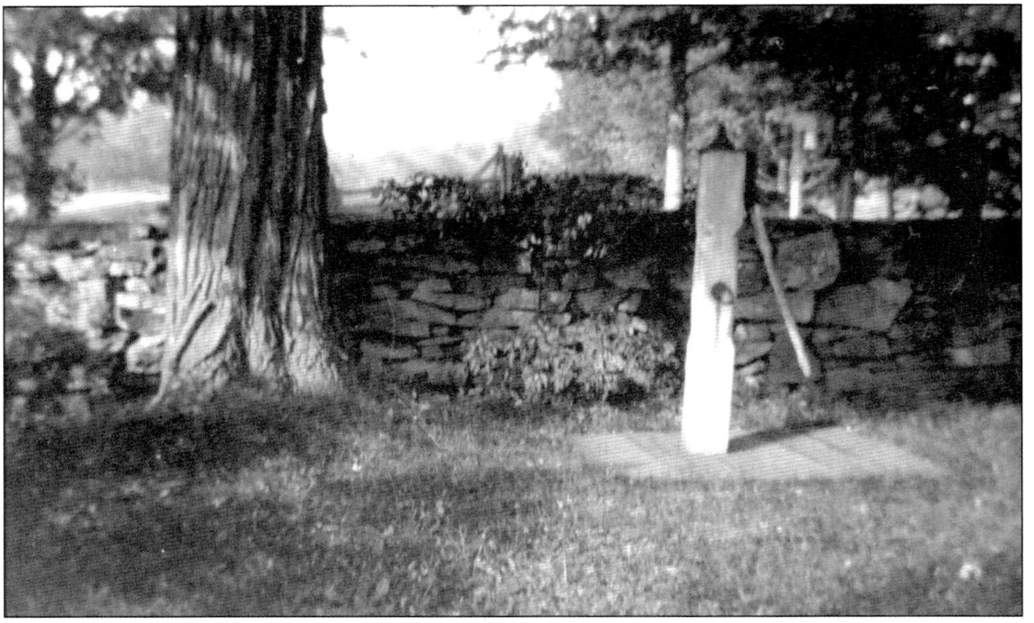

**A Furber Pump, 1914.** A company started by John S. Furber made this pump in north Londonderry. His factory and home were located across from Crowell's Corner on Mammoth Road, on the present site of a mobile-home park. These "improved" wooden pumps were for sale in north Londonderry, and it was claimed they could fill a barrel of water in one minute.

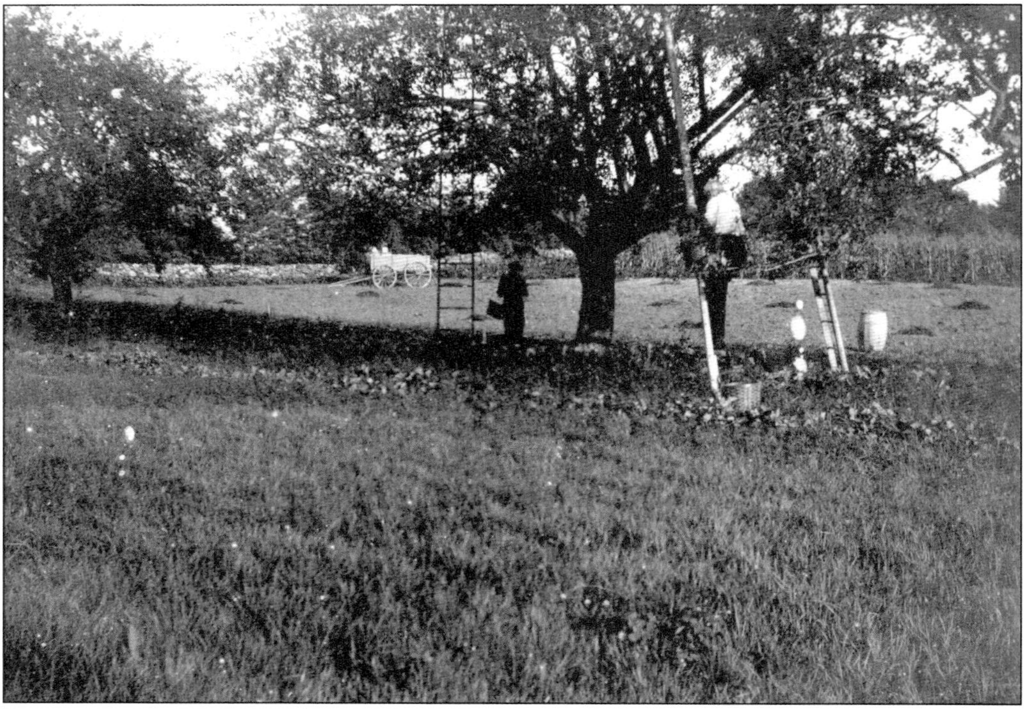

**Picking Apples, 1902.** The people in this photograph are picking apples at an orchard near Stonehenge.

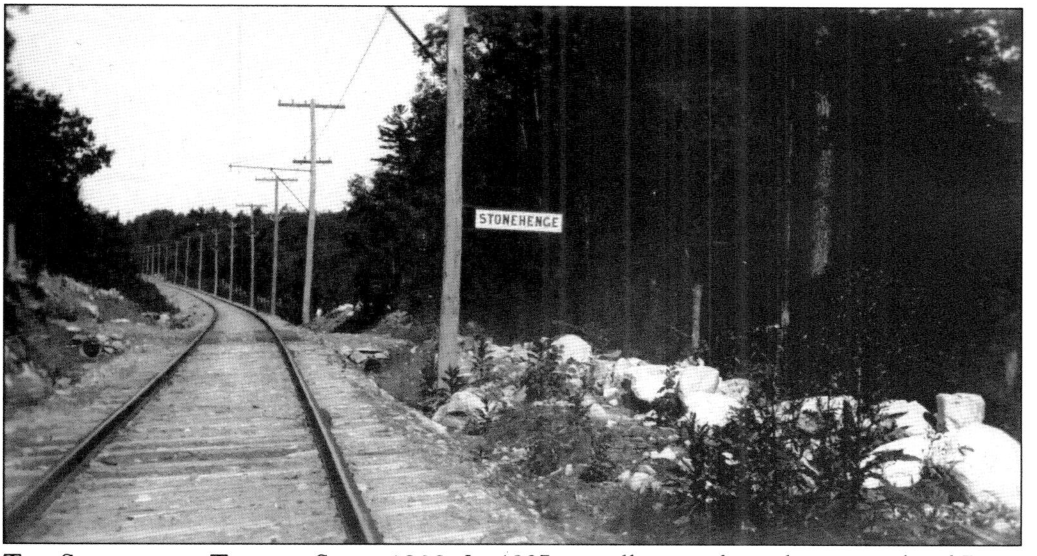


**The Stonehenge Trolley Stop, 1908.** In 1907, a trolley ran from the west side of Derry through the north end of Londonderry to Manchester. After running for a little less than 20 years, the trolley ceased operation on August 31, 1926.

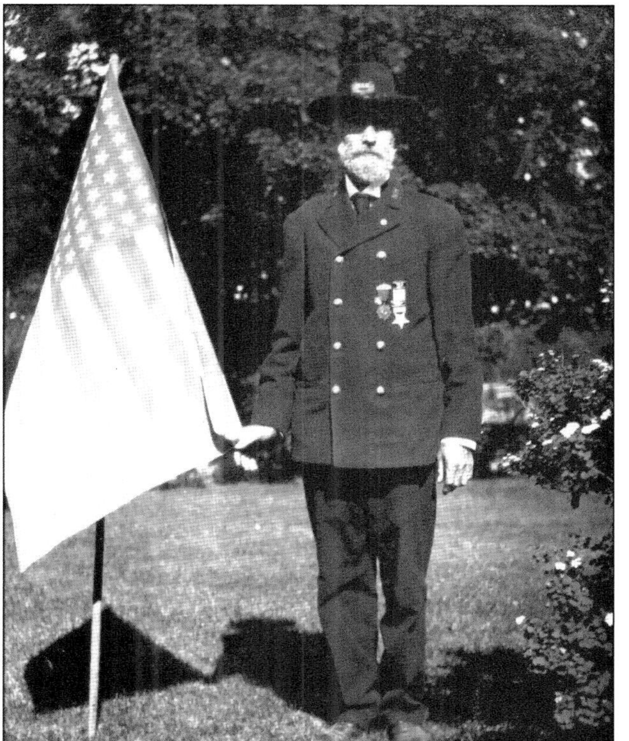

**William Clark, 1911.** William Clark is seen here wearing the same uniform he wore 46 years earlier while serving as a corporal in the Civil War as a member of Company D of the 1st New Hampshire Heavy Artillery. Clark returned home and followed his father's farming vocation. He was an important member of the community and served at various times as a legislator, deputy sheriff of Rockingham and Hillsborough Counties, a justice of the peace, and a school board member. He was also instrumental in organizing Grange No. 44. Clark married Alice McIntire on August 23, 1876, and they had two sons, Reed Paige and Ralph. Clark died in 1916 during a flu epidemic.

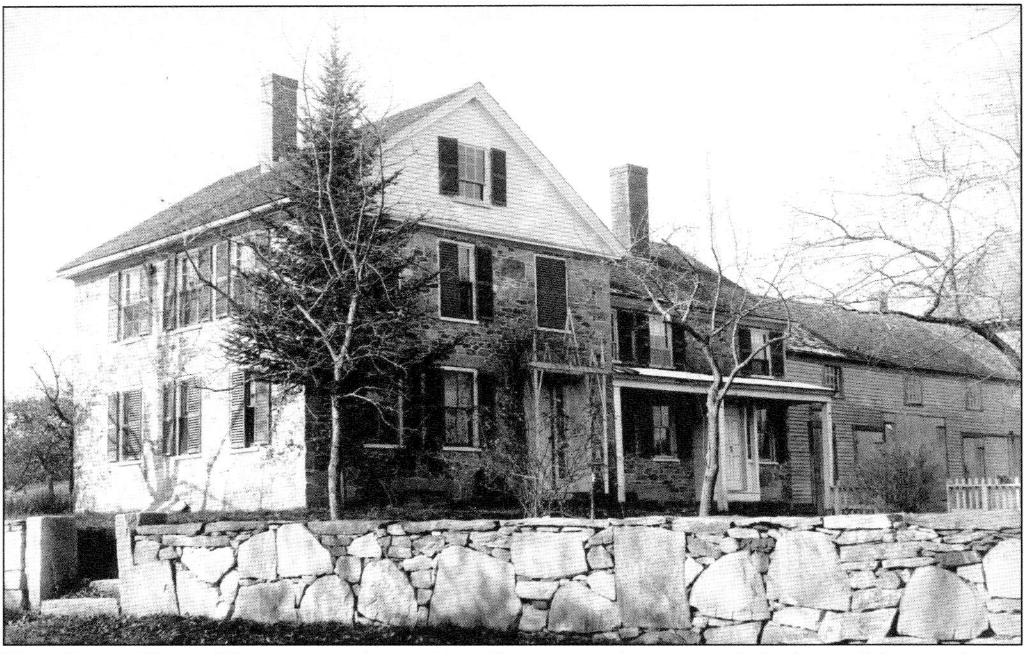

**THE CLARK HOME (STONEHENGE) C. 1910.** Here is another view of the beautiful stone home built by Reed Paige Clark Sr. in 1844, located on the corner of Stonehenge and Perkins Roads. Reed Clark II worked in public and foreign service for 40 years. He graduated from law school in 1898 and was a clerk to various senate committees, a general receiver of customs in Liberia, and a consul in many foreign countries. The home continues to be occupied by members of the Clark family, Reed Paige Clark III and his wife, Phyllis.

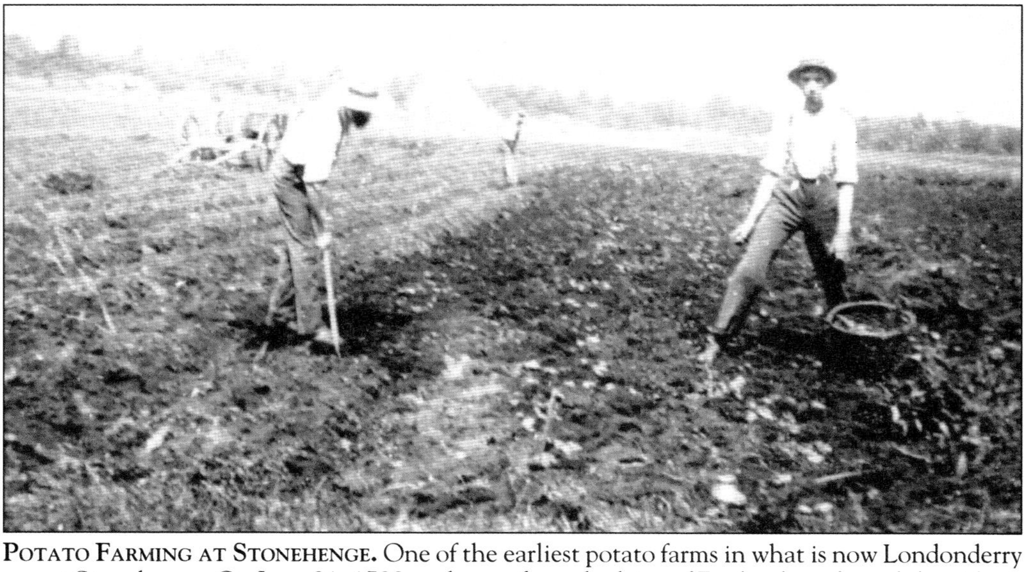

**POTATO FARMING AT STONEHENGE.** One of the earliest potato farms in what is now Londonderry was at Stonehenge. On June 21, 1722, a charter from the king of England confirmed the title to the town of Londonderry but stated that once a year, forever, they should pay the king a quitrent of one peck of potatoes.

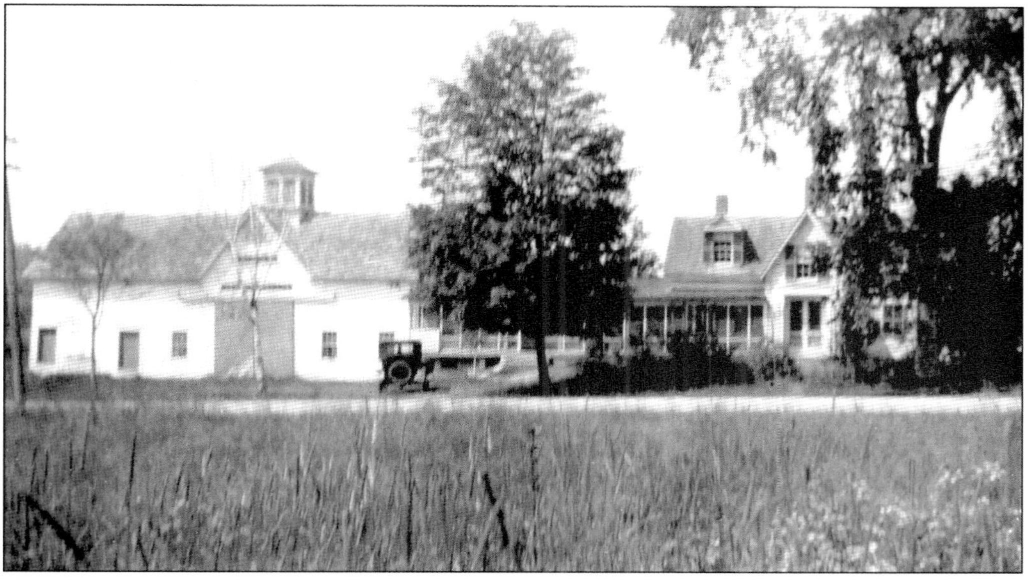

**The Crowell Home at Crowell's Corner c. 1920.** David Crowell settled in Londonderry before 1775. His grandson Henry married Judith Plummer in 1850, and they lived on the southwest side of the corner of Mammoth and Litchfield Roads. Together, they ran an 85-acre farm while Henry worked as a traveling salesman for Dunn Edge Tool Company. When Henry Crowell died in 1906, the house was occupied by his granddaughter Mary Crowell Brown. She added a large porch and a new chimney and fireplace.

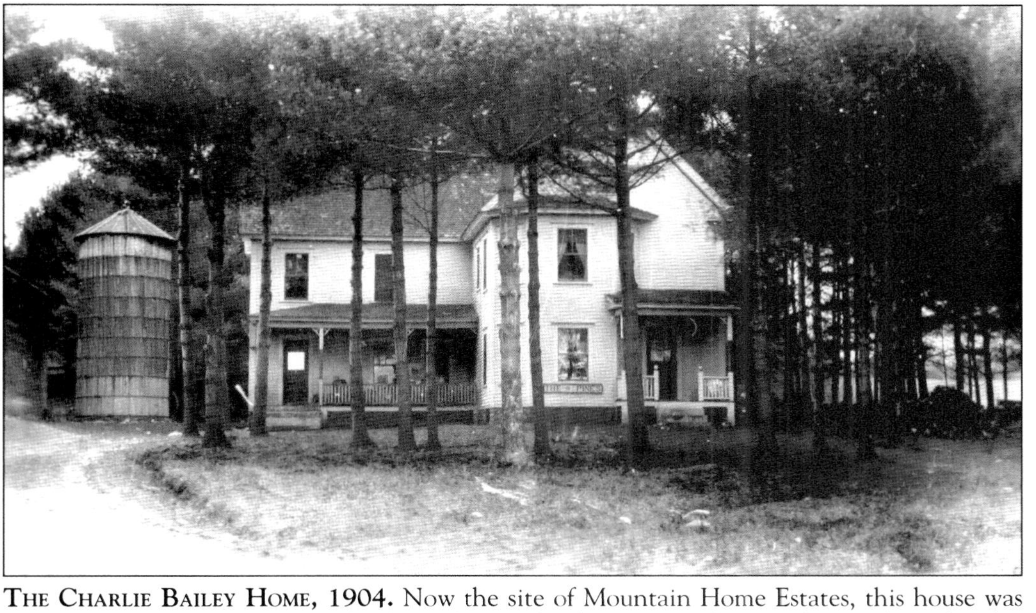

**The Charlie Bailey Home, 1904.** Now the site of Mountain Home Estates, this house was built on Mammoth Road after Charlie Bailey's earlier home on Kelley Road burned. Carl Bailey was the last of the family to live here.

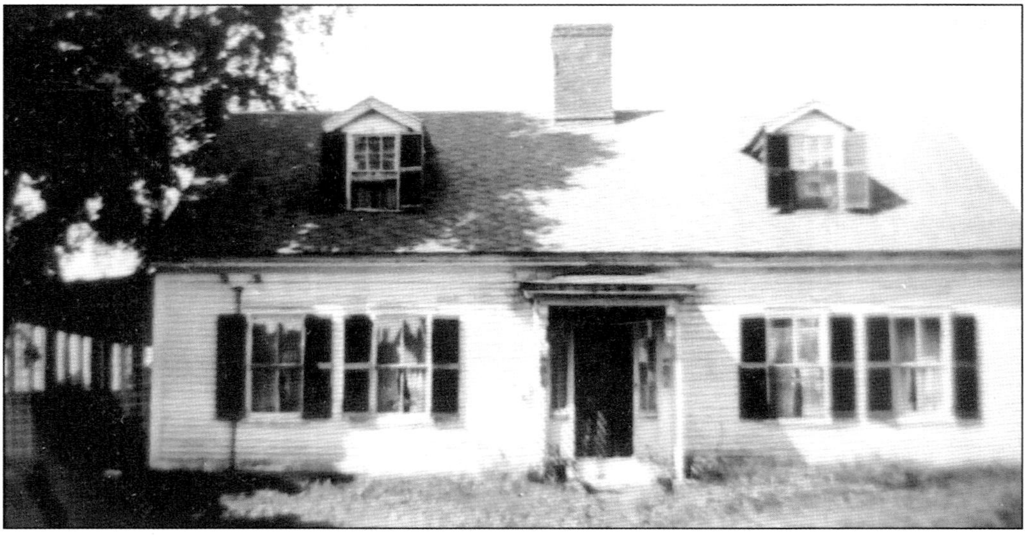

**THE WATTS-COLBY-KIDDER HOUSE.** Moses Watts built this home on Mammoth Road in 1752 and lived here with his wife, Peggy, and their 13 children. Four of his sons fought in the Revolutionary War. In 1792, the home was given to his son James. In 1857, it became the home of Ebenezer Colby, and during the mid-20th century, it became the property of the Kidders, who sold antiques. They uncovered the kitchen fireplace to find an old crane, early S hooks, and a Dutch oven hidden by an old pine door.

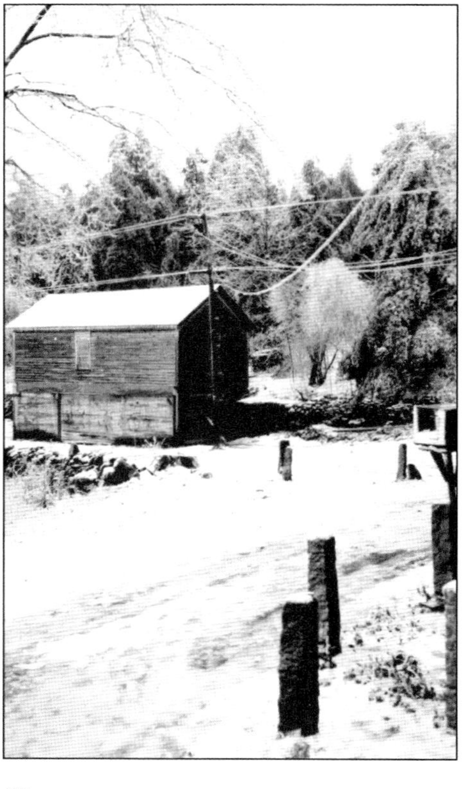

**THE COBBLER SHOP ON BLODGETT FARM.** This shop was located on Rockingham Road near Stonehenge on the farm of Isaac Blodgett, which was called Echo Farm. Young men, usually under the age of 30, made shoes in similar cobbler shops throughout New England. Colonel Pillsbury and Aaron Hardy both started as shoemakers. Echo Farm burned in October 1916.

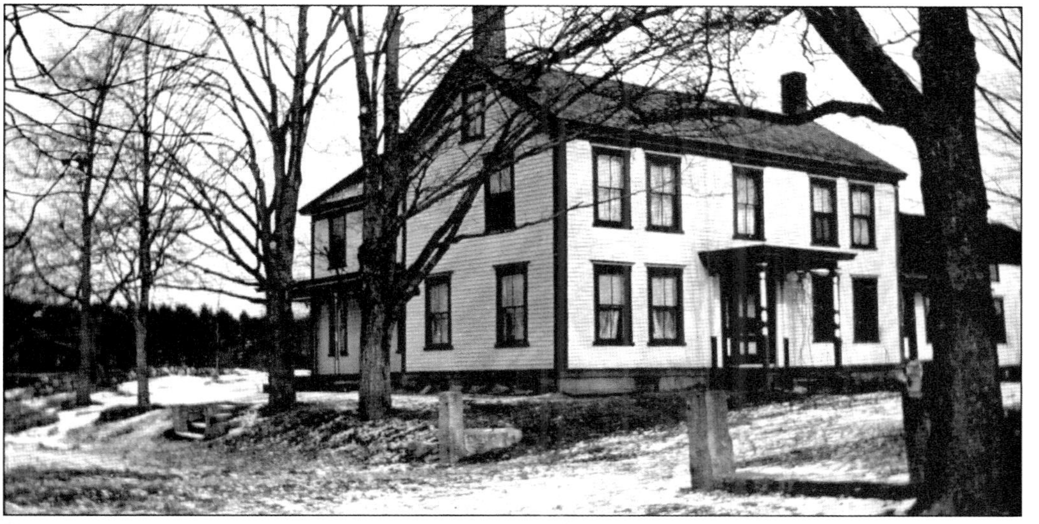

**THE PLUMMER HOUSE ON PERKINS ROAD.** During the late 18th and early 19th centuries this was the home of Jonathan Griffin, a cooper, deacon, and selectman. Upon his death, his wife, Hannah, sold the home to Edmund Adams, and it remained in the Adams family for about 75 years. Originally a Cape Cod–style house, the Plummer House was rebuilt and enlarged in 1873. At some point an ell was added and a cobbler shop was joined to the house by a shed. Alfred Plummer bought the house in 1904.

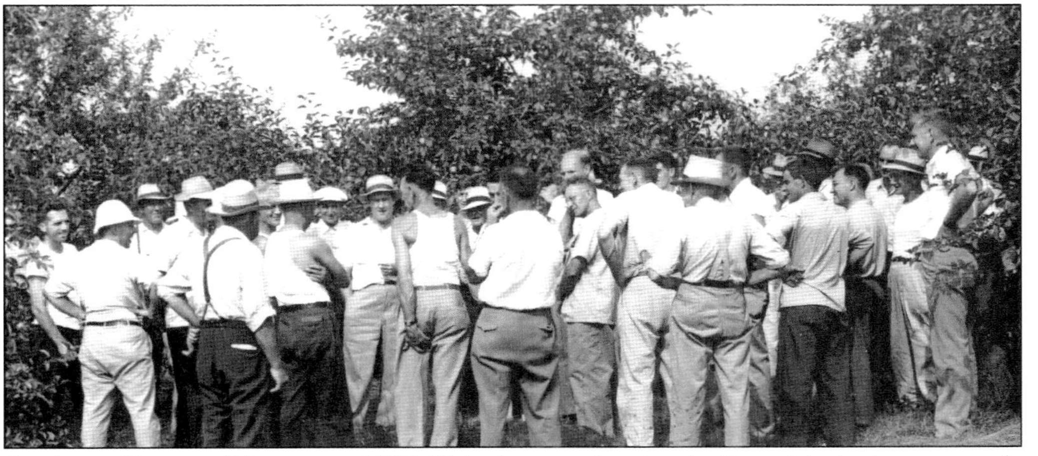

**AN APPLE GROWERS MEETING C. 1950.** This photograph, taken by Grace Mack, shows an apple growers meeting at Moose Hill Orchard. Pictured are local apple growers, who are probably discussing such topics as pest control, disease control, and the health of the year's apple crop.

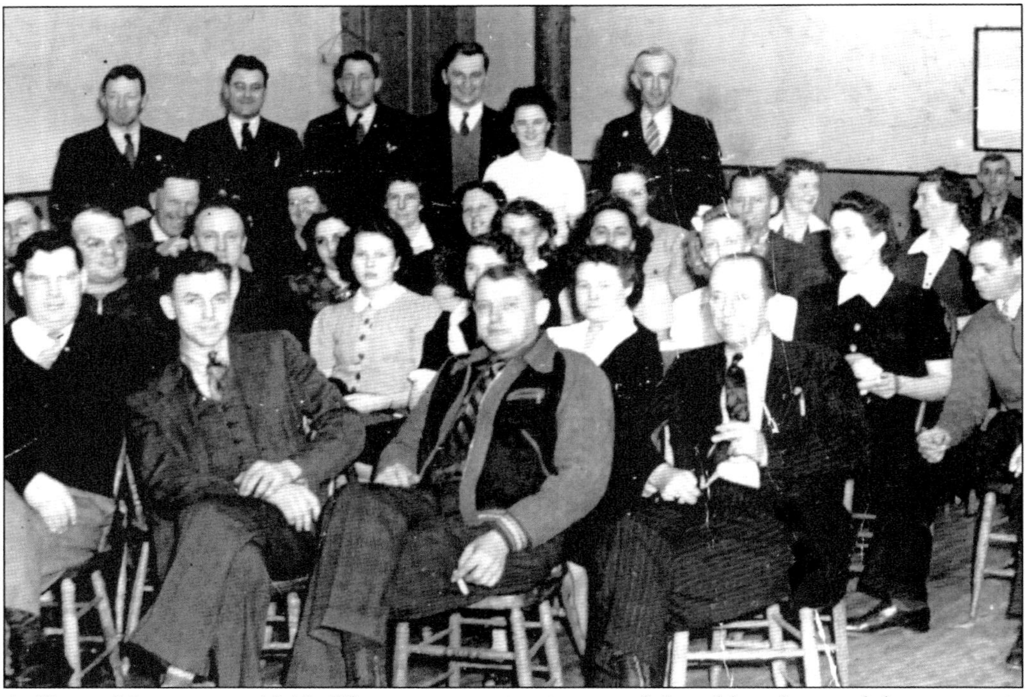

**A Town Meeting c. 1948.** The town meeting is one of the oldest forms of democracy in North America. These gatherings ensure that townspeople have a direct voice in the governing of the town. Here, Londonderry citizens attend a meeting in the old town hall, now the Lions Hall.

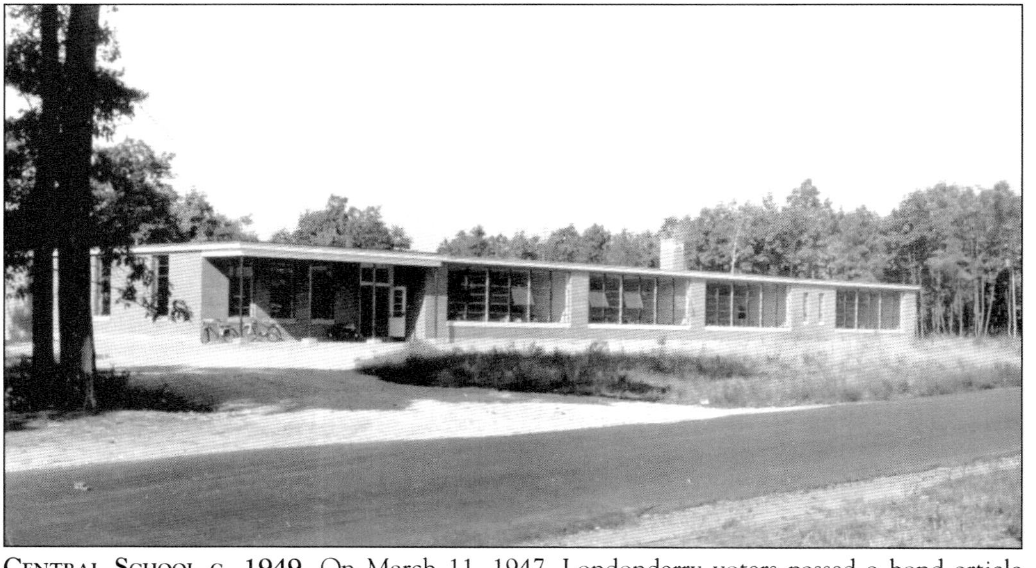

**Central School c. 1949.** On March 11, 1947, Londonderry voters passed a bond article authorizing the district to spend $90,000 for the construction of Londonderry Central School. It opened its doors on September 9, 1949, to 268 students. Over the next 30 years, additions were made to Central School to accommodate the ever-increasing student population and its needs. In the 1975–1976 academic year, it became known as Matthew Thornton School.

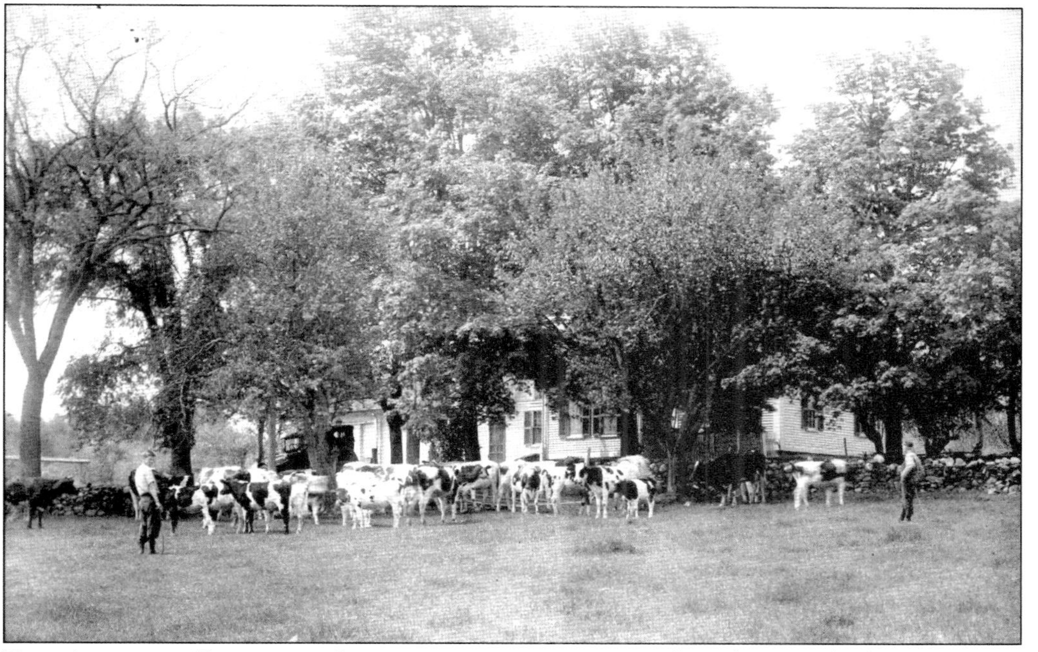

**The Anderson Farm and Slaughterhouse c. 1930.** This photograph shows cows at Anderson Farm.

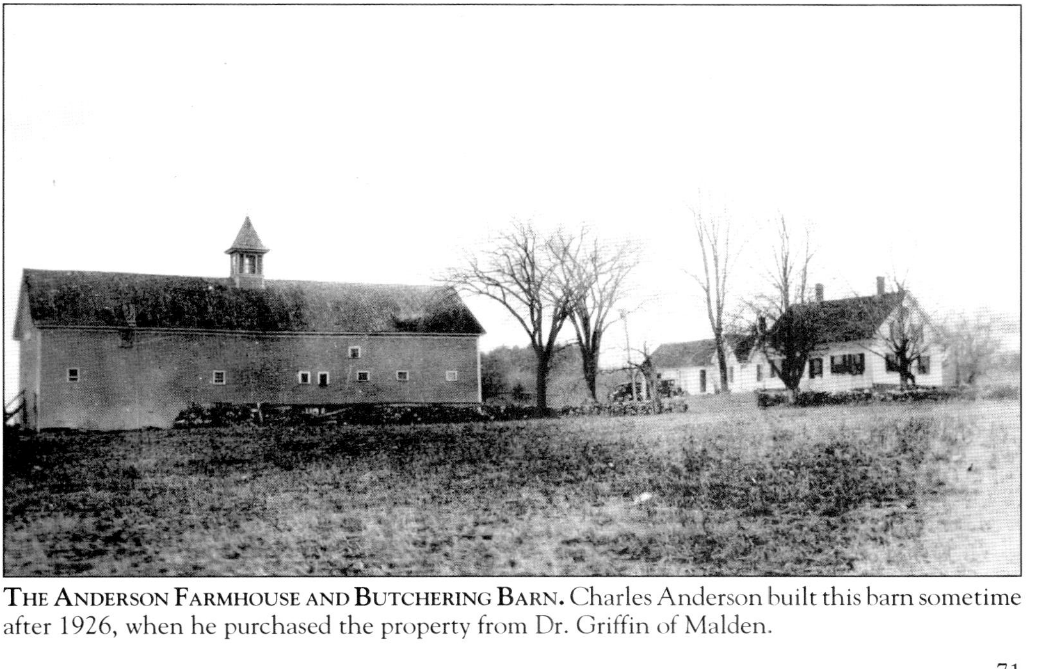

**The Anderson Farmhouse and Butchering Barn.** Charles Anderson built this barn sometime after 1926, when he purchased the property from Dr. Griffin of Malden.

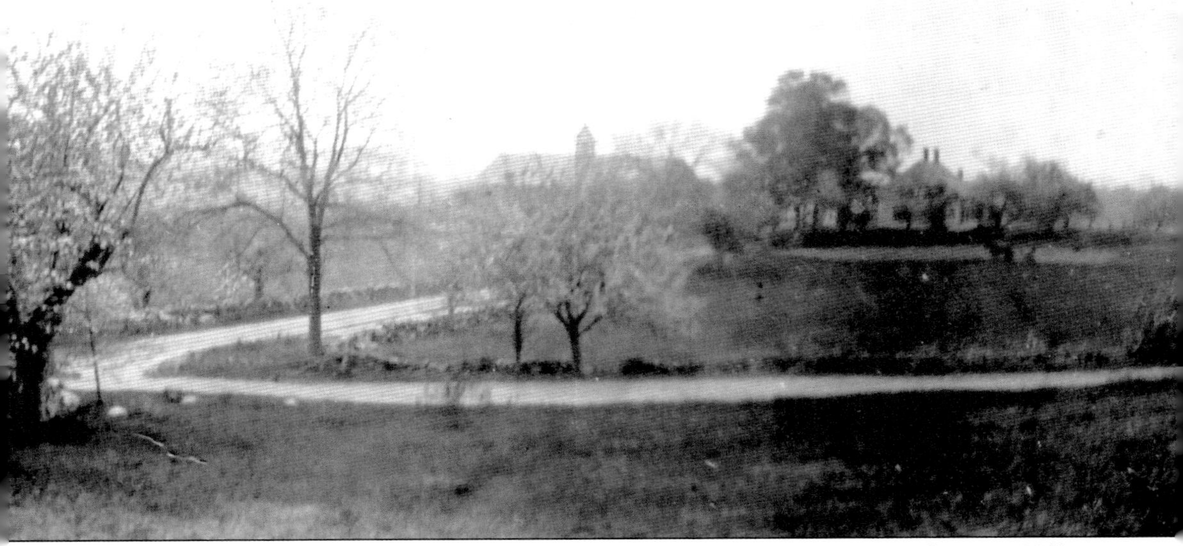

**Anderson Farm.** This farm, ideally situated behind the protective crest of Moose Hill, was located on Anderson Lane off Pillsbury Road. It was bought by Samuel Dickey, whose parents came to Londonderry before 1730. He married Martha Taylor in 1732 and later left the farm to his two sons, Adam and Robert, when he moved to Greenfield. It remained in the family until unmarried family members died and the property was willed to Dr. Griffin of Malden. Charles Anderson bought it from Dr. Griffin in 1926. Here, he ran a dairy, sold vegetables, and had a butchering business.

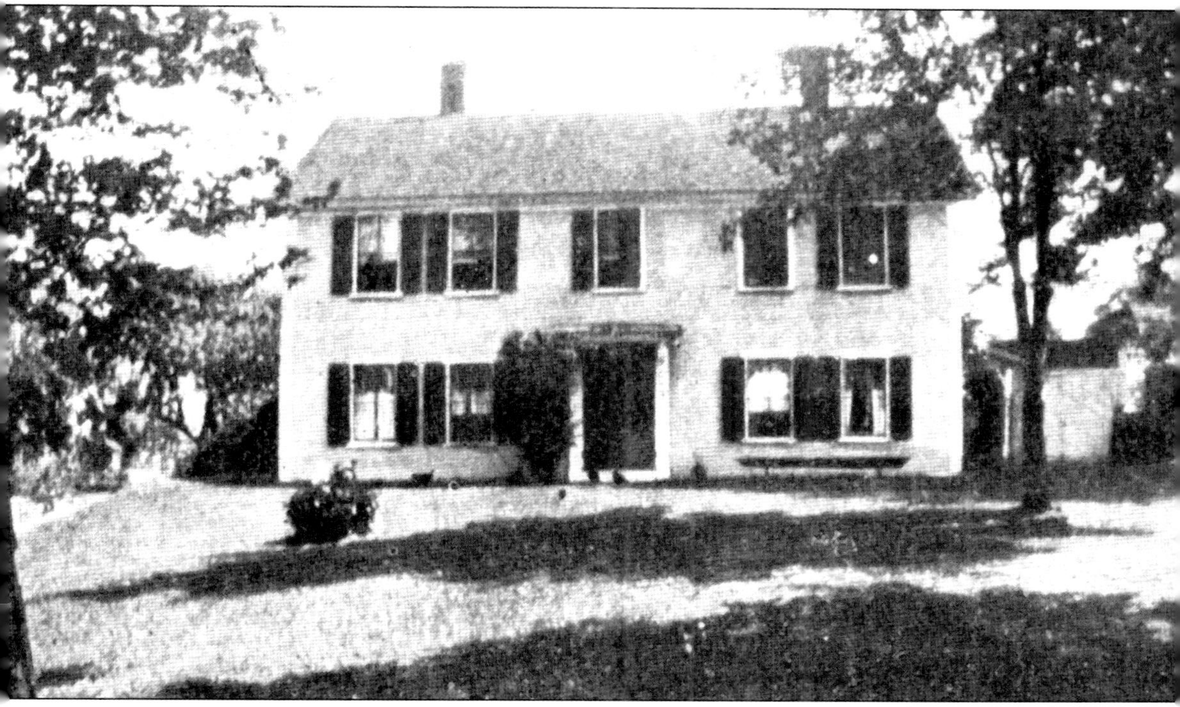

**Sunset View Farm.** Mattie Woods married Charles Adams in 1885 and returned to her parents' home on Mammoth Road to care for them. Adams operated her farm, also known as the Mattie Woods Adams Farm, as a boardinghouse. She also served as town clerk of Londonderry for many years, running the office from her home.

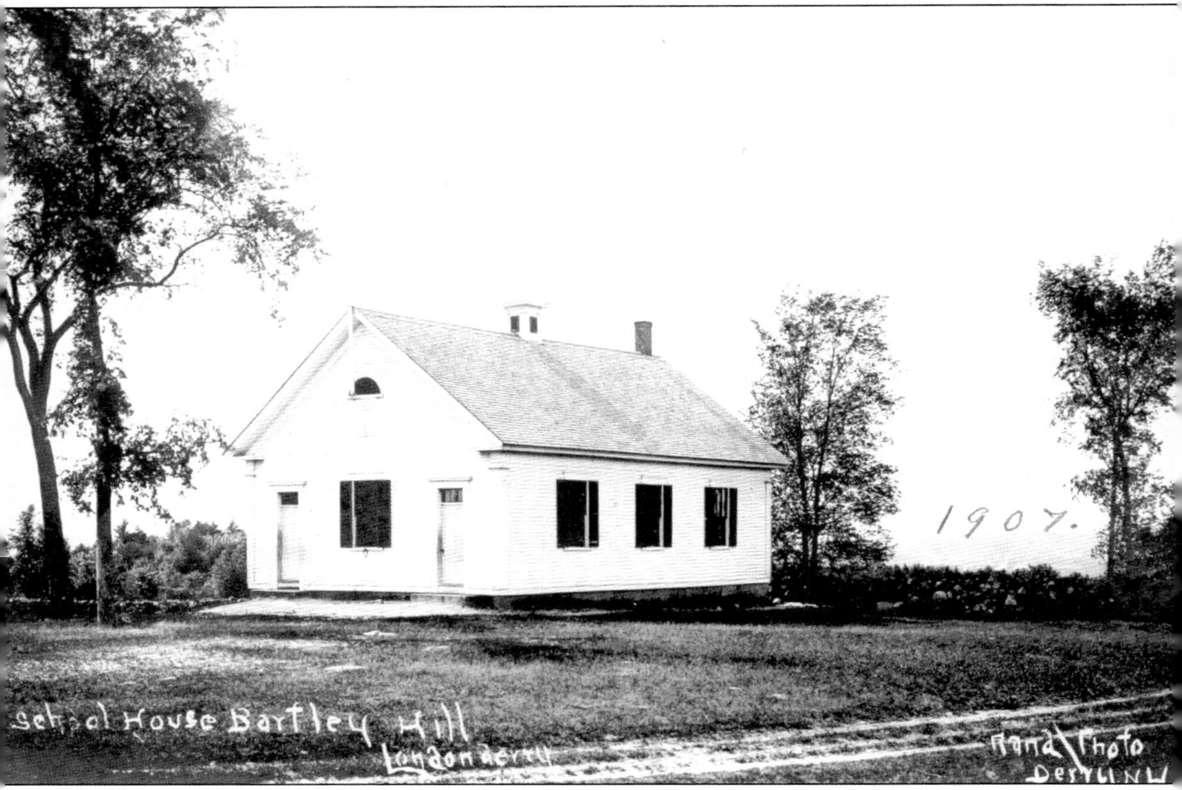


**SCHOOLHOUSE NO. 8.** Before the Revolutionary War, New England towns were required to provide tax-free schools. By the early 1800s, towns where divided into districts. Schoolhouse No. 8, located on Bartley Hill Road, replaced an old red 25-foot-by-17-foot schoolhouse that was built in 1794. This newer building was finished sometime in 1858, and a belfry was added in 1912. The building burned in 1931 and was replaced in 1932. Since they were often the only public buildings in their neighborhoods, schoolhouses served multiple purposes for the community, providing a place to hold events such as singing school, spelling competitions, and religious revivals.

# *Five*

# SCOBIE POND

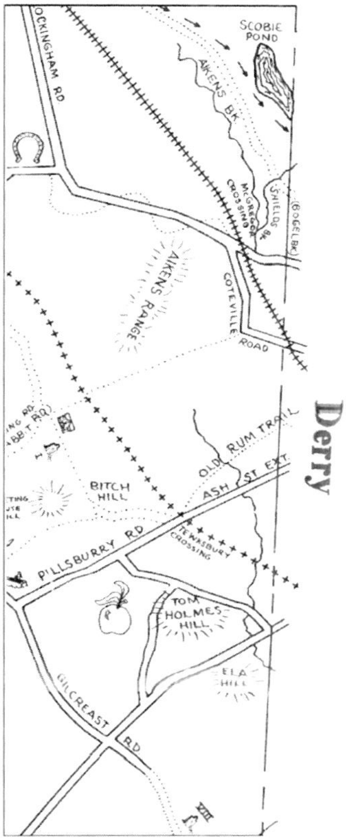


**EAST.** This eastern section of Londonderry is now the location of Exit 4 of Interstate 93.

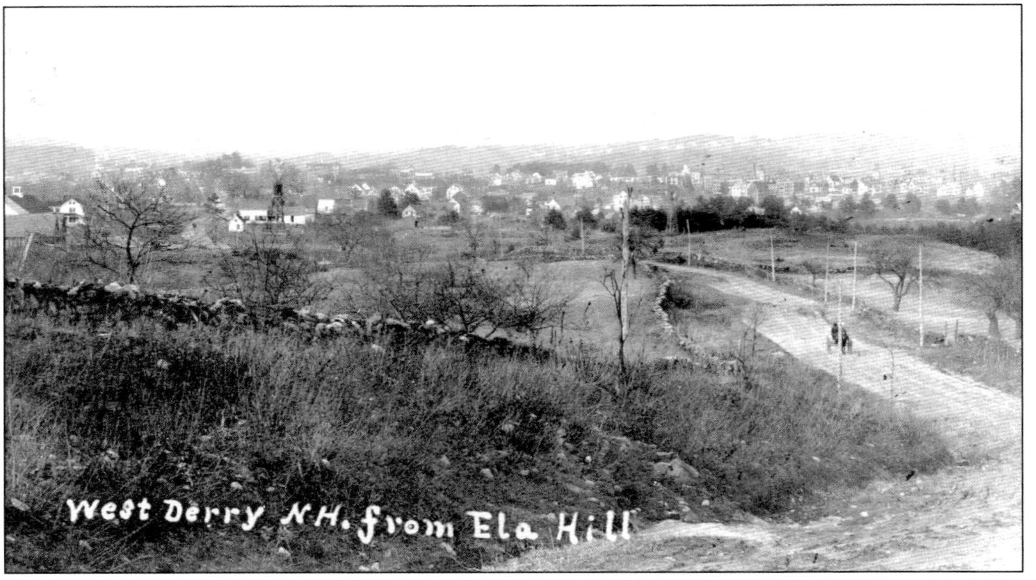


**DERRY, SEEN FROM ELA HILL IN LONDONDERRY C. 1920.** Looking east to Derry from Londonderry, at right we see a horse and buggy traveling the dirt road known as Old Nashua Road. Today, the horse would be on Route 102 crossing the bridge over Interstate 93. To the left of the stonewall are peach and apple trees and an open hay field. The 5,000-gallon tank in the distance furnished spring water to the Ela farm.

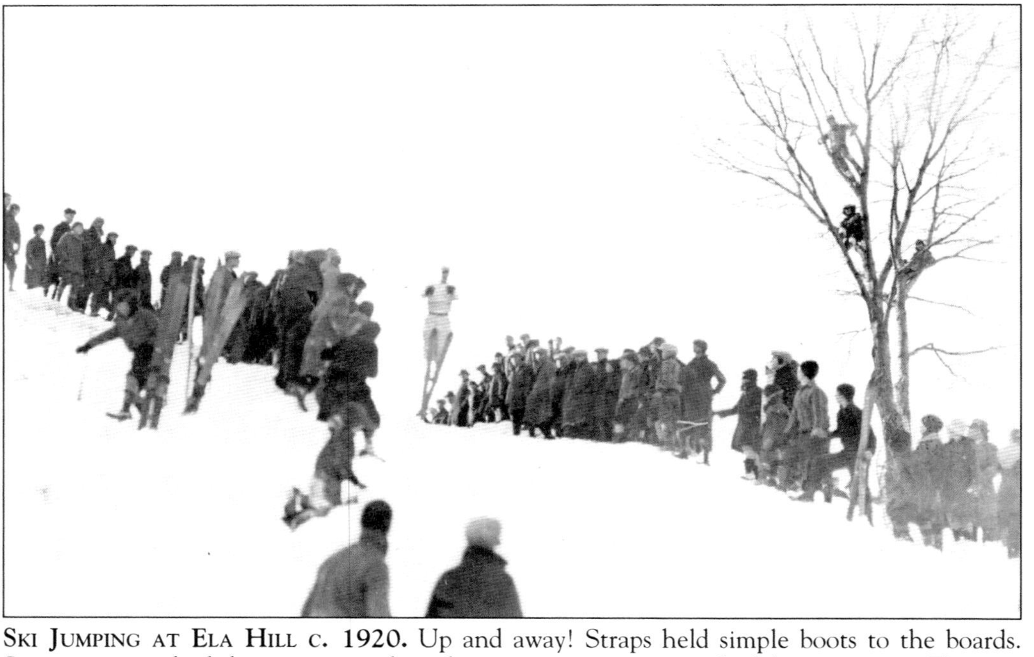

**SKI JUMPING AT ELA HILL C. 1920.** Up and away! Straps held simple boots to the boards. Spectators watched the jumpers with enthusiasm; some even watched from treetops. The area is now Exit 4 off Interstate 93.

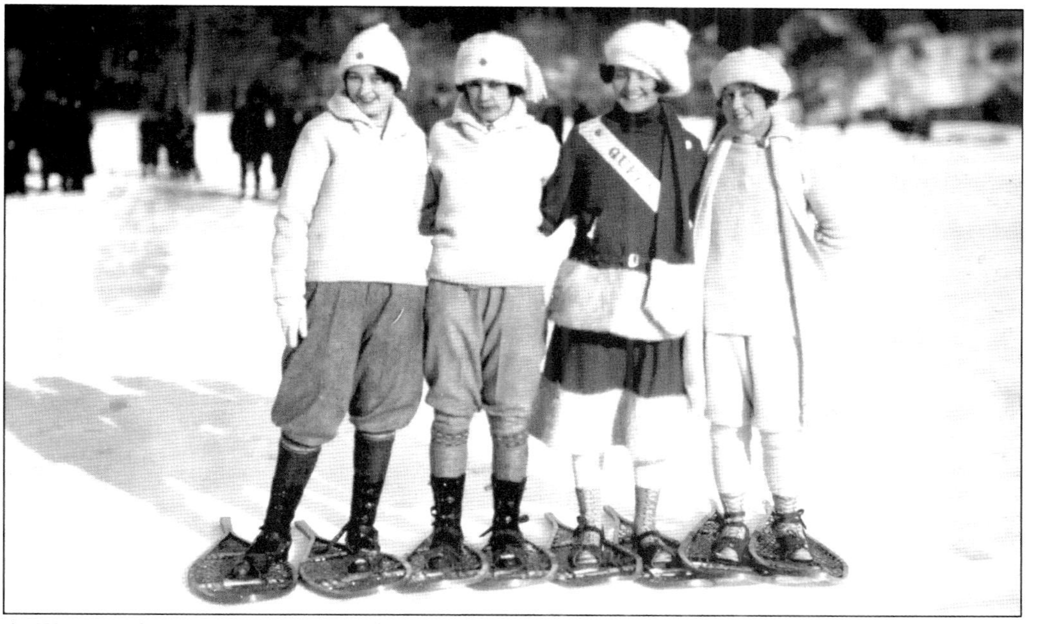

**A Winter Carnival c. 1926.** The Carnival Queen and her three smiling court attendants pose on the ice at Ela Pond. Warmly dressed and sporting their fashionable snowshoe footwear, they probably cannot wait to enter the little warming house at the right for hot chocolate. Note the skaters in the left background. Two restaurants and a gas station on Route 102 now surround the pond, which was once a great area for winter recreation.

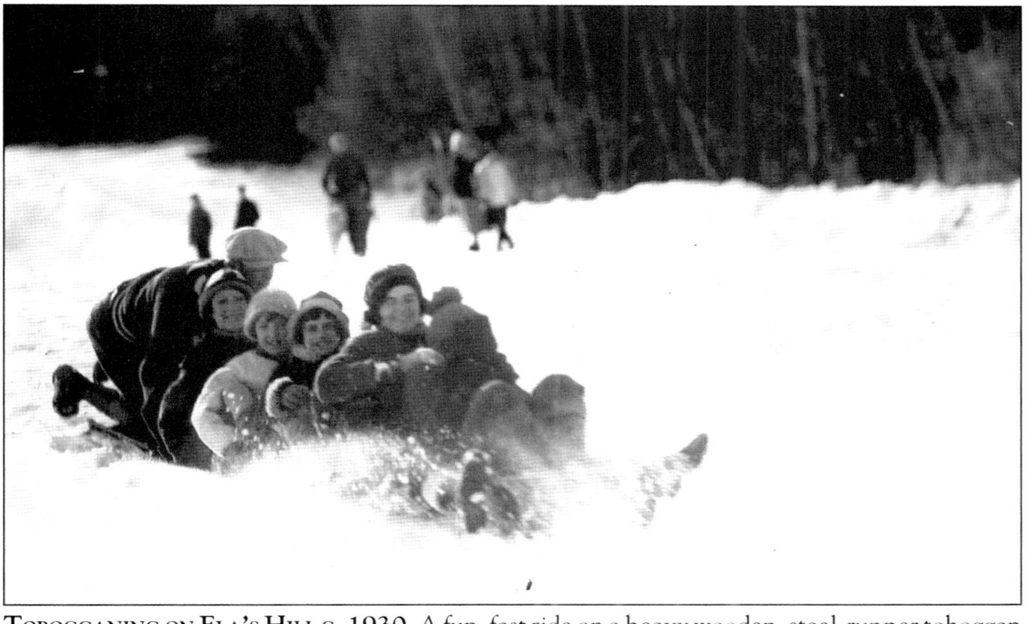

**Tobogganing on Ela's Hill c. 1930.** A fun, fast ride on a heavy wooden, steel-runner toboggan gave these children a thrill. After sledding down the hill, the kids hitched onto a horse-drawn log sled and were pulled back up. The area is now part of Exit 4 off Interstate 93.

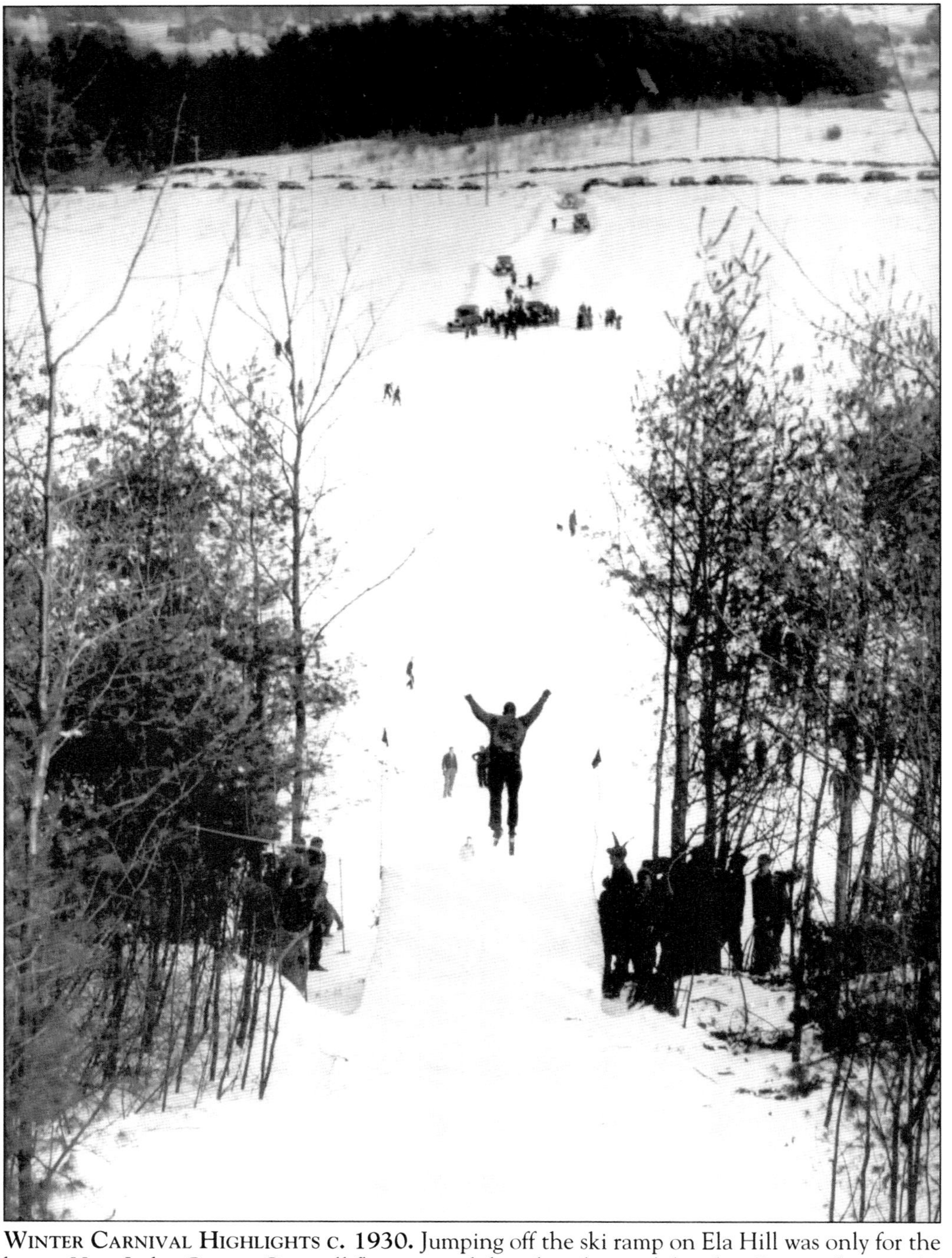

**Winter Carnival Highlights c. 1930.** Jumping off the ski ramp on Ela Hill was only for the brave. Here Judge George Grinnell flies not with his plane but with his skis. Six carefree youths once tobogganed down this ski jump, hoping to sail to a soft, snowy landing. Instead, they dropped like a rock to a bone-rattling jolt. Now they are 70-year-old survivors. The cars in the distance are parked on Old Nashua Road (Route 102). Today, Judge Grinnell and the youths would have landed on the southbound lanes of Interstate 93 near Exit 4.

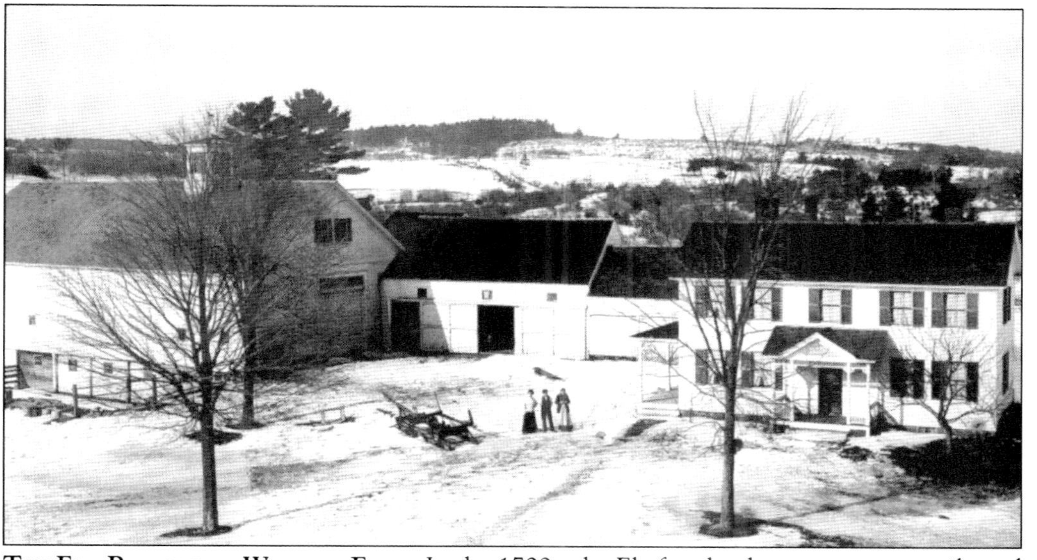

**The Ela-Parmenter-Wheeler Farm.** In the 1700s, the Ela farmland was one square mile and provided flax for Londonderry linen. The immense barn held 47 cows, 3 horses, and many chickens and pigs. The nearby pond was dammed for ice-cutting operations. The Parmenter family purchased the farm to grow and sell produce to the farmers' market. People enjoyed the plums, asparagus, potatoes, squash, pumpkins, and strawberries (which sold for only 5¢ a box). Mr. Wheeler owned the land when all of these old buildings were razed to make way for the Derry Plaza (Route 102) at the Londonderry-Derry line. He also built Spacetown Motel, which was razed in the 1980s. The construction of Interstate 93 in 1963 dramatically changed the area forever.

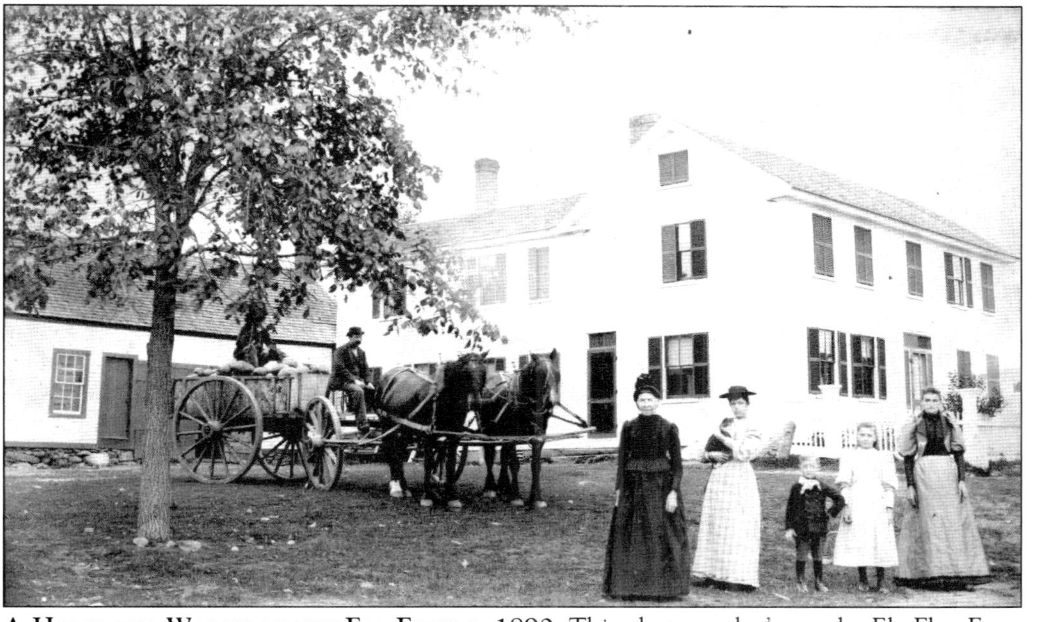

**A Horse and Wagon at the Ela Farm c. 1890.** This photograph shows the Ela Flax Farm near the Londonderry-Derry town line on Old Nashua Road (Route 102). The children in the photograph are Edward Ela and Mildred Ela (Pinkham).

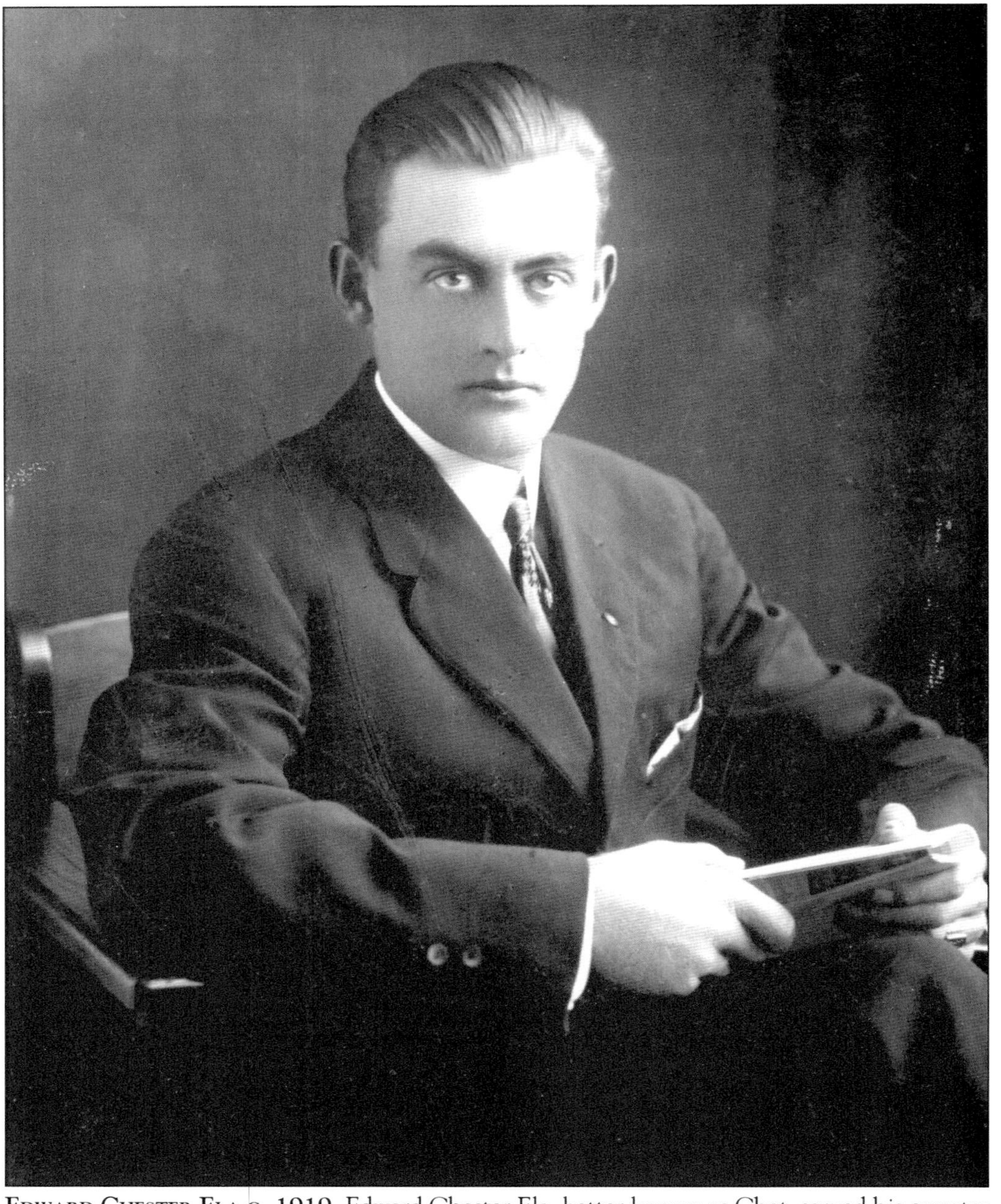

**EDWARD CHESTER ELA C. 1919.** Edward Chester Ela, better known as Chet, served his country in Europe during World War I. While stationed in England, he met his bride, Florence Davies. After the war, they returned to the United States and raised two daughters, Dorothy Ela (Ross) and Marilyn Ela (Moore). In his youth, Chet Ela lived on the large Ela Farm on Route 102. His daughter Dorothy provided this handsome portrait.

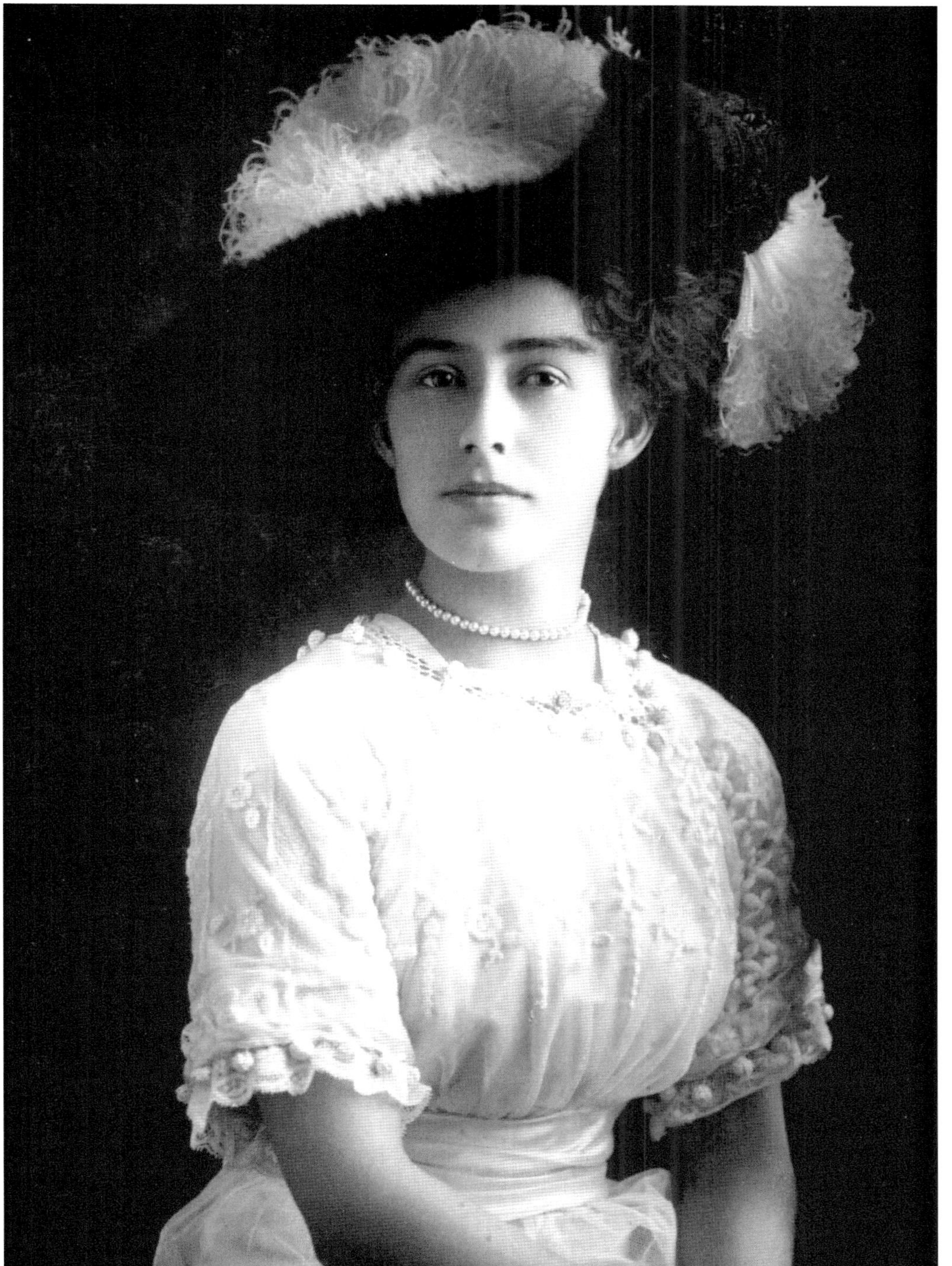

**FLORENCE DAVIES ELA C. 1919.** The lovely Florence Davies Ela was a World War I English war bride brought to the United States by her soldier husband, Edward Chester Ela. Her daughter Dorothy provided this beautiful portrait.

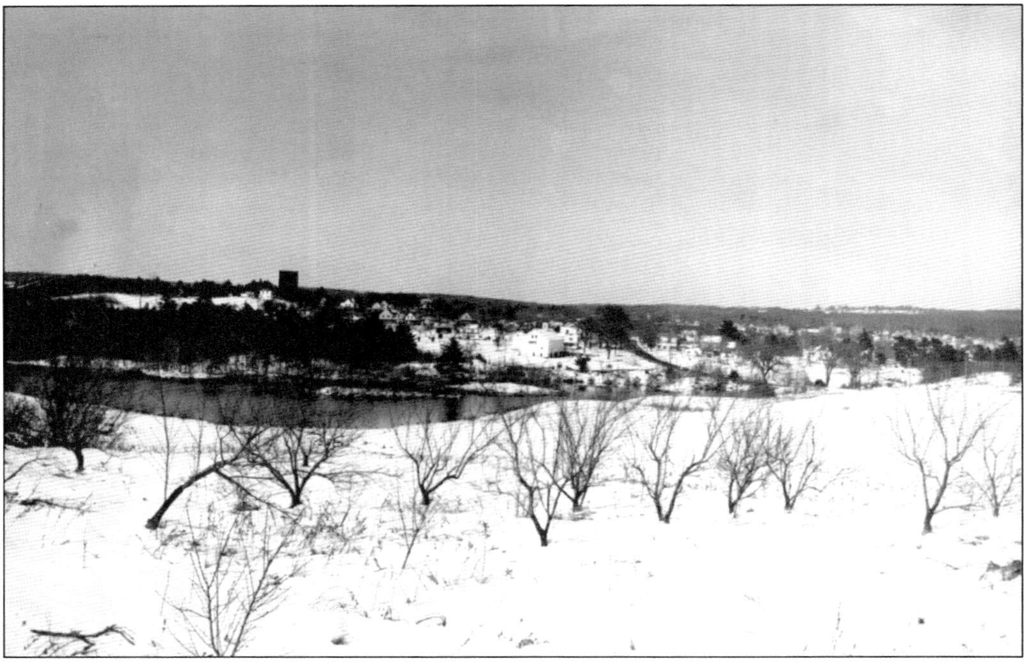

**ELA POND AND ELA FARM c. 1900.** This photograph, taken from Ela Hill, shows Old Nashua Road leading to the Ela property. This is now the site of Exit 4 off Interstate 93.

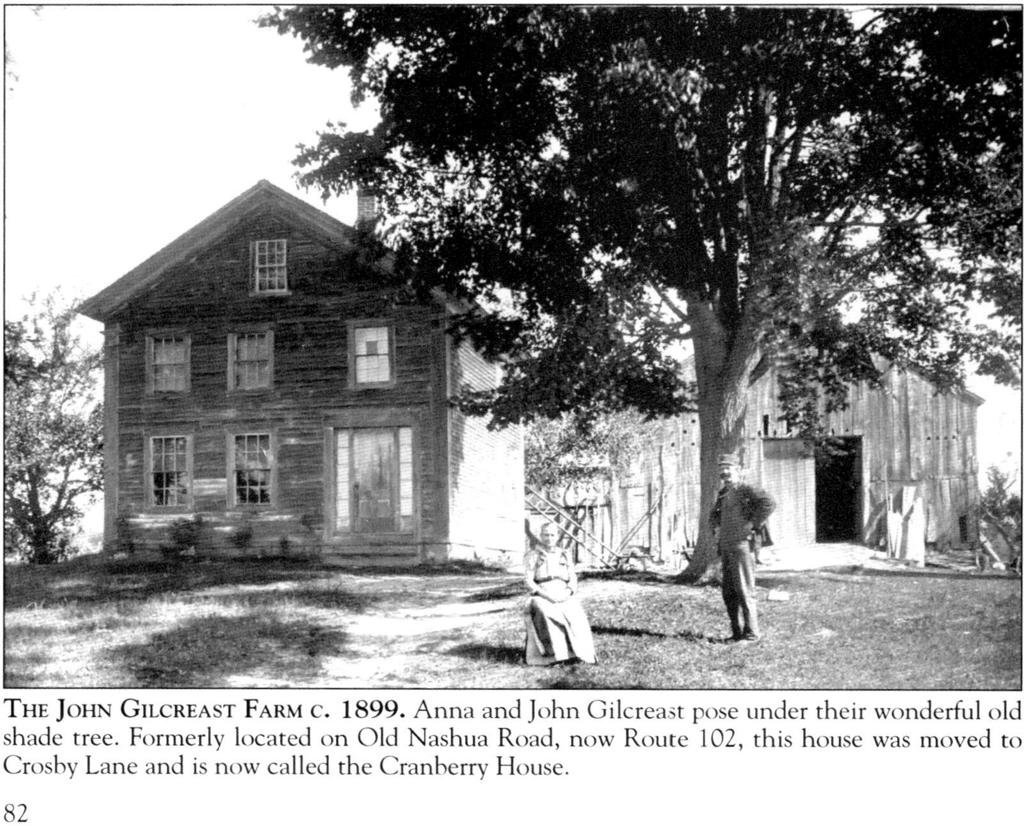

**THE JOHN GILCREAST FARM c. 1899.** Anna and John Gilcreast pose under their wonderful old shade tree. Formerly located on Old Nashua Road, now Route 102, this house was moved to Crosby Lane and is now called the Cranberry House.

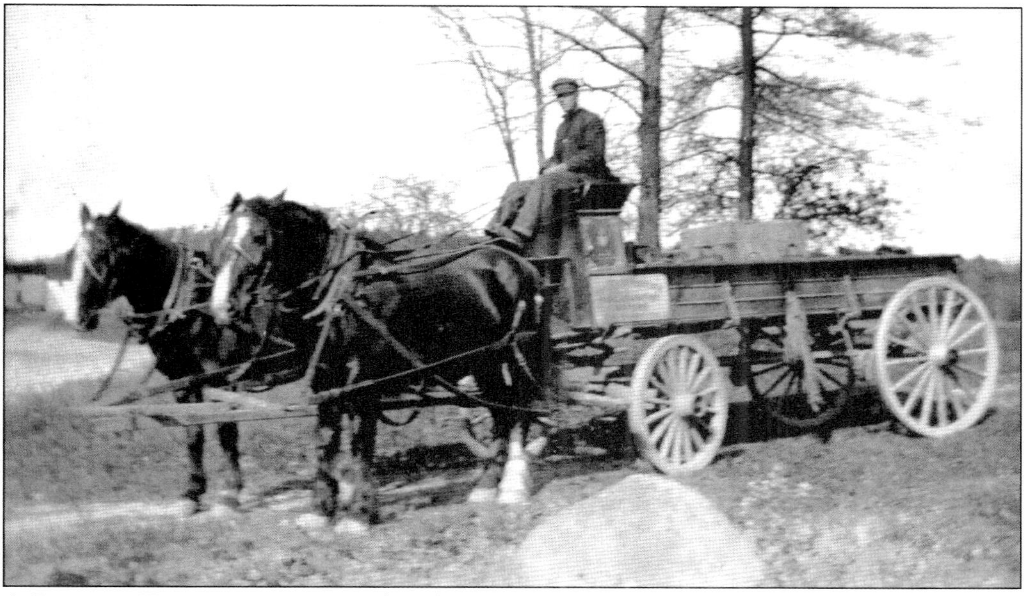

**A Delivery Wagon c. 1890.** Frank Gilcreast returns to the farm with grain and dry goods.

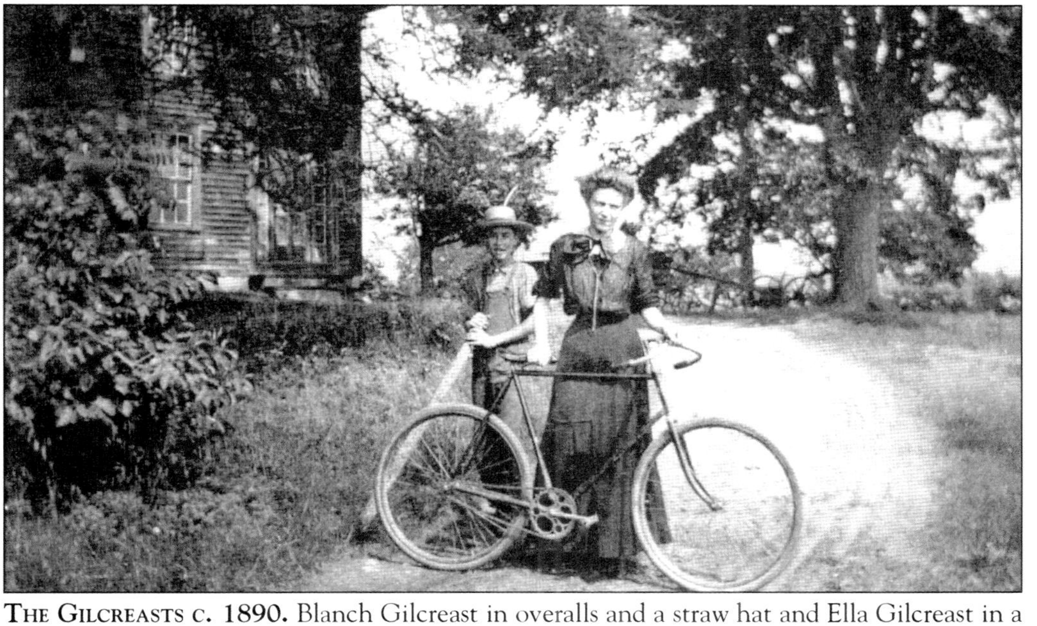

**The Gilcreasts c. 1890.** Blanch Gilcreast in overalls and a straw hat and Ella Gilcreast in a dress and bouffant hairdo stand outside their home off Old Nashua Road, now Route 102. This area was consumed by a large shopping center.

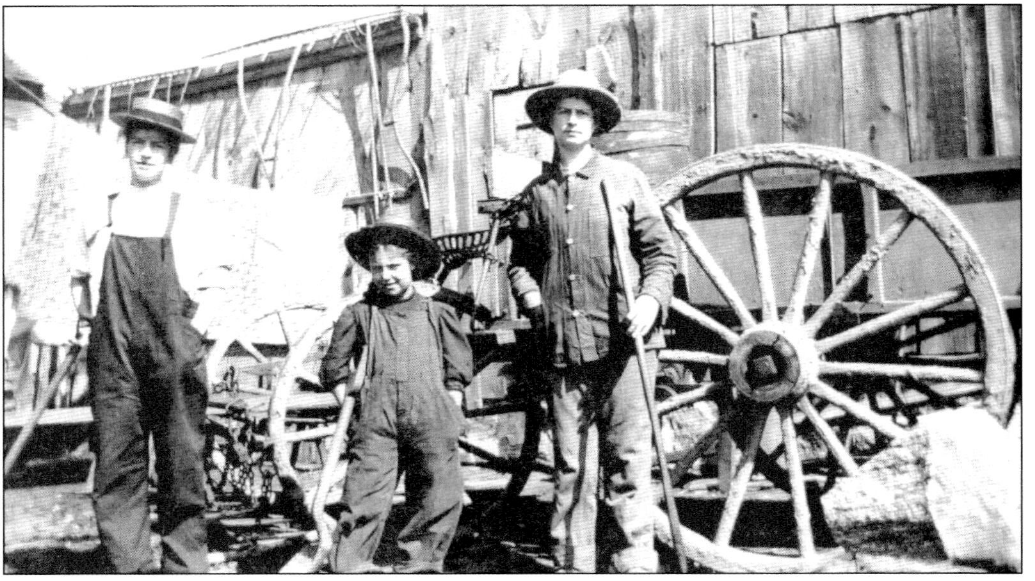

**TAKING A WORK BREAK.** Ella, Raymond, and Blanch Gilcreast take a rest before digging more potatoes.

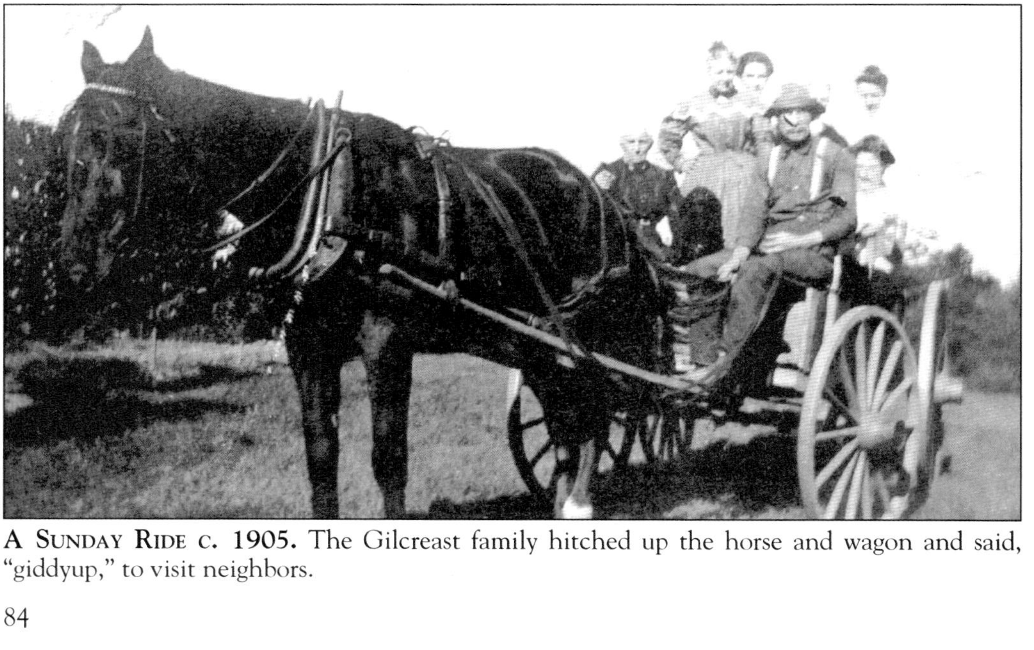

**A SUNDAY RIDE C. 1905.** The Gilcreast family hitched up the horse and wagon and said, "giddyup," to visit neighbors.

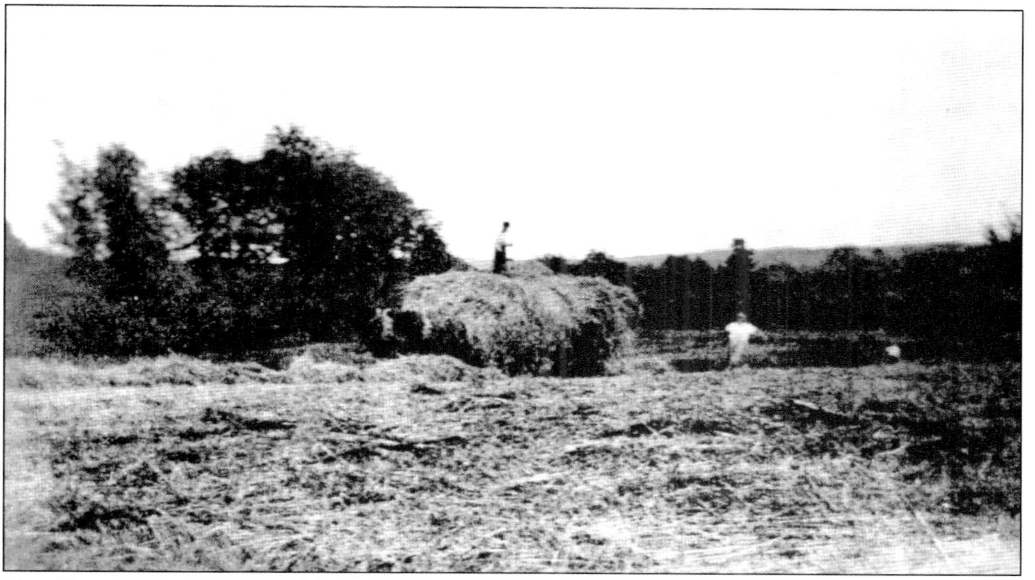

**HAY FARMING C. 1930.** Building a load of loose hay was an art form. Farm hands cut the hay by hand with scythes, formed it into rows with a hay rake, and then pitched mounds of dry hay up to the person on the horse-drawn, wooden wagon. In July it was hot, hard work. This Gilcreast farm field is now a shopping center along Route 102.

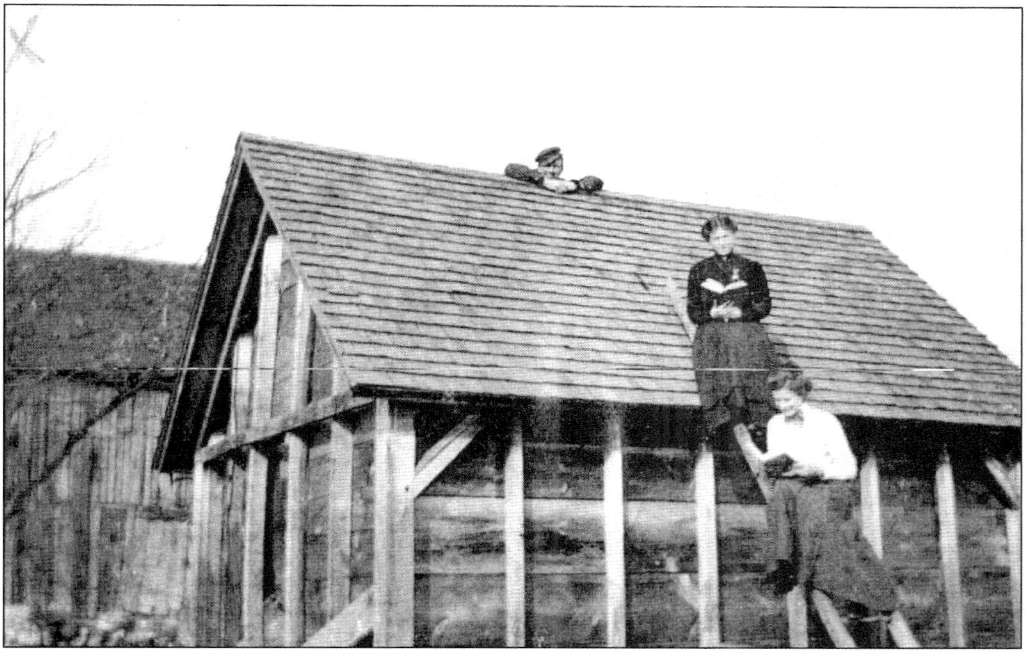

**THE ICEHOUSE C. 1929.** The icehouse became a Sunday retreat for reading and a little brotherly interference at the Gilcreast farm. During winter months, ice was cut at Ela and Kendall Ponds and brought here by horse and wagon. The ice was packed in sawdust. Iceboxes were the refrigerators of the time.

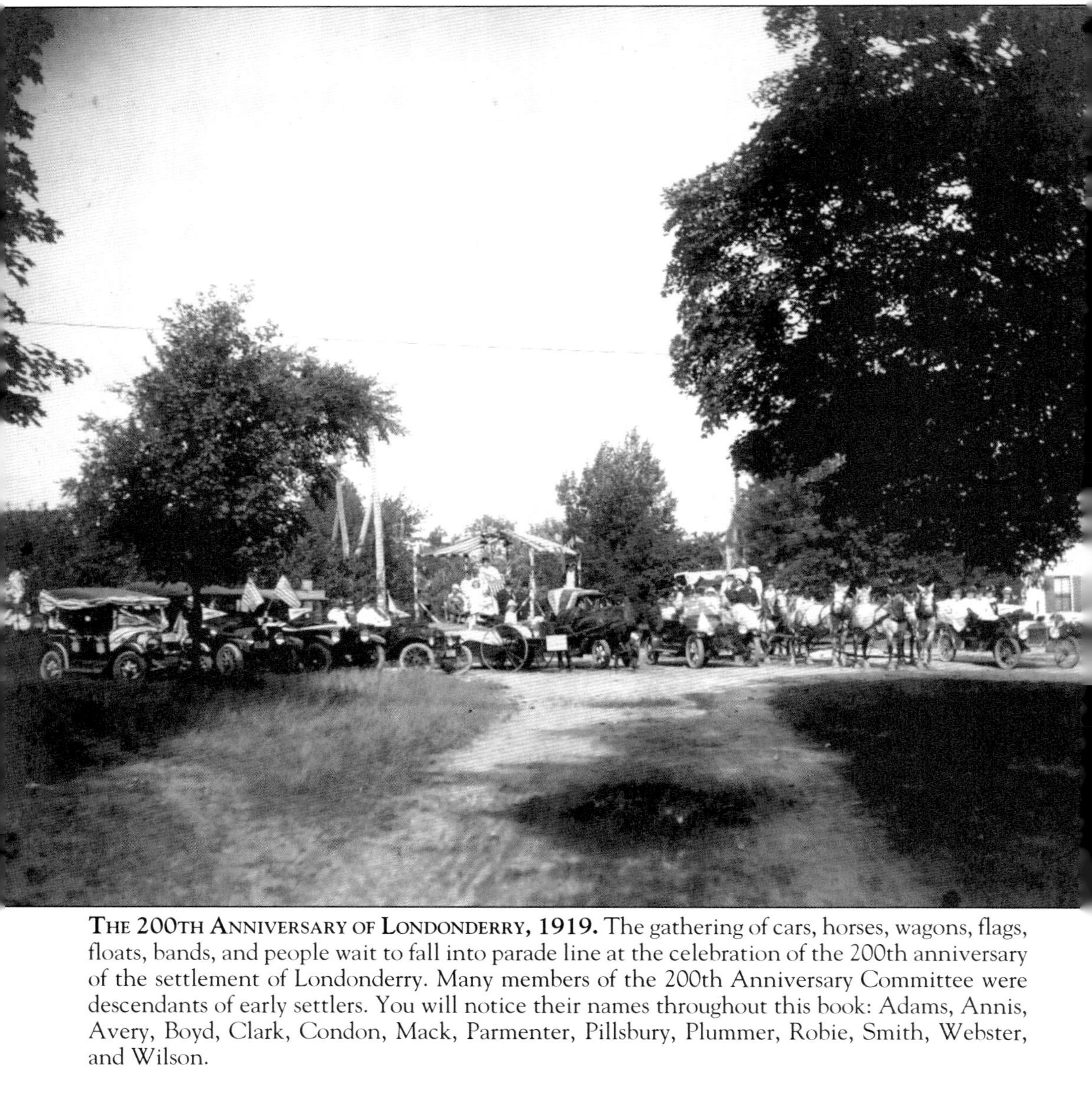

**THE 200TH ANNIVERSARY OF LONDONDERRY, 1919.** The gathering of cars, horses, wagons, flags, floats, bands, and people wait to fall into parade line at the celebration of the 200th anniversary of the settlement of Londonderry. Many members of the 200th Anniversary Committee were descendants of early settlers. You will notice their names throughout this book: Adams, Annis, Avery, Boyd, Clark, Condon, Mack, Parmenter, Pillsbury, Plummer, Robie, Smith, Webster, and Wilson.

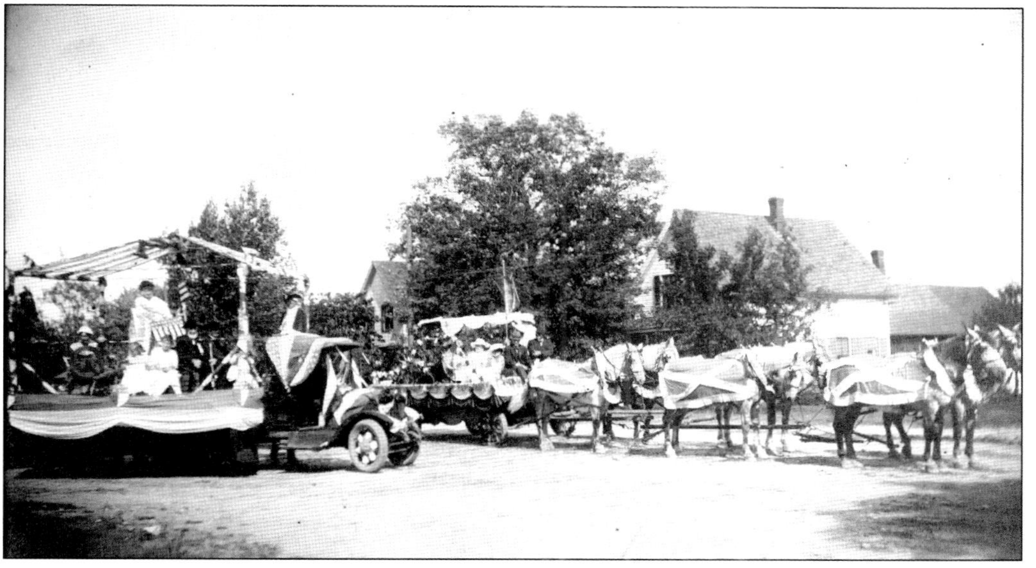

**Parade Floats at the 200th Anniversary of Londonderry, 1919.** Of the eight divisions of the parade, this is the second, showing the decorative floats of the Derry and Londonderry Granges. They wait at the corner of West Broadway (Route 102) and Londonderry Road for two blasts from the Derry fire whistle, which will signal them to begin. There were thousands of cheering people lining the two-mile parade route.

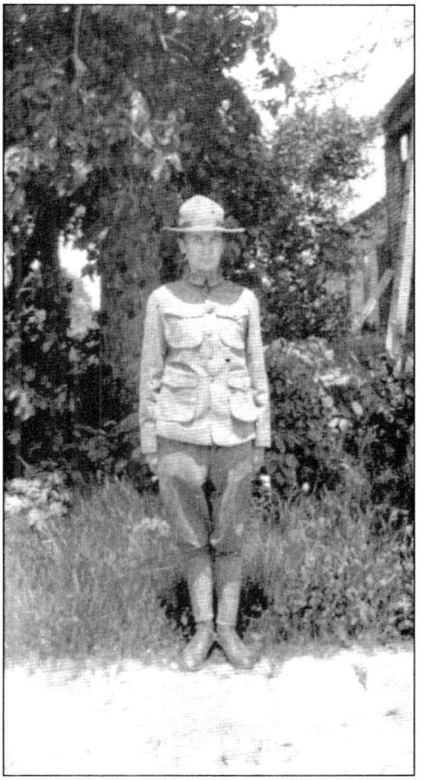

**James Martin, World War I.** James Martin was one of eight children. His father, Cyrus, built their home in 1905. His mother, Effie (Gilcreast) Martin, gave music lessons and played the church organ. Their house, at the right of the photograph, later became the Palmer Riding Camp. The area is now the Londonderry Commons. Years ago, Martin and his siblings used to climb a sycamore tree by their home. Today, the giant old tree stands next to a pizza restaurant—holding onto the past, observing the present, and awaiting the future.

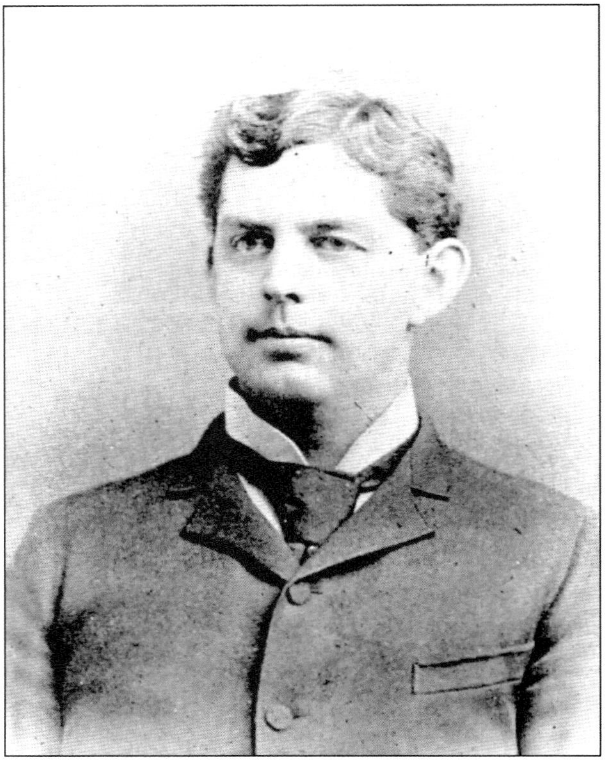

**Rosecrans W. Pillsbury c. 1895.** Rosecrans Pillsbury was born in Londonderry in 1868, one of eight children of Col. William and Martha S. Pillsbury. Educated at Pinkerton Academy and Dartmouth College, he became a prominent lawyer, industrialist, banker, apple grower, and politician, having served in the New Hampshire State Legislature. He was a trustee of the University of New Hampshire and was president of the First National Bank of Derry. His career took him into the newspaper business, and he took control of the *Manchester Union* in 1906. Pillsbury was married in 1885 to Annie E. Watts. They had three children. One can still approach the large rambling Victorian home that he built and lived in by going up the circular driveway across from the Woodmont Orchard buildings on east Pillsbury Road.

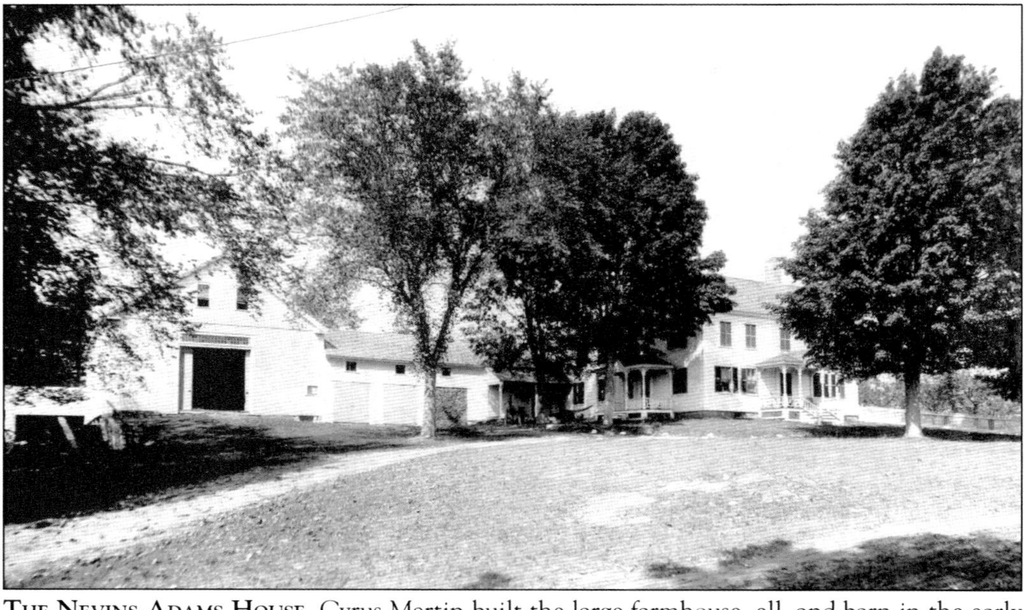

**The Nevins-Adams House.** Cyrus Martin built the large farmhouse, ell, and barn in the early 1900s. This was the home of Wesley Adams and Mabel (Nevins) Adams. Both were very active in town and state affairs. Wesley was a senator, and his portrait hangs in the state house. This farm on Old Nashua Road (Route 102) was later demolished to make room for the park-and-ride roadway.

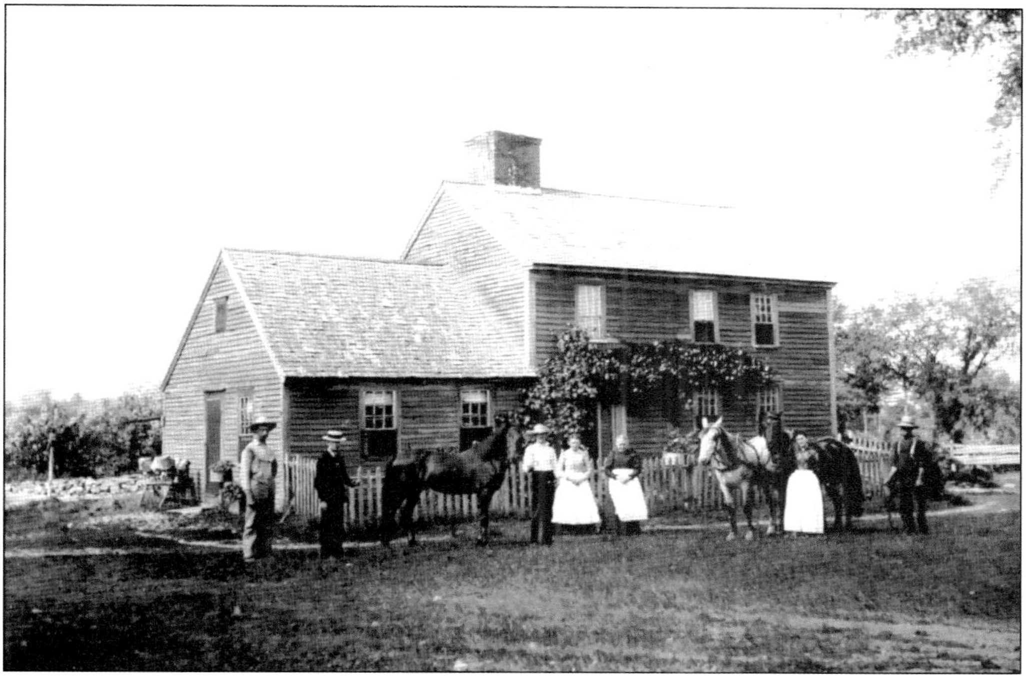

**The First Boyd House, Gilcreast Road.** The man holding the horse is Frederick Augustus Young, father of Mason J. Young Sr. The other individuals are not identified. The Young family still resides in Londonderry.

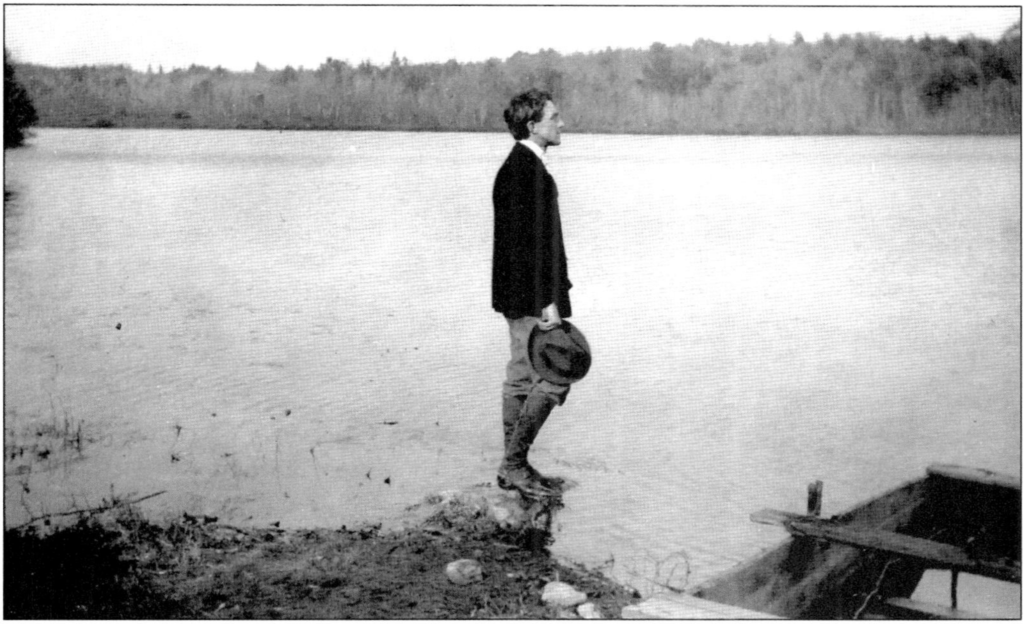

**Scobie Pond, 1902.** Reed Paige Clark II, with hat in hand, looks across the quiet waters and forested shores of Scobie Pond. Here, the selectmen yearly "walked the boundary" between the eastern edge of Londonderry and Derry, as decreed by early records. An old Native American dugout canoe was recovered from this pond and resides at the Manchester Millyard Museum.

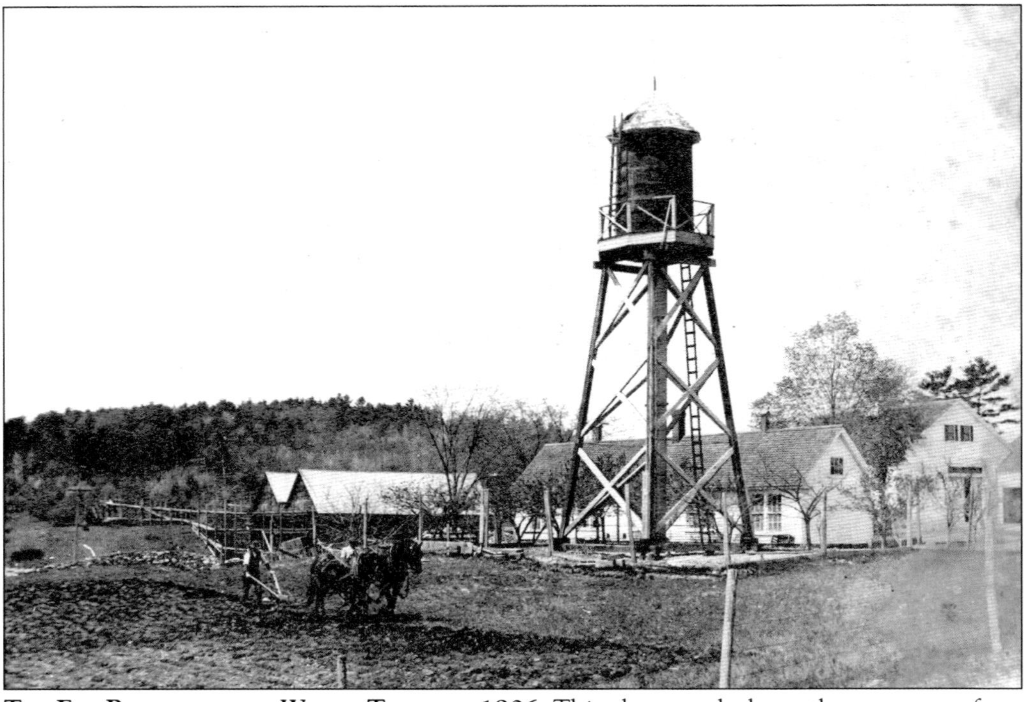

**THE ELA PLACE AND THE WATER TOWER c. 1906.** This photograph shows the area across from the Ela Farm on Old Nashua Road (Route 102). The water tower could hold upwards of 6,000 gallons. Notice that the gentleman in this photograph is using a plowshare pulled by a horse to turn the soil over for planting.

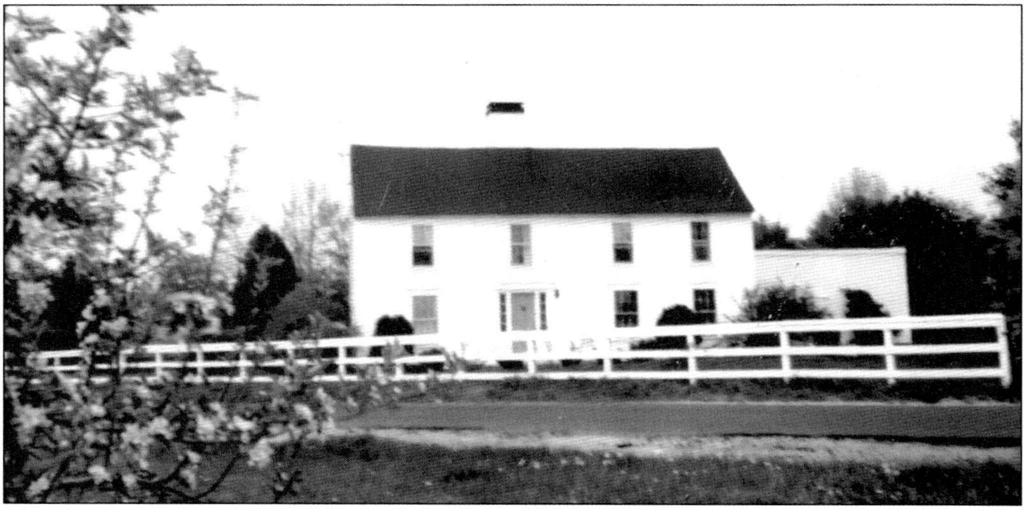

**THE REVEREND DR. WILLIAM MORRISON HOUSE.** This salt-box home, built in 1725 by Edward Proctor on land granted to him in 1722 by the king of England, is the oldest house still standing in Londonderry. In 1786, it became the home of the Reverend Dr. Morrison, the second pastor of the Presbyterian Society. In 1822, Mrs. Morrison brought back a few pounds of tomatoes from a visit to Pennsylvania. Tomatoes in our town gardens date from that time. This house, located on Gilcreast Road south of Route 102, remains in remarkable condition.

*Six*

# Musquash

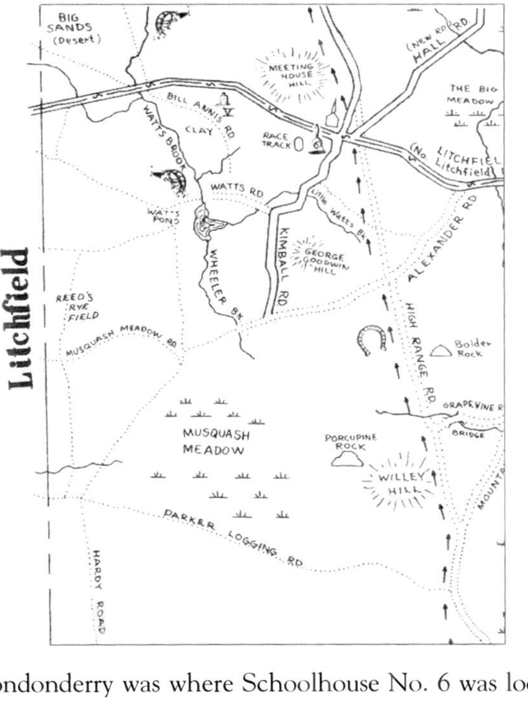


**West.** This area of Londonderry was where Schoolhouse No. 6 was located on Kimball Road near Litchfield Road.

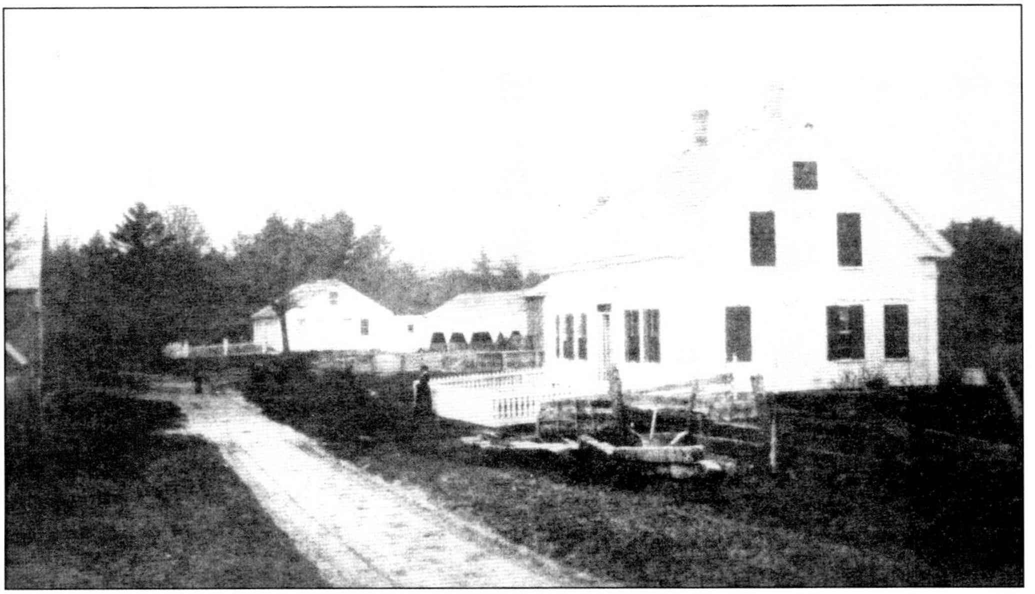

**The Watts Homestead.** At the end of Watts Road stands the Moses Watts Homestead, originally built in 1790. The home has undergone extensive restoration since a fire in the 1980s destroyed the carriage sheds, barn, and part of the house. Six generations of the Watts family lived on the homestead, including Melvin Watts, who was at one time the Londonderry town historian. The area is listed in the site files of the New Hampshire Division of Historical Resources, Archeology Division. The home was recently sold out of the family after Mr. Watts's death.

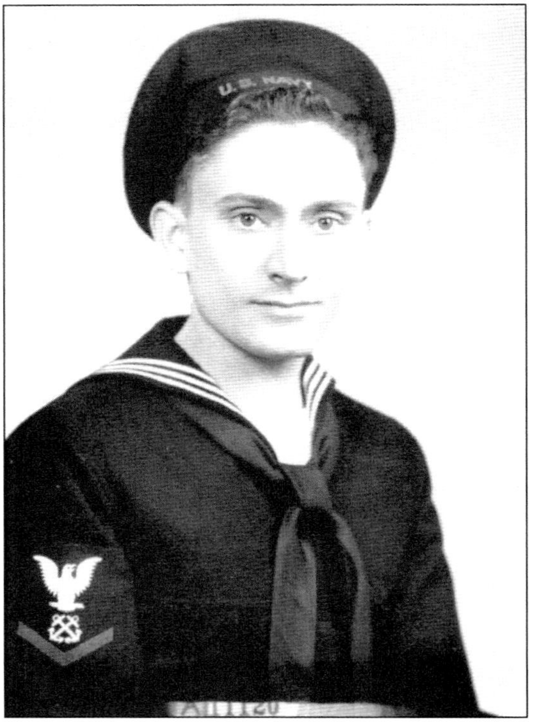

**Melvin E. Watts (1916–2003).** Melvin was born in Londonderry. He was the sixth generation of the Watts family to live on the original homestead on Watts Road. He was educated at Schoolhouse No. 6 in Londonderry, Manchester Central High, the Manchester Institute of Arts and Sciences, and Harvard University. He served in the U.S. Navy during World War II. He married Ruth Gilkerson and together they raised two daughters, Elizabeth and Delight. Melvin was curator of the Currier Gallery of Art in Manchester for more than 40 years and was the first president of the Londonderry Historical Society in 1956. He co-edited with Jessie Beckley the second volume of the *History of Londonderry* and assisted with the writing of the five volumes of *Early Londonderry*.

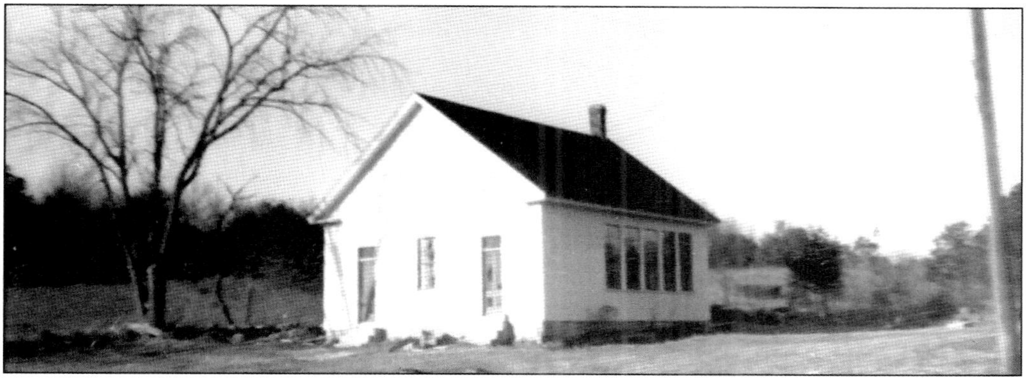

**Schoolhouse No. 6.** This 1940s photograph was taken after Central School, now Matthew Thornton, was constructed. At that time, the old schoolhouses were abandoned. The 1858 School Register of Schoolhouse No. 6 indicates that they did not have reference books, a globe, a clock, or any maps or charts. Francis Parker, the teacher, received $10 a month and board with a scholar's family. The school building, on its original site, is now a private home on Kimball Road near Litchfield Road.

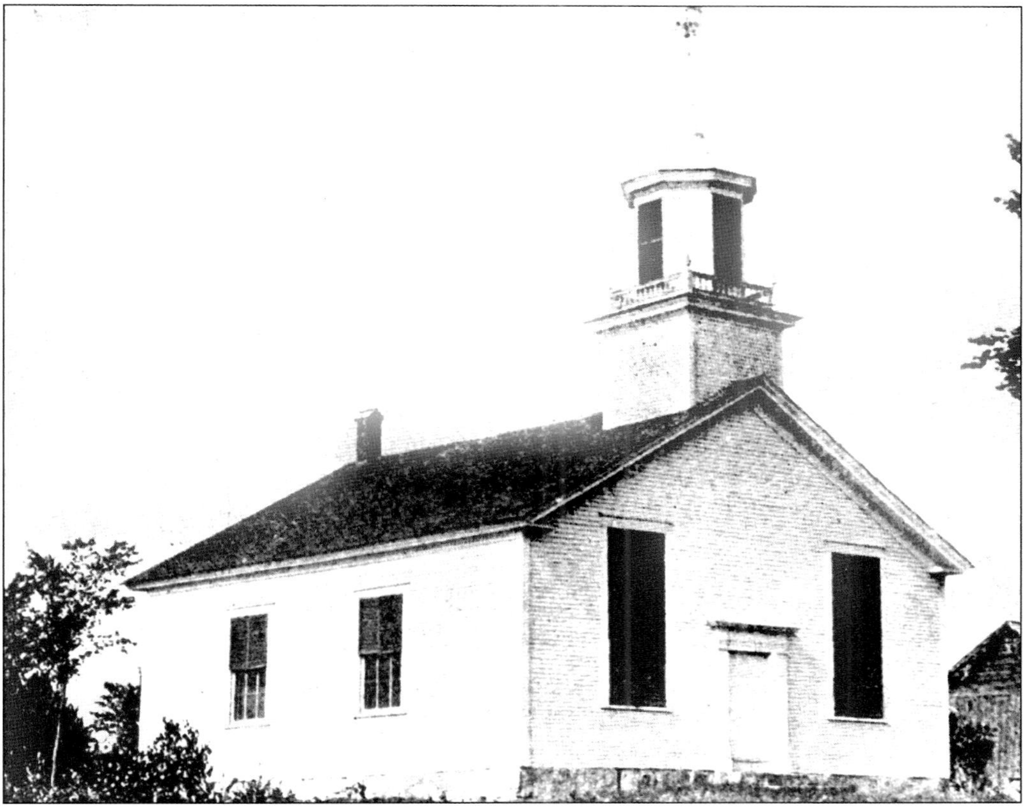

**The Old Baptist Meeting House.** Built in 1829, the Old Baptist Meeting House was situated on High Range Road, north of the five corners. It was sold in 1910 for the sum of $1 and was then torn down. The old deed read, "It shall stand as a church while grass grows, and water runs," but this decree was not followed. However, a new Londonderry Calvinist Baptist church was built in the north village due to the population growth in that area.

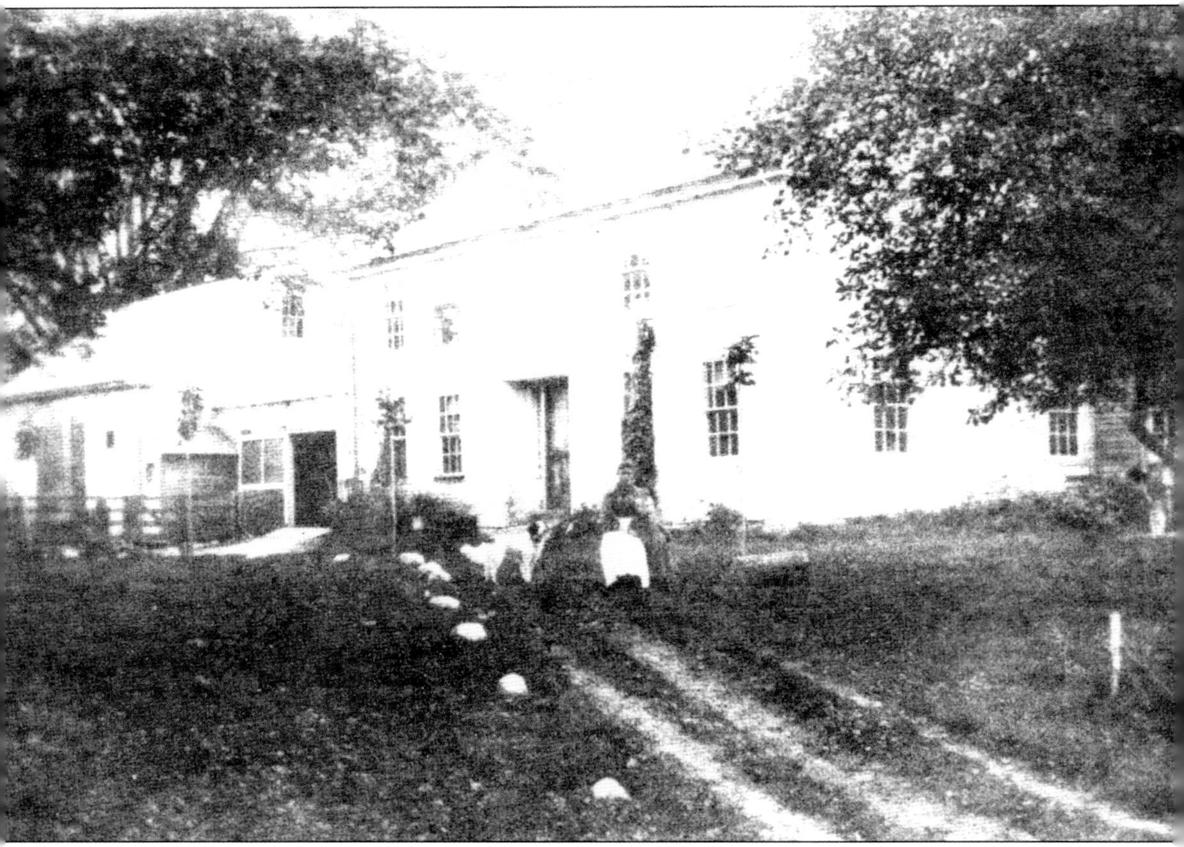

**The Annis-Reynolds Farm.** This photograph shows the Annis-Reynolds farm on Litchfield Road *c.* 1850. The old Mulberry tree on the right now stands bent with age. In 1944, Ned Reynolds and Helen (Annis) Reynolds came to live in the Annis family homestead. Ned was a jack-of-all-trades and a great storyteller. He loved working with horses in the woods, on his trotting track behind the farm and at the sulky races at Beaver Lake. Helen was an authority on birds, taught piano and organ, and was accomplished at rug braiding and quilt making. The 1976 bicentennial quilt of Londonderry hangs in the Leach Library as a tribute to her talent. Ned and Helen's warm and friendly home is now surrounded by new houses.

*Seven*

# KENDALL POND

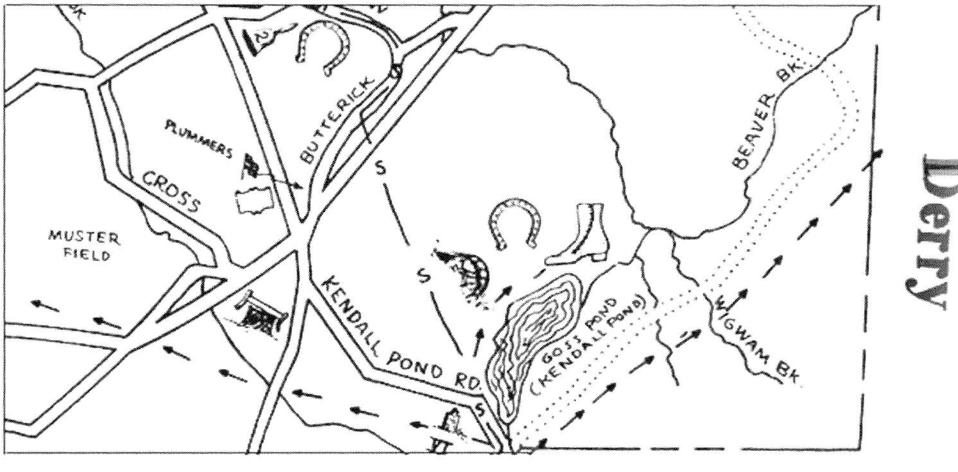


**SOUTHEAST.** This area of Londonderry is where Schoolhouse No. 2 was located at the intersection of Peabody Row and Mammoth Road.

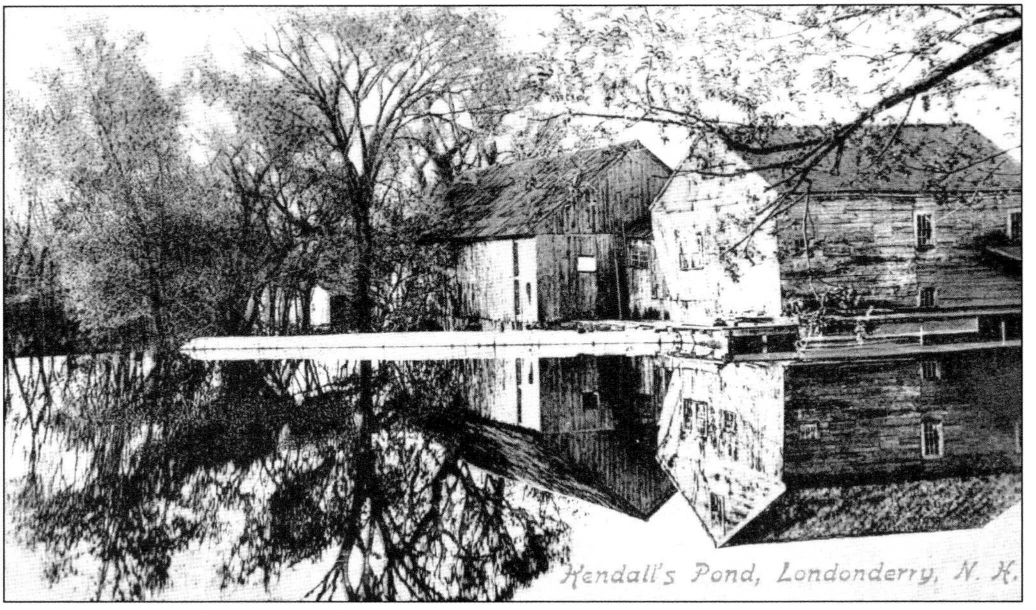


**KENDALL POND, 1910.** Located in south Londonderry, Kendall Pond was the site of a thriving mill business. In 1731, rights to establish a mill were granted to Benjamin Wilson, who built the first mill on this location. At various times, it has been called Goss's, Moor's, and Kendall's mills. In the late 1800s and early 1900s, Kendall Pond furnished most of the ice in Londonderry for home iceboxes and milk coolers.

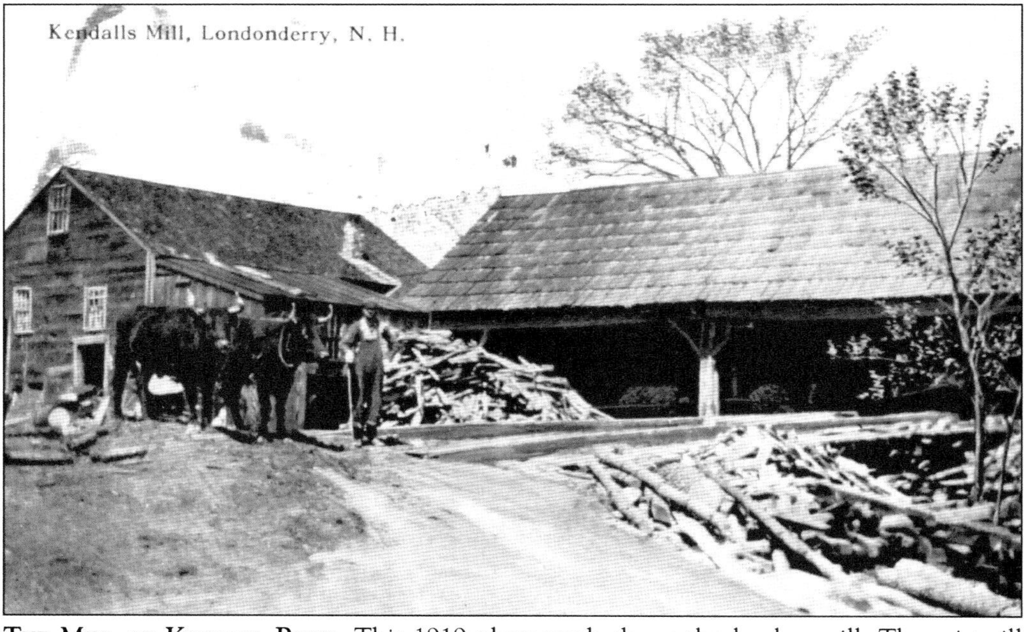


**THE MILL AT KENDALL POND.** This 1919 photograph shows the lumber mill. The gristmill operated under a state charter that required grist to be ground the same day. At the mill, logs were sawed, grain was ground, and apples were pressed. A farmer could then cross the bridge to have his horses shod and spend the waiting time fishing in the pond to catch dinner.

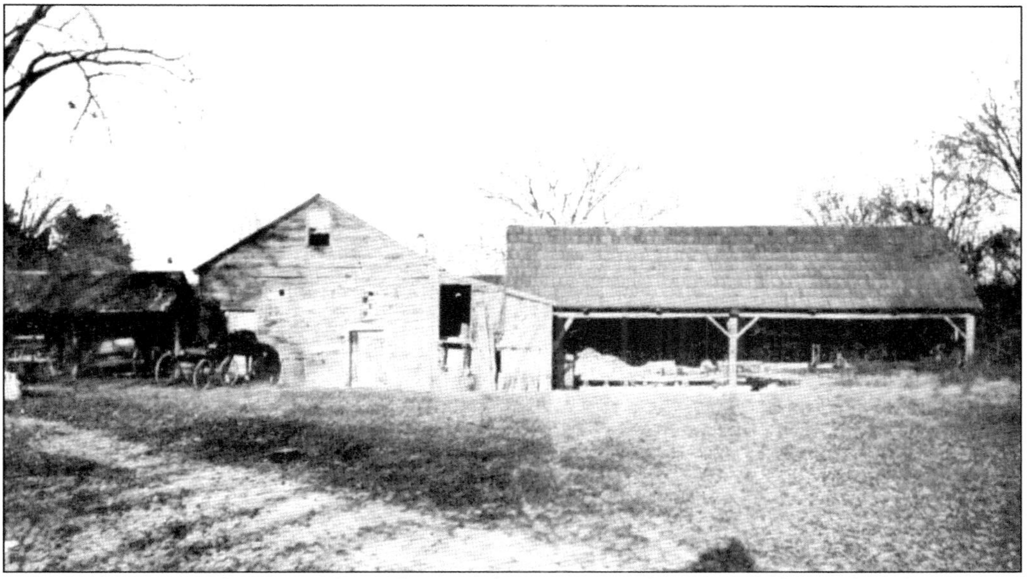

**Kendall's Mills.** There was a large farm on the property, a barn across the road, and a separate building to store and age cider. In 1866, approximately 700 barrels of cider were made at Kendall's. When Mr. Kendall died, his daughter Ida lived in the home and later sold it. The mill buildings and barn burned in October 1924.

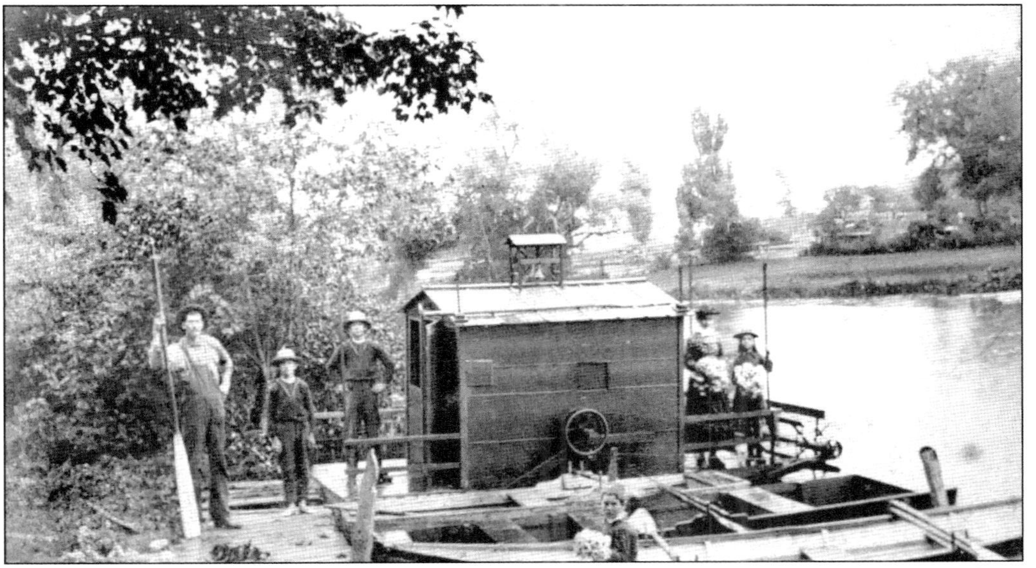

**A Robie Boat on Kendall Pond.** In 1895, boat owner Frank Robie took people for boat rides by appointment to pick pond lilies. Notice the boy in the front boat holding a bouquet of lilies.

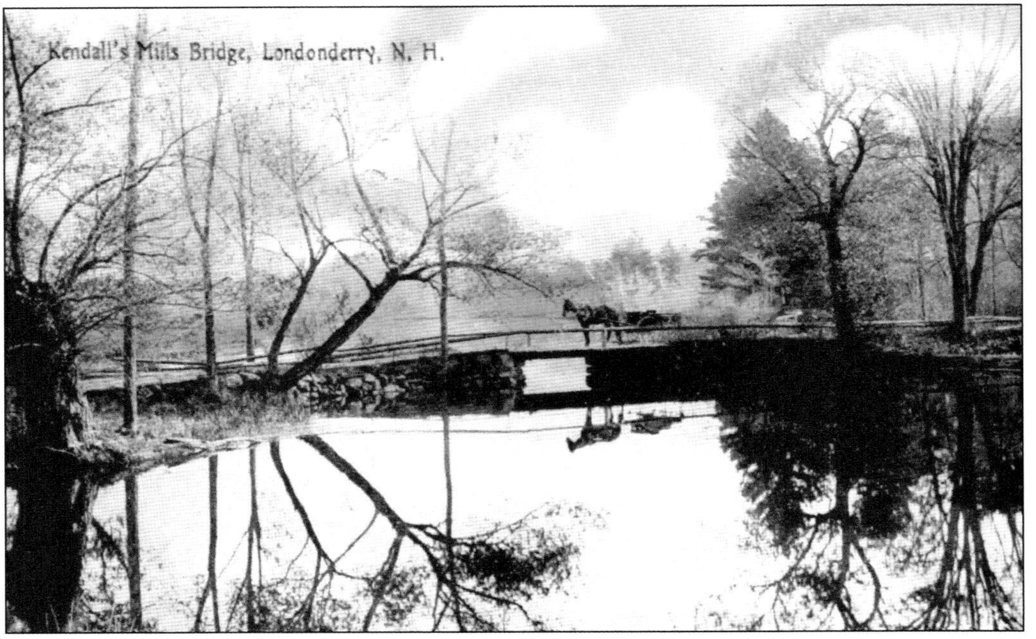


**THE KENDALL'S MILLS BRIDGE, 1909.** The original bridge, built in 1760, connected Kendall Pond to several roads leading to present-day Derry and Windham, then a part of Londonderry. Standing on the bridge looking north, one could see both Kendall Pond and the dam, whereas the mill was visible looking south. A repair of the pond's dam took one day to drain the pond, another to make the repairs, and a third day to refill the pond.

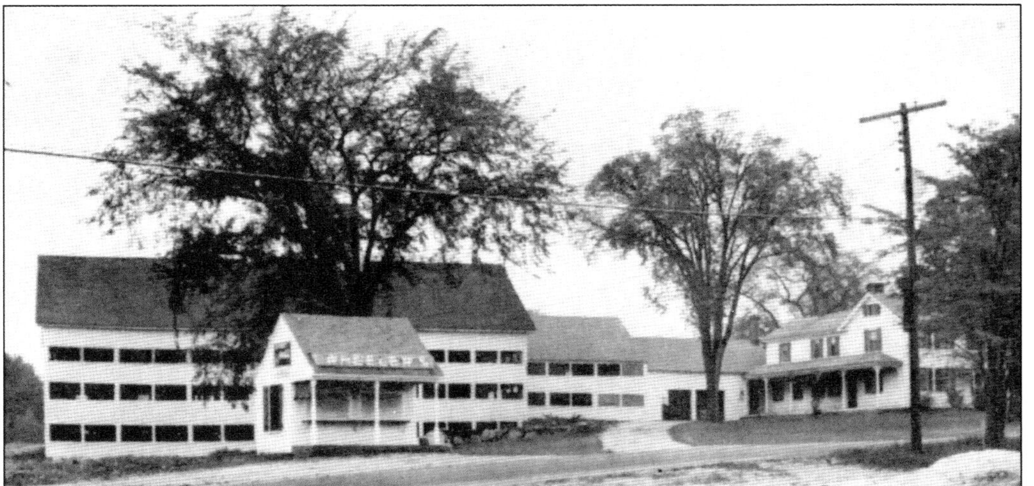

**THE WHEELER FARM.** Located along the east end of Old Nashua Road (currently Route 102), this farm was representative of the large chicken farms in the town. The Wheeler family also operated a farm stand for many years. Previously, this farm was owned by the Ela family.

**COLLECTING MAPLE SYRUP ON GILCREAST FARM.** In the late 1930s, Ralph Dutton of Gilcreast Farm tapped the sugar maples in Londonderry. The syrup was sold at the farmers' market. It takes 25–40 gallons of sap to make a gallon of maple syrup. The spile (the spout inserted into the tree to draw sap) shown here is hand-carved of alder. The wooden bucket, made of ash, was kept in the brook to keep it from shrinking.

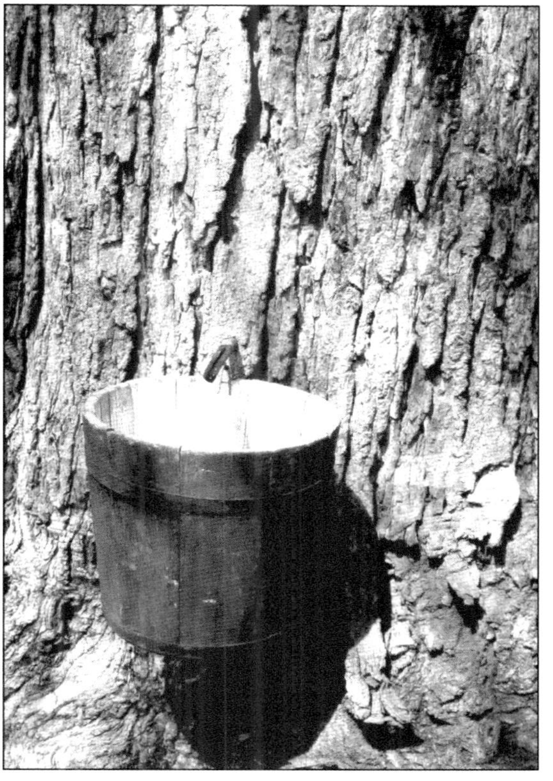

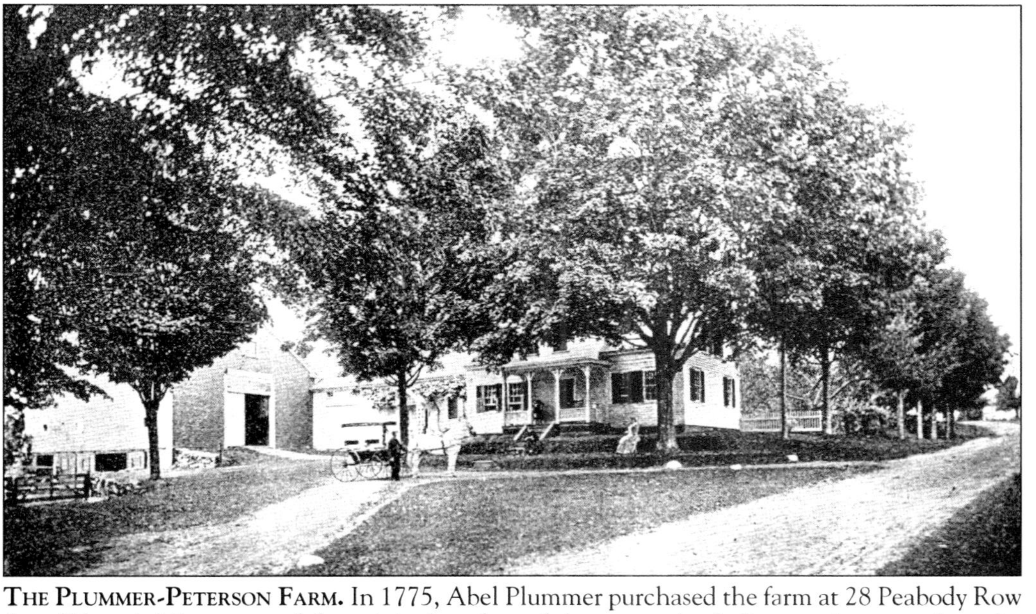

**THE PLUMMER-PETERSON FARM.** In 1775, Abel Plummer purchased the farm at 28 Peabody Row from Edward Aiken, one of the original settlers of the town. An Indian garrison stood on the property, as well as a large barn for storing hay. Capt. John Anderson Plummer lived on the farm for more than 80 years. His great-grandson Granville Plummer was the fifth generation to live there. The present owners are the Petersons, who operate a sugarhouse.

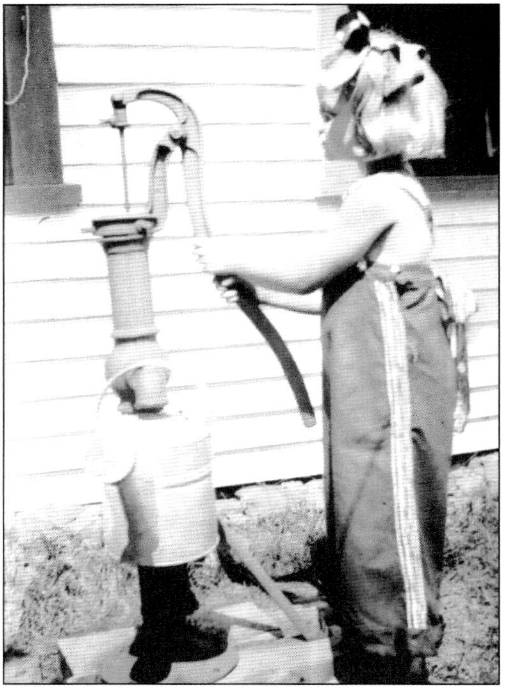

**PUMPING WATER, 1934.** In this photograph, Marilyn Ham is pumping water outside of her childhood home. All children had regular chores, and on this morning, Marilyn was watering the plants. She and her husband, Chester, now live in the Jonathan Warren Peabody home. Marilyn is the current Londonderry town historian.

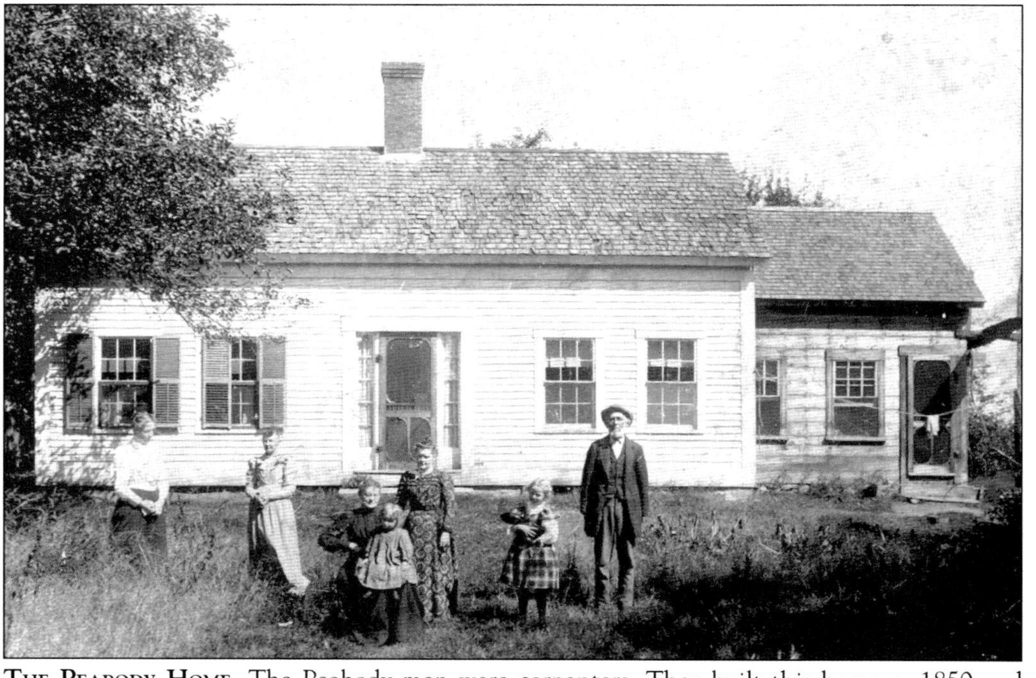

**THE PEABODY HOME.** The Peabody men were carpenters. They built this home *c.* 1850 and two earlier homes on Peabody Row. "Row" meant right of way and is an old stagecoach term. Pictured in this 1899 photograph are four generations of the Peabody-Tenny-Roach family: Mary Tenny Peabody (seated in center) and Jonathan Warren Peabody (right), and their children, grandchildren, and great-grandchildren.

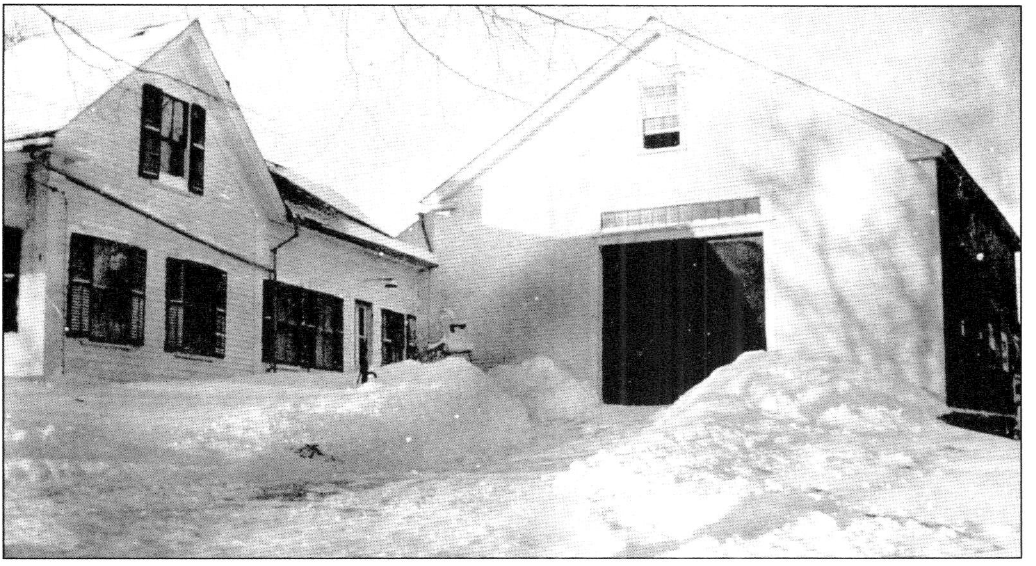

**The Misty Meadow Farm.** Orville A. Peabody built this farmhouse in 1857. Subsequent owners raised vegetables, chickens, and hay. In the 1930s and 1940s, it was a working dairy farm known as Maple Shade and owned by Warren Pinkham. Robert Webber and his wife bought the farm in 1964. The present owners, the Joudreys, are the second generation of the Webber family to live there.

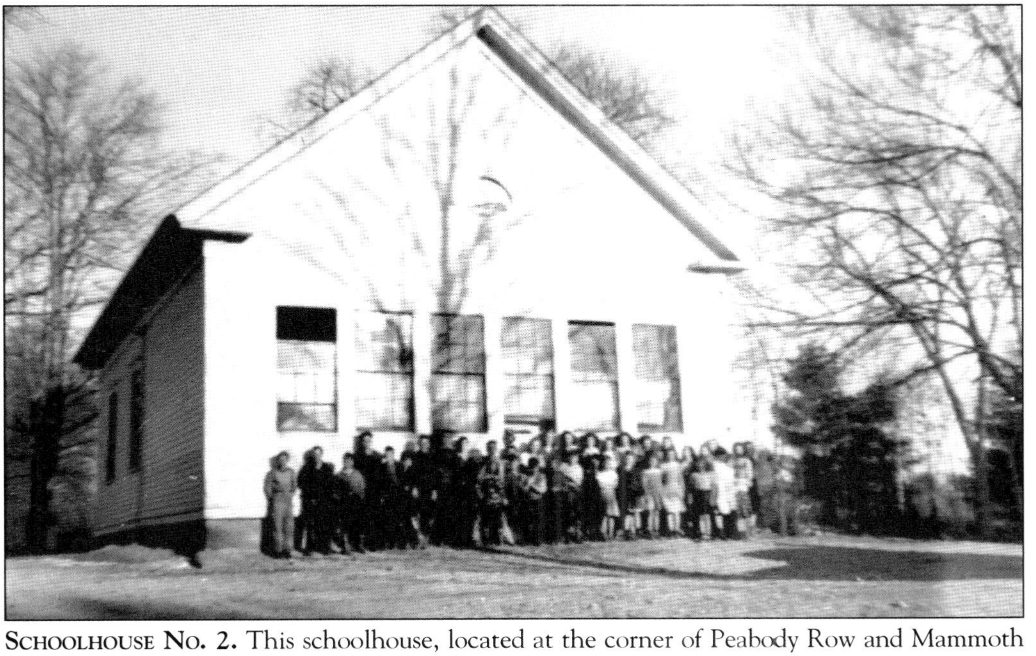

**Schoolhouse No. 2.** This schoolhouse, located at the corner of Peabody Row and Mammoth Road, was built prior to 1784. It was originally a one-room schoolhouse with separate entrances for girls and boys. A large stove near the front of the room provided heat; male students chopped the wood and stoked the fire. The schoolhouse was remodeled and is now a private home.

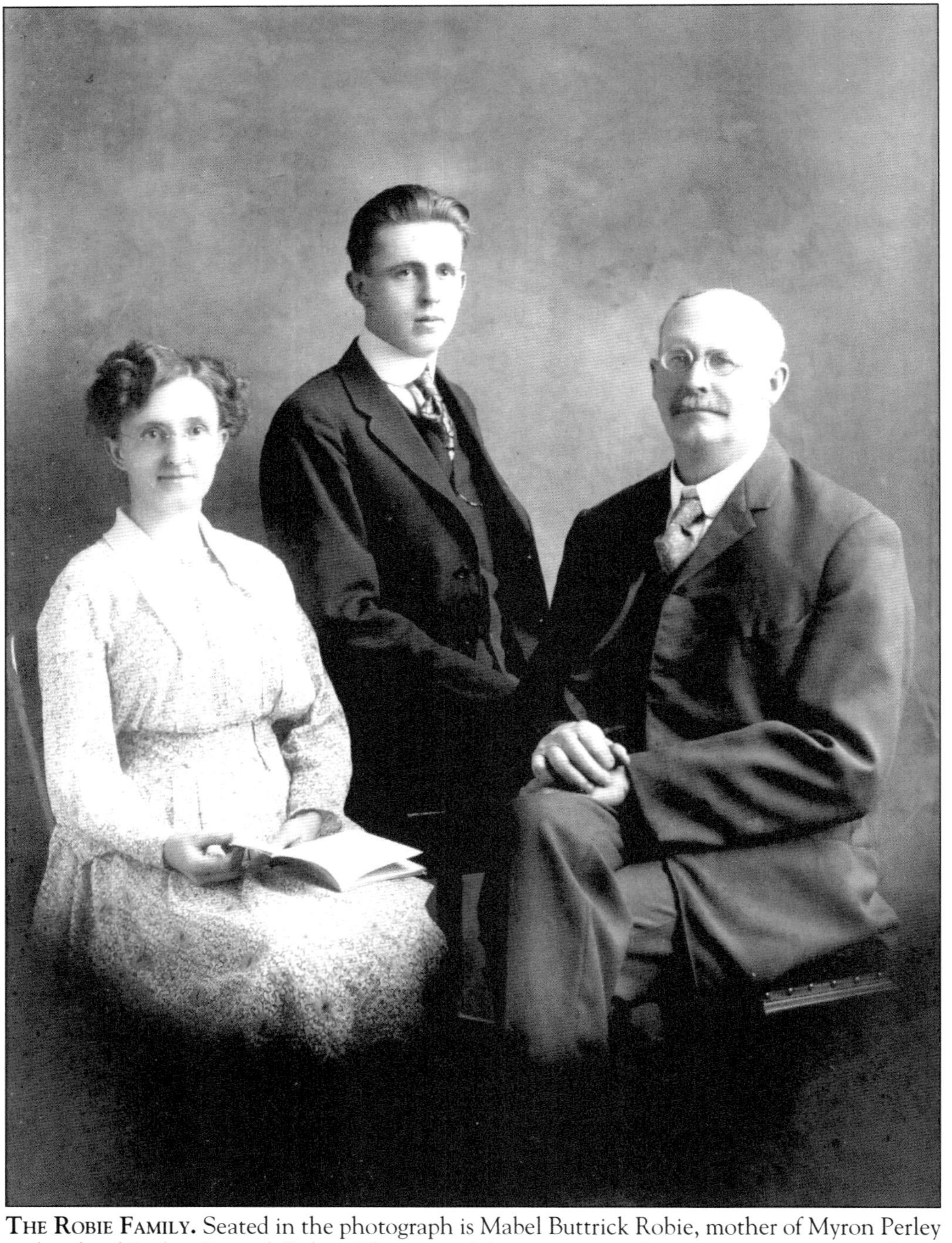

**The Robie Family.** Seated in the photograph is Mabel Buttrick Robie, mother of Myron Perley and wife of Perley Samuel Robie. Their son, Myron, seen in the center, never married and continued to live in the family home until his death in 1998.

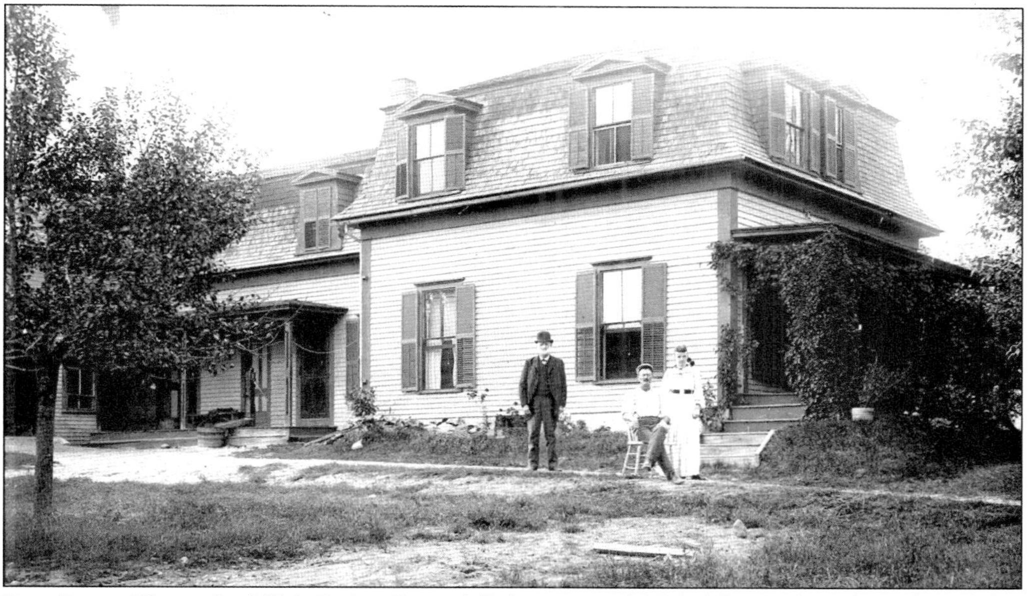

**The Robie Home.** In 1894, Perley Samuel Robie married Mabel Buttrick and purchased this lovely Victorian home with a mansard roof and wraparound porch. The property included a two-story carriage barn with a cupola. A country store located just south of the home, near the junction of Mammoth and Old Nashua Roads, was also the first post office in Londonderry. The contents of the Robie home were sold at auction in 1998. The house has been well preserved and is now a business.

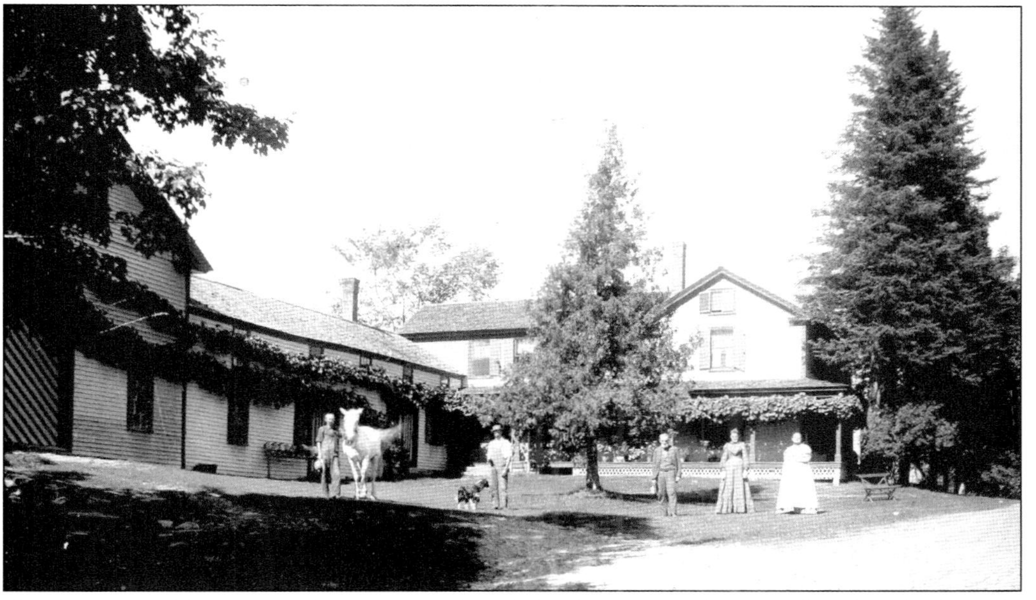

**The Buttrick Farm.** Isaac Buttrick purchased this farm when he moved to Londonderry in 1876. The original Colonial home was connected to the barn by a carriage shed. At one time, there was a cobbler shop on the hill. This was one of the large dairy farms in Londonderry; it later became primarily a poultry farm. Currently, it is a horse farm where horses are bred and boarded and riding lessons are offered.

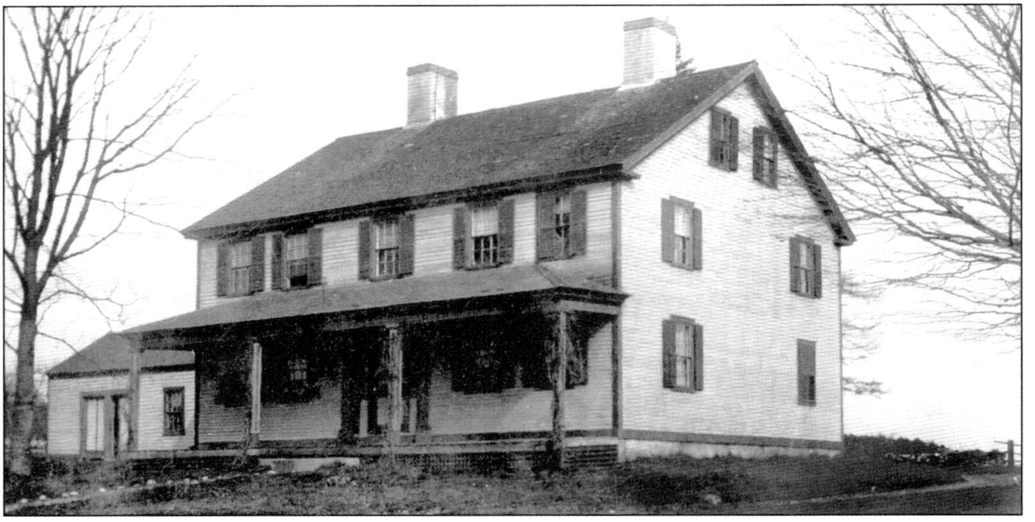

**PLUMMER'S TAVERN.** Built in 1810 by Dr. Watson, this large Colonial home had 12 rooms and 9 fireplaces. Located on the northeast corner of Mammoth Road and the Old Nashua Road (Route 102), the tavern was a regular stop along the stagecoach line from Boston to Concord and from Nashua to Exeter. Fresh horses were exchanged for the weary ones. Mail was also exchanged here. In the stagecoach days it was called Shepard Tavern after the great-great-uncle of Alan Shepard. Currently, it is a popular restaurant.

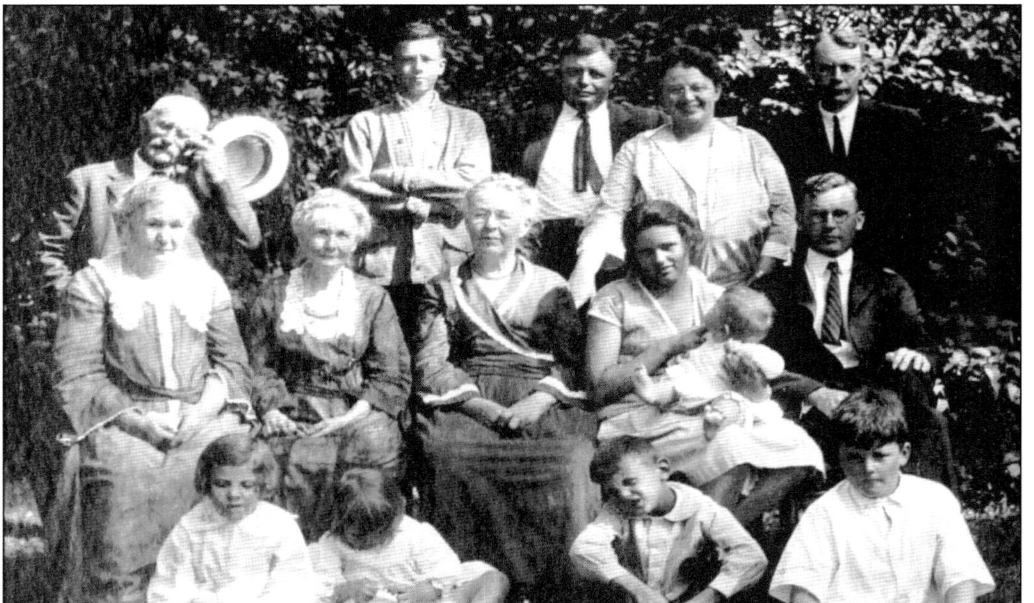

**THE YOUNG AND CROWELL FAMILIES.** Seen in this family photograph are, from left to right, the following: (first row) Agatha A. Young, Priscilla D. Young, David Crowell, and Edward Crowell; (second row) Abby Boyd Crowell, Emma Boyd Young (mother of Mason J. Young Sr.), Margaret Boyd, Dorothy Crowell Hyde (holding Mason J. Young Jr.), and an unidentified man; (third row) Frank S. Crowell, Frank P. Crowell, Clarence Crowell, Mary Crowell Jones, and Maurice Young.

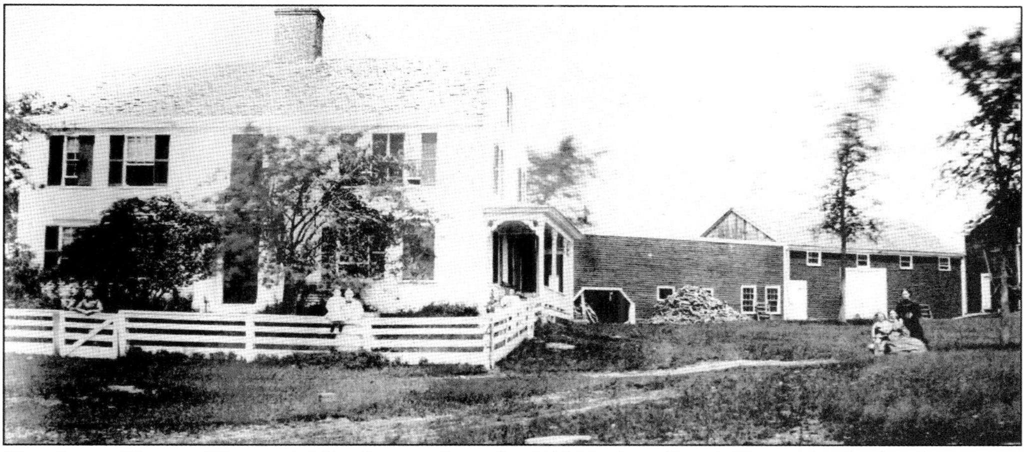

**THE BOYD-YOUNG HOME, 1863.** Situated on the Old Nashua Road (Route 102), this home was built in early 1802 by Capt. William Boyd. The large barns and connecting sheds were built a few years later. Captain Boyd's father, William, who came from Northern Ireland and whose family was of Scottish heritage, originally purchased the property in 1757. In 1841, the property was divided between the two sons of William Boyd and his second wife, Martha Dickey, and a wall was built separating the sons' properties. The older son, Calvin, (Mason was the younger son) built the house that is now known as "the Grey Goose"; it was sold in 1918. The home descended through the Boyd family to become known as the Young homestead. The Young homestead has the distinction of being the only home in Londonderry placed on the National Register of Historic Places by the U.S. Department of the Interior.

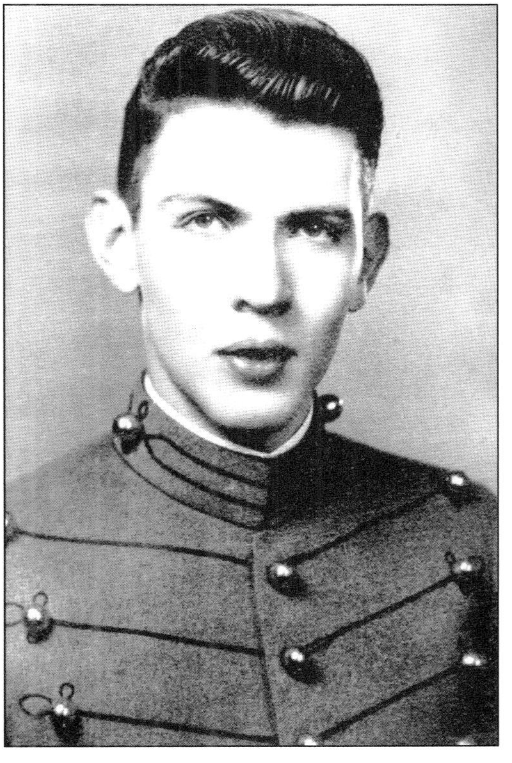

**COL. MASON J. YOUNG JR.** He was the great-great-grandson of Capt. William Boyd, who was an officer in the Revolutionary War. Young was a 1944 graduate of the U.S. Military Academy at West Point and was a veteran of World War II, the Korean War, and the Vietnam War. His father was a 1915 West Point graduate, and his son, Mason J. Young III, was a 1970 graduate.

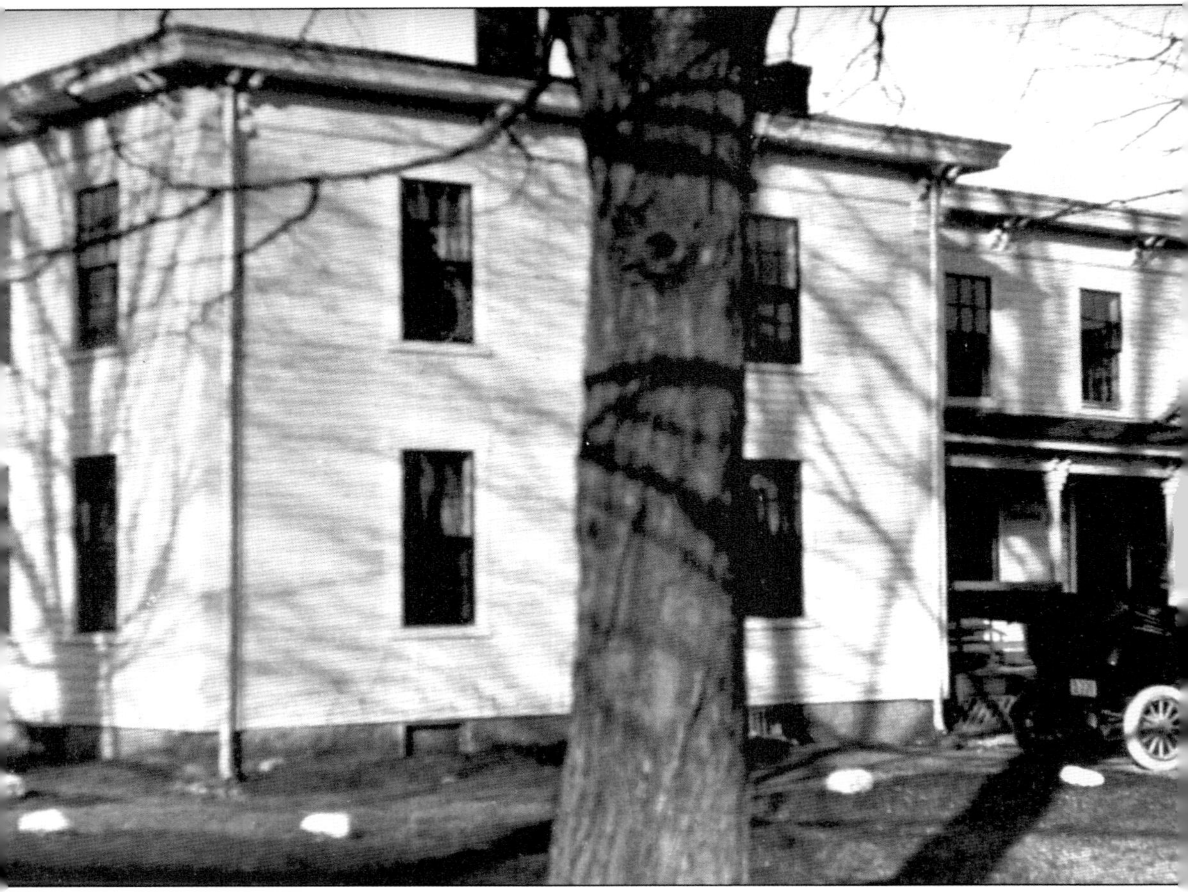

**The Barrett House.** This photograph of the left-hand side of the Wilbur and Georgietta Knight Barrett home was taken before the home burned in 1917. Their only son George and his wife, Ann, built their home from the timber on the land. Ownership then passed to the Denningers, and later the home was moved to Young Road.

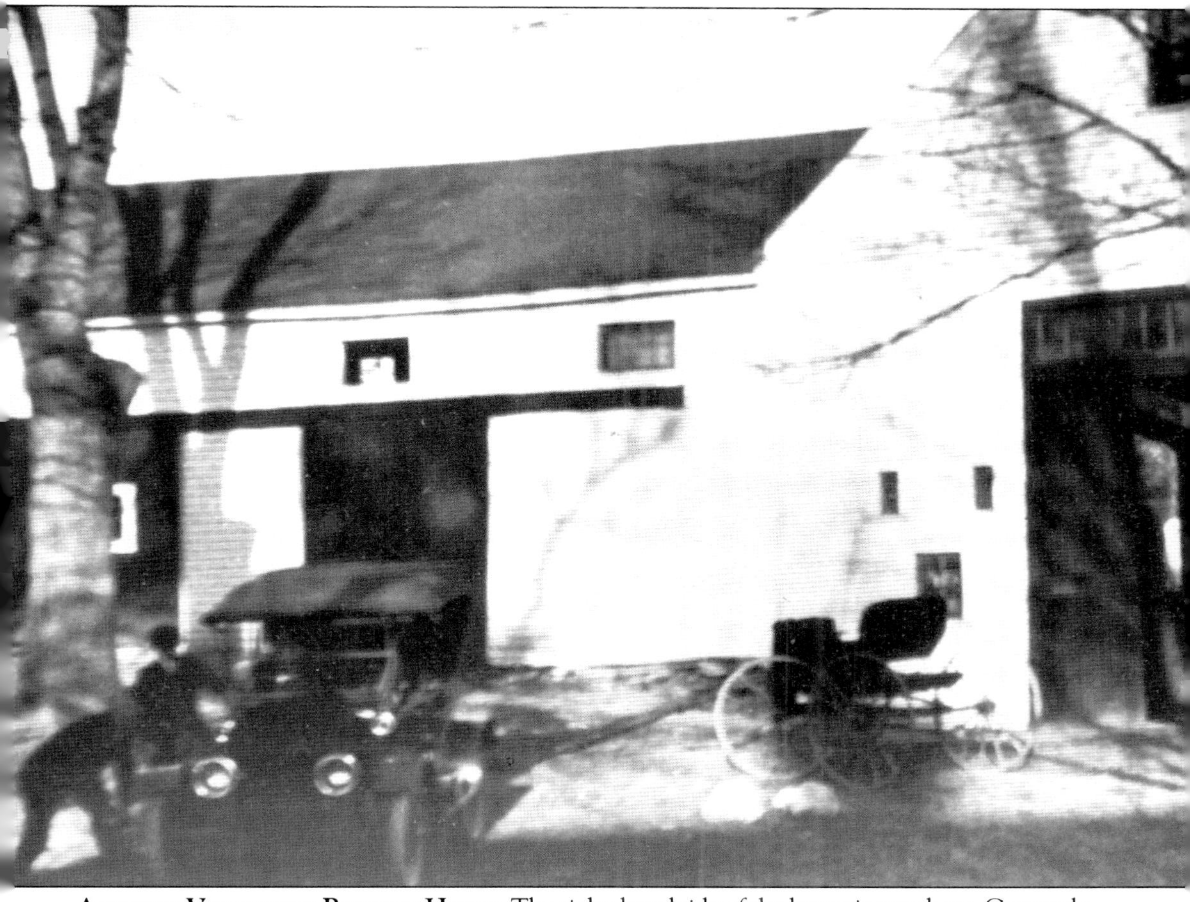

**Another View of the Barrett House.** The right-hand side of the home is seen here. Currently, the corporate headquarters of Blue Seal stands where the Barrett home once stood.

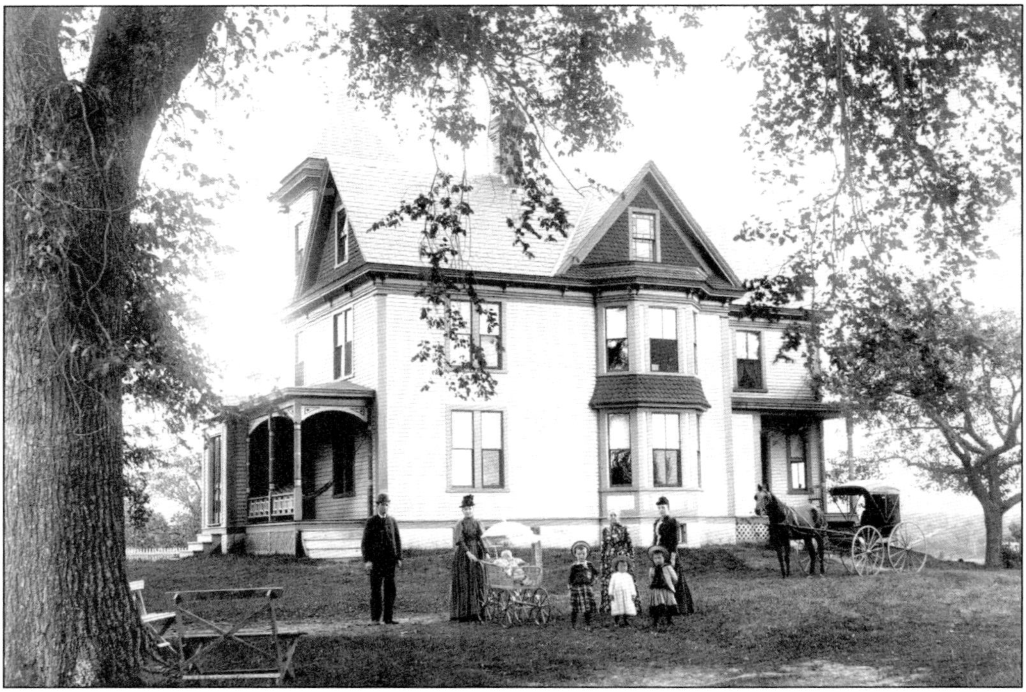

**The McAllister House and Family.** Carl and Mary Smith moved to the Dickey farm in Londonderry *c.* 1916 with their children, Ina, Roscoe, and Bushrod. The Smith family bought this home in the early 1930s and lived there until 1952. The home was located where the shopping mall now stands at the corner of Mammoth Road and Route 102. Carl Smith and his son Roscoe ran a sawmill at this location. In this 1939 photograph, Roscoe Smith's son Warren is pulling cousin Carlton in a wagon.

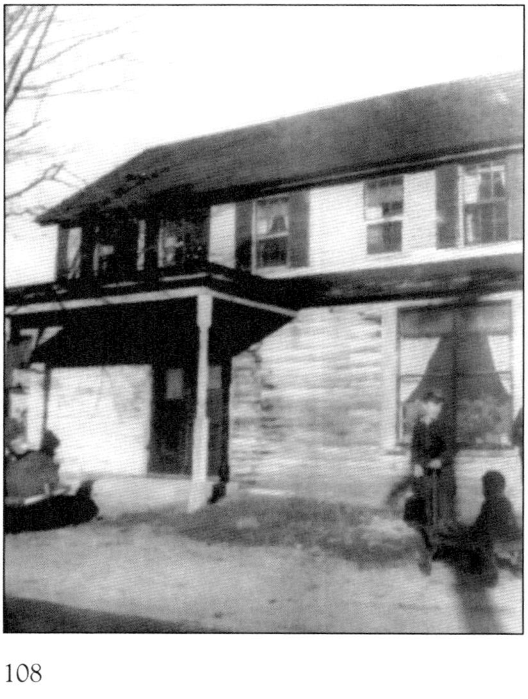

**The Smith Residence.** Charles McAllister, born in 1852, moved to this home when he was 14 years old and lived there until his death in 1905 at the age of 52. Charles was an apple buyer for Seavern and Company of Boston for 25 years. He served as town selectman for two years and as a member of the school board for three years.

*Eight*

# LITHIA SPRINGS

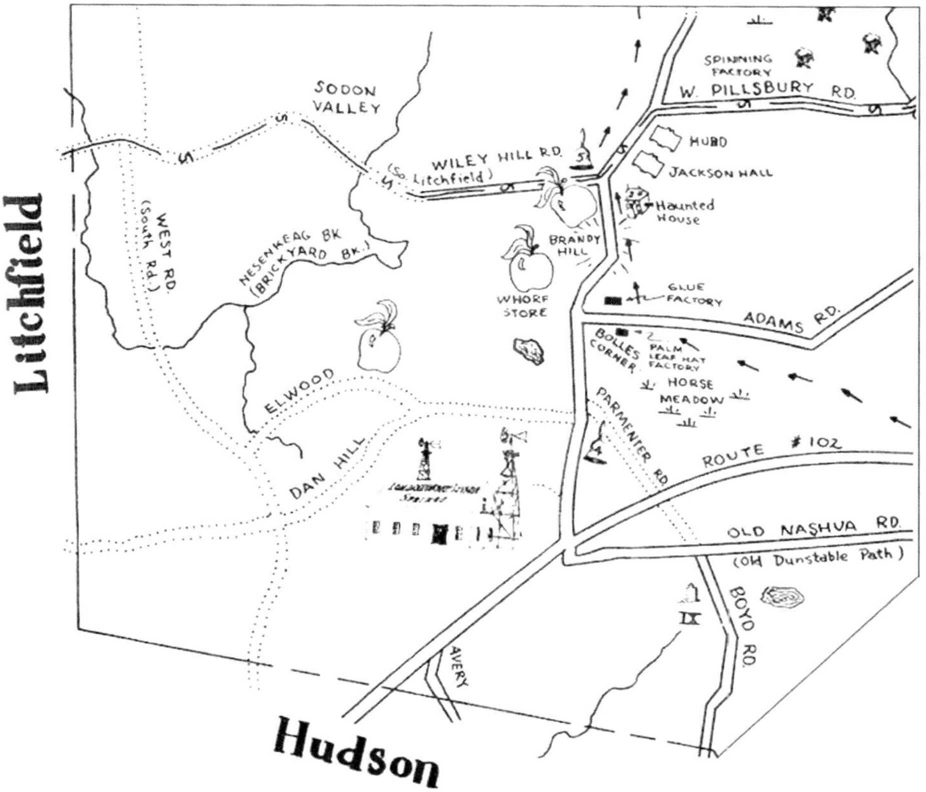


**SOUTHWEST.** This area of Londonderry contained two early schoolhouses: Schoolhouse No. 4, located at the intersections of High Range and Parmenter Roads, and Schoolhouse No. 5, located on Wiley Hill Road near High Range Road.

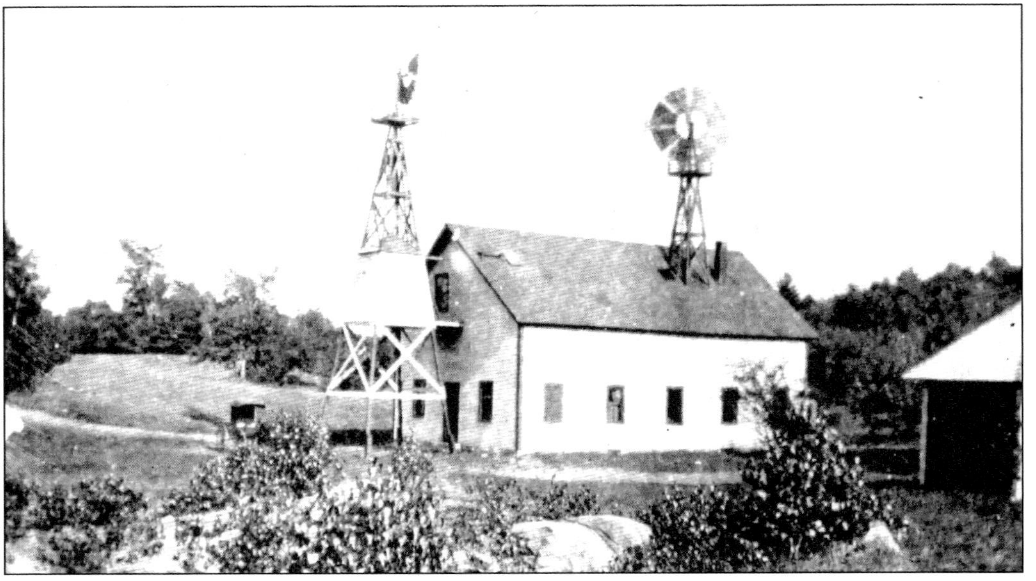

**LITHIA SPRINGS.** In 1882, Londonderry Lithia Springs was discovered on the Avery farm in south Londonderry. In search of a new source of water when the family well went dry, Frank Avery used the dowsing method and found the location of the spring-water source from the nearby granite hill. The water was known for containing lithium, which was considered a cure at the time for many health problems.

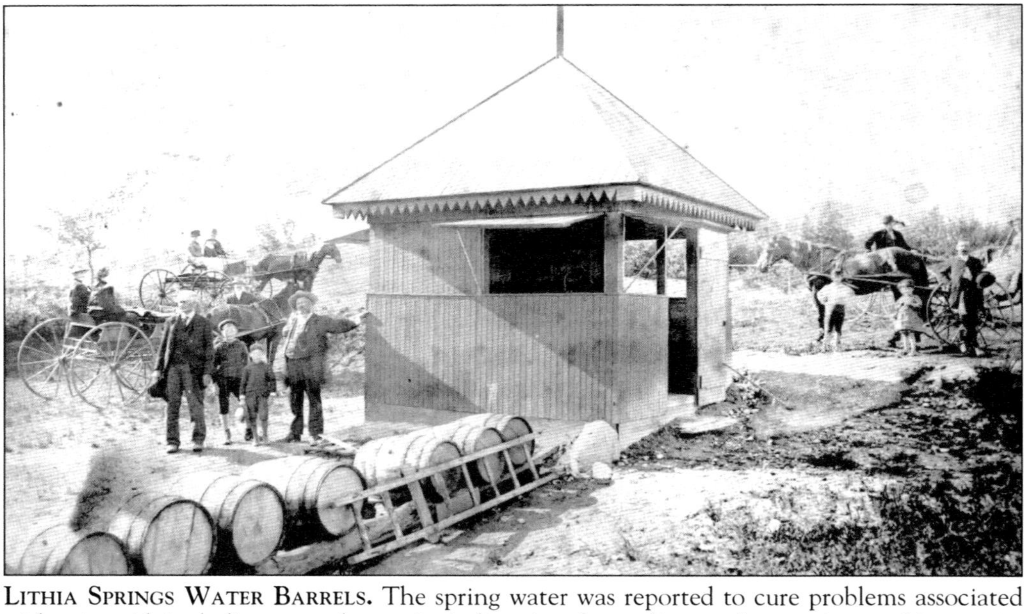

**LITHIA SPRINGS WATER BARRELS.** The spring water was reported to cure problems associated with uric acid, including gout, dyspepsia, indigestion, heart disease, rheumatism, and insomnia. An 1896 advertisement stated "Uric acid is the bane of all the people who live well. . . . By a thousand tests, the *Londonderry* has been proven the best, in fact, the only absolutely safe and sure solvent of this deadly crystal. . . . Londonderry Lithia removes the great cause of disease; nature does the rest."

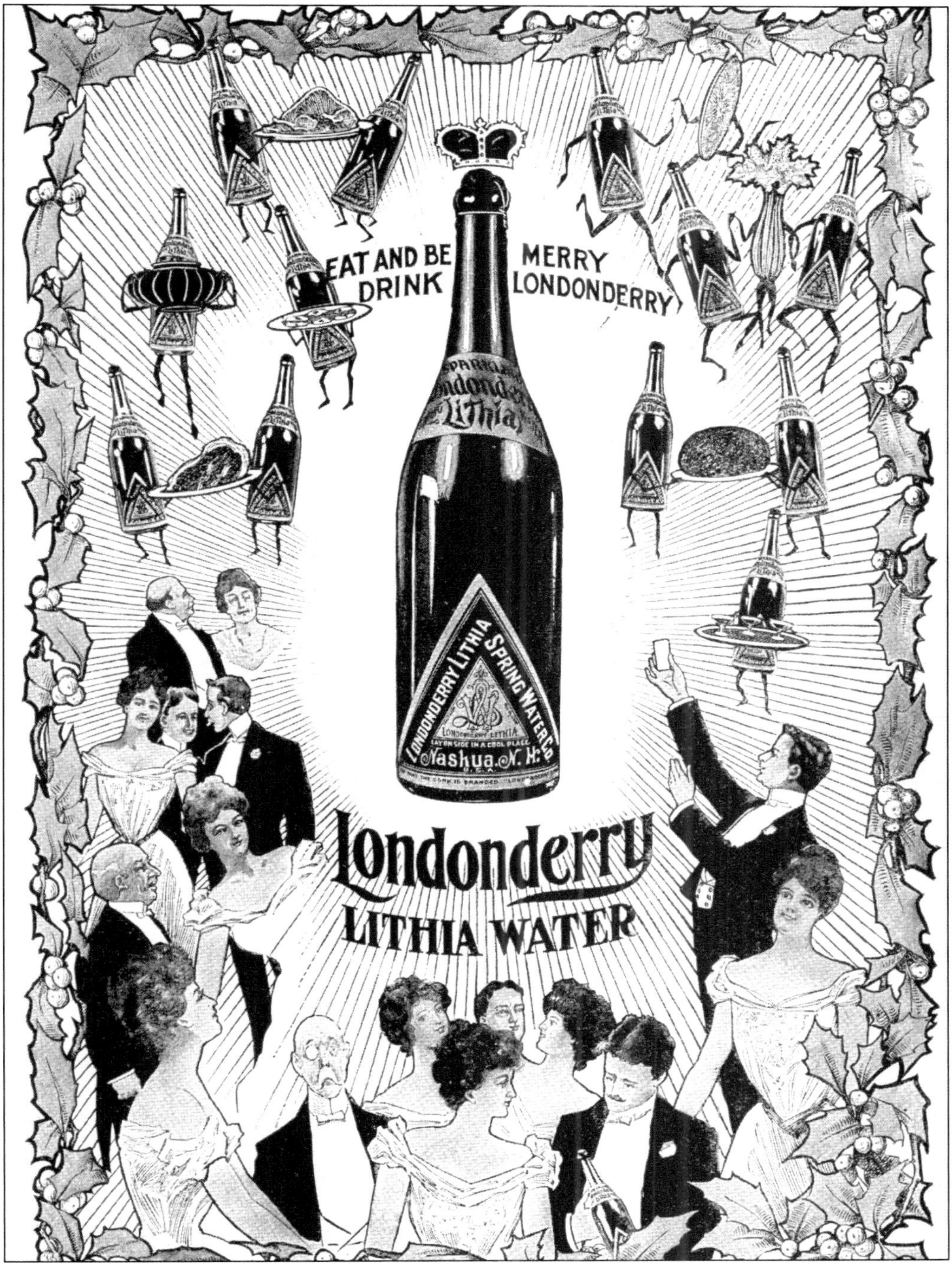


**A Lithia Springs Water Advertisement.** An 1896 advertisement for Londonderry Lithia Springs Water claimed the spring water "has a record of cures that would make any physician eminent." There was tremendous marketing of the product and many advertisements appeared, such as this one featuring the quart-sized bottle. Lithia Water was available in both still and sparkling varieties. It was also used as a mixer for cutting spirits.

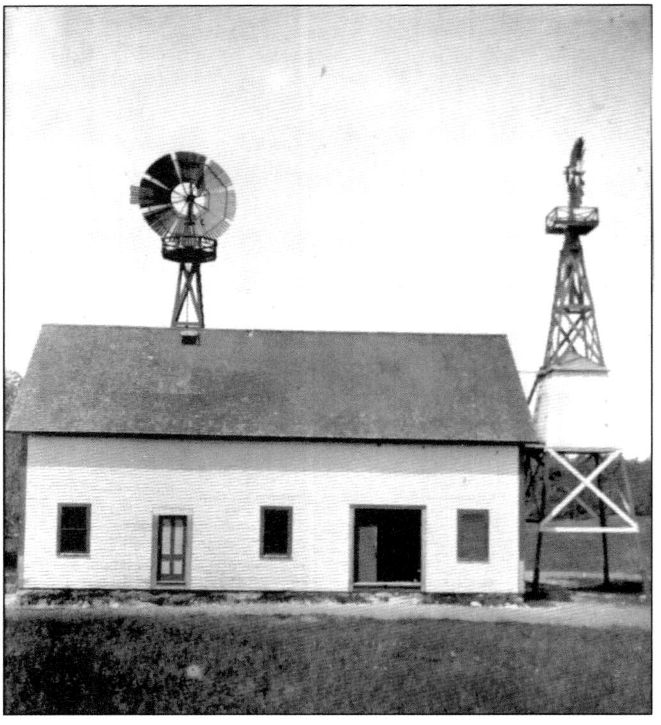

**The Lithia Springs Pump House.** The pump house held the spring well, which was lined with marble. The spring water was prescribed by doctors and used by hospitals all over the country. Lithia Springs was of such significance in state history that it is listed in the the site files of the New Hampshire Division of Historical Resources, Archeology Division. The pump house is no longer standing.

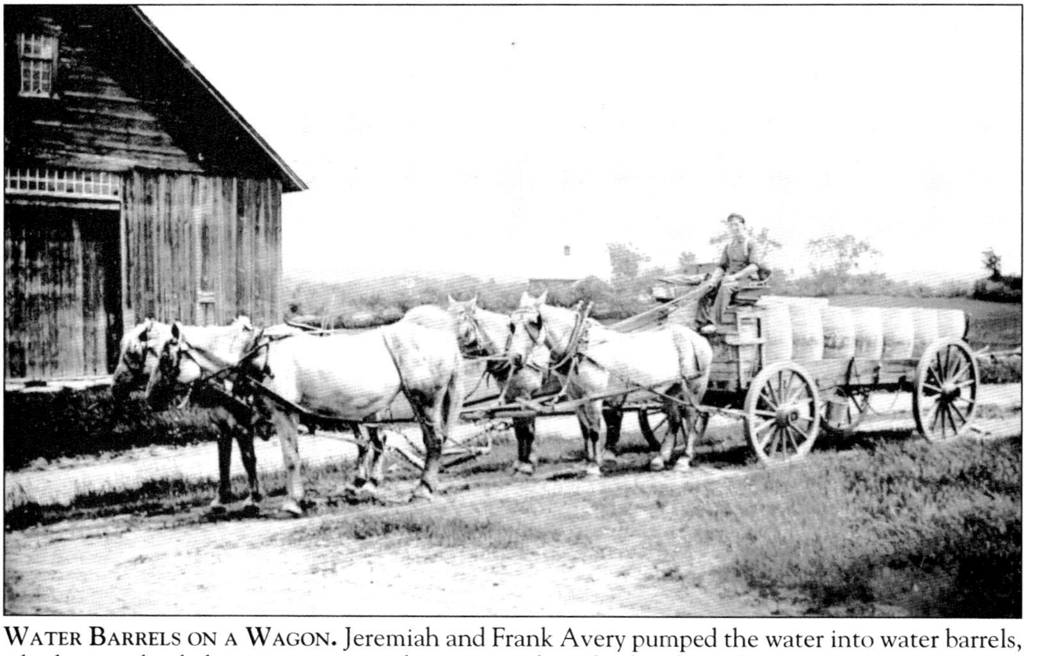

**Water Barrels on a Wagon.** Jeremiah and Frank Avery pumped the water into water barrels, which were loaded onto wagons and transported to the bottling plant in Nashua. To guard against imitation, the glass bottles were sealed and the corks were branded with trademarks. The three-gallon stoneware jugs that were used when the business opened in 1882 had the company name printed on them in blue.

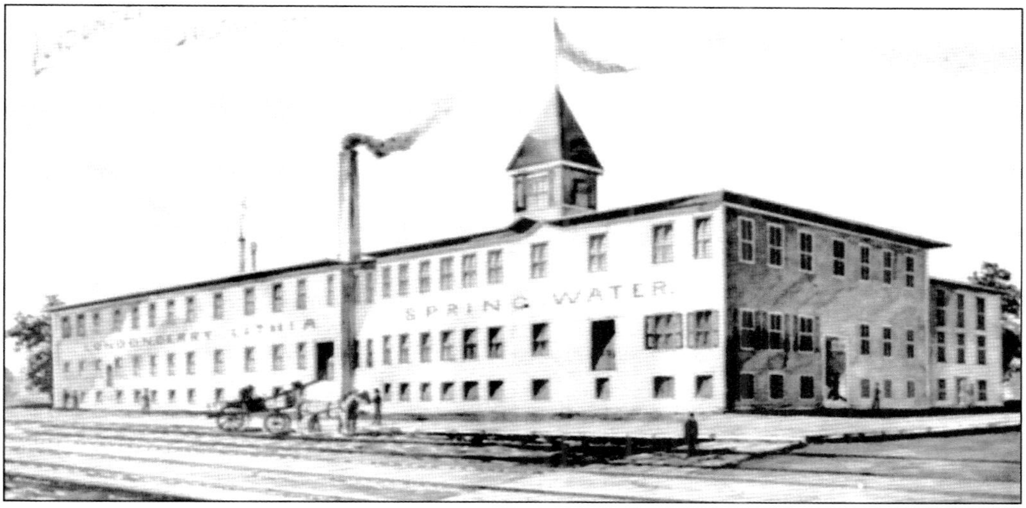


**THE LITHIA SPRINGS BOTTLING PLANT, NASHUA.** Because of its supposed medicinal properties, Lithia Springs Water was in high demand in the late 1800s to early 1900s and was distributed throughout North America and Europe. However, marketing of the spring water stopped before 1920, when the U.S. government determined that the amount of the mineral contained in the water was not sufficient to continue using the description "lithia" on the label. In addition, the influence of prohibition contributed to the demise of the company. The bottling plant was sold and was later torn down.

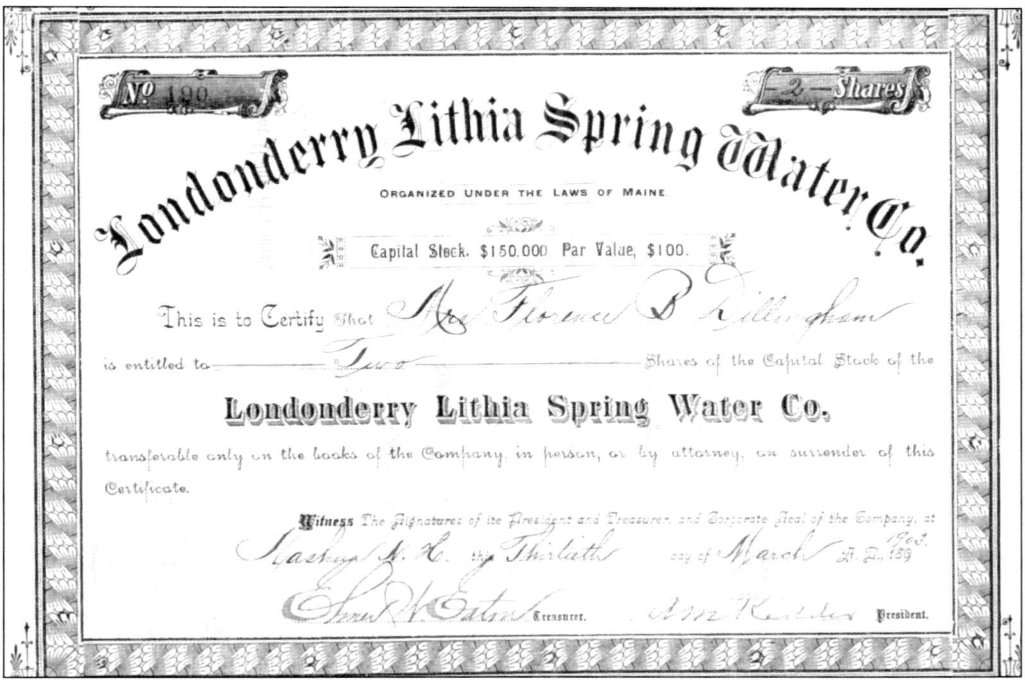


**A LITHIA SPRINGS STOCK CERTIFICATE.** Two doctors from the Nashua area who hailed the benefits of Lithia Springs Water formed a stock company to bottle and market the product. This certificate is signed by Elmer W. Eaton. Jeremiah Avery, owner of the property where the spring was located, and his only son, Frank, were hired by the stock company to operate the spring.

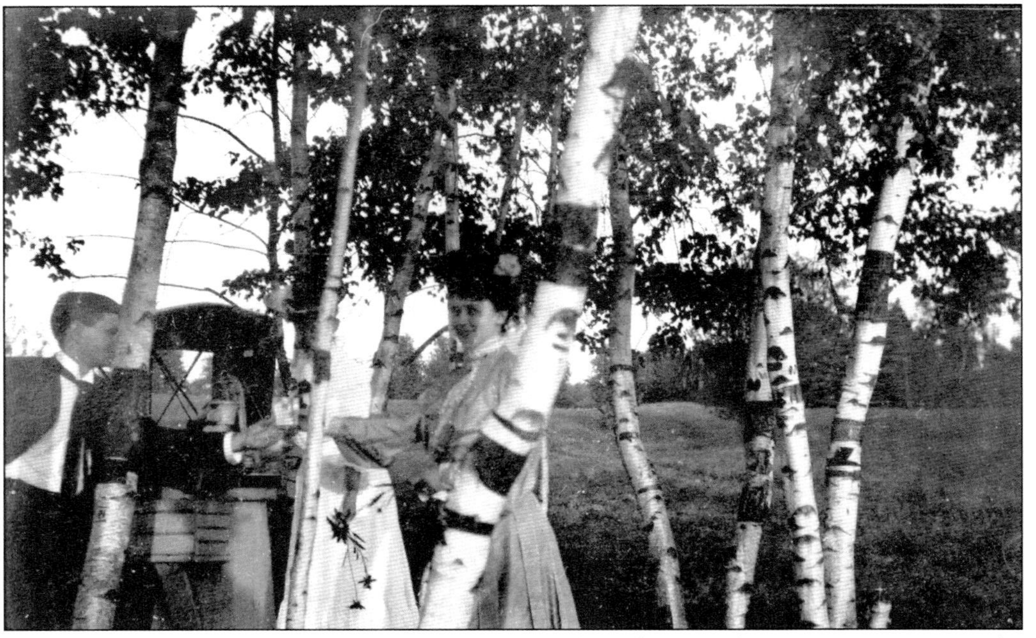

**GETTING WATER AT LITHIA SPRINGS, 1903.** It was a fun adventure for many visitors to stop by Lithia Springs. This photograph is of Reed Clark, Sara Lamborne, and Harriet Tag, who came by horse and buggy to get water from the spring.

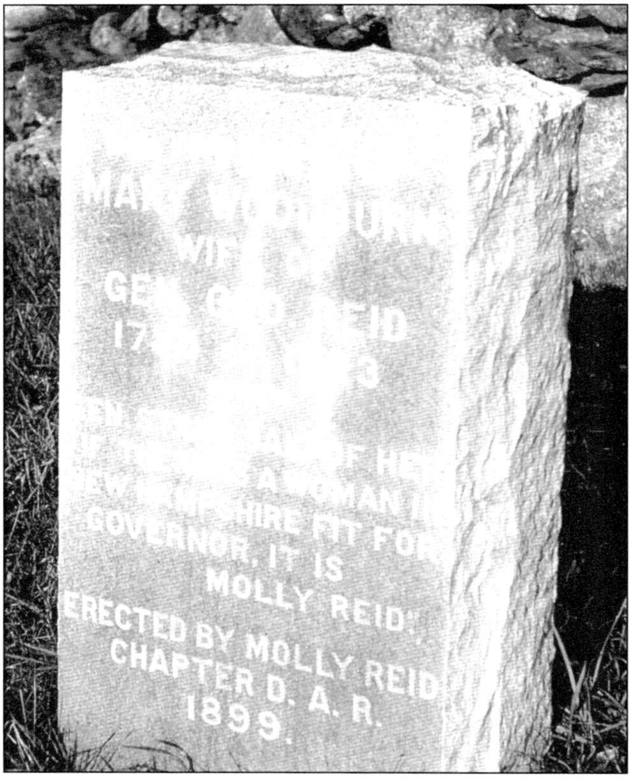


**THE MARY WOODBURN MONUMENT.** On July 10, 1899, this granite marker was erected at the birthplace of Mary Woodburn Reid on High Range Road. The Molly Reid Chapter of the Daughters of the American Revolution, named after Mary Reid, organized the dedication ceremony. Reid was one of four daughters of John Woodburn and his first wife, Mary Boyd. In 1757, she married George Reid and settled in Londonderry. George Reid was a celebrated soldier at the battle of Bunker Hill and later survived the brutal winter of 1777 at Valley Forge. Mary Reid died in 1823 at the age of 88. General Stark's tribute to her was engraved on the monument: "If there is a woman in New Hampshire fit for governor, it is Molly Reid."

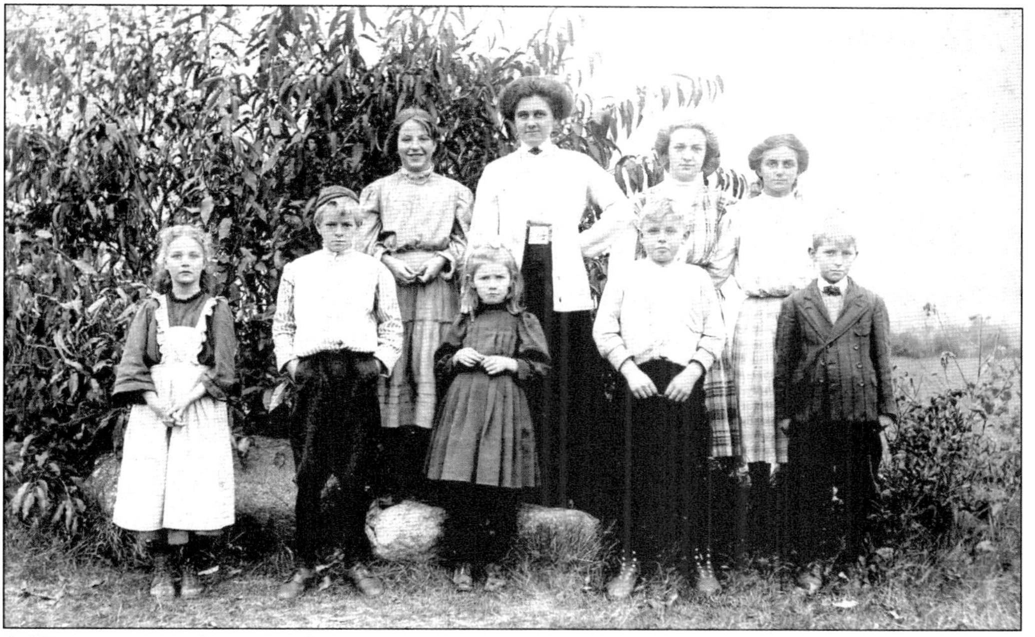

**A Teacher and Class at Schoolhouse No. 4.** Pearl Reid, the teacher (center), is pictured in this 1909 photograph along with her class, which included Draper Parmenter (front row, second from left) and Vera Pillsbury Ralston. Horace Greeley, the famous newspaperman who started the *New Yorker*, attended school here when he was visiting his Woodburn grandparents in Londonderry.

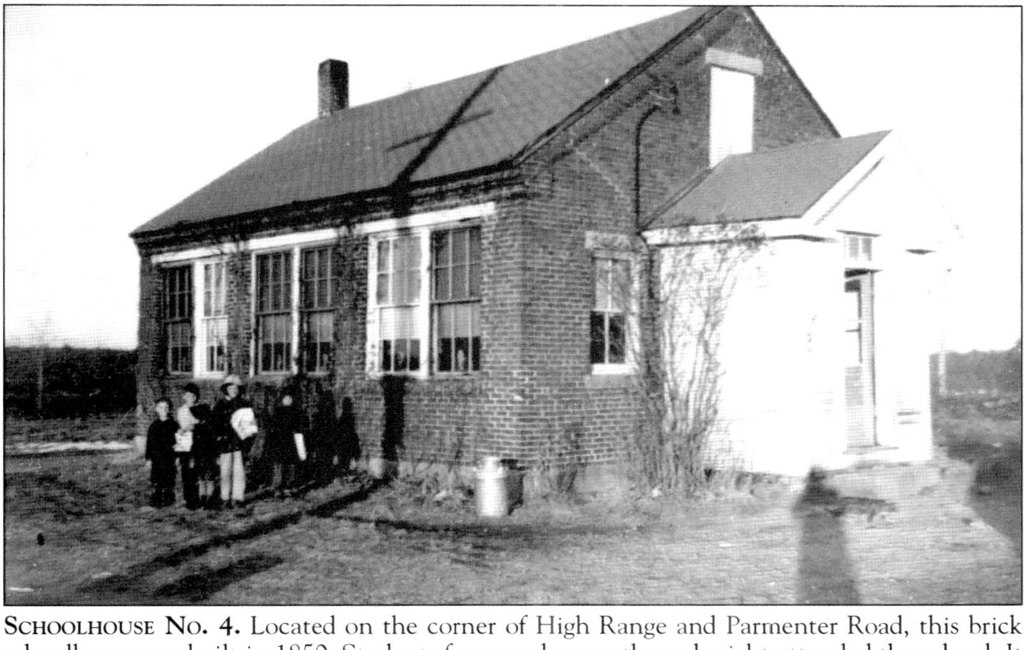

**Schoolhouse No. 4.** Located on the corner of High Range and Parmenter Road, this brick schoolhouse was built in 1850. Students from grades one through eight attended the school. It is now a private residence.

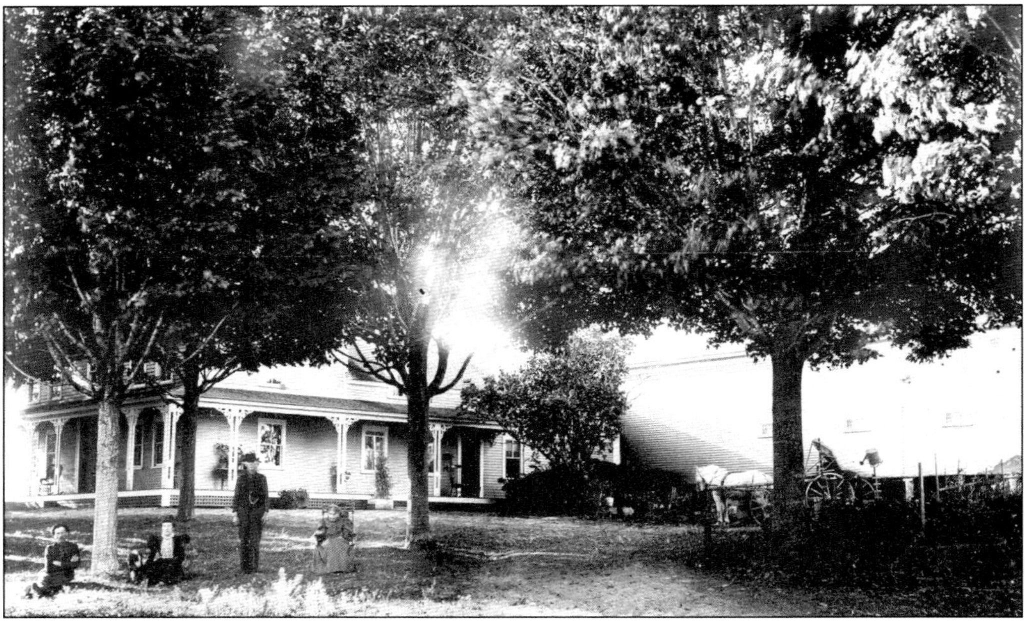

**THE PLUMMER FARM.** This *c.* 1906 photograph is of the Plummer home and farm, originally owned by Nathan and Charlotte Plummer. The Plummers raised two sons, Robert and George Nathan. George married Eliza Annis in 1898, had four children, and continued to live on the farm. It was primarily a dairy farm, but the Plummers also raised apples and vegetables. Between 1890 and 1910, the Plummers used part of their home as a boardinghouse and welcomed summer boarders from Boston and New York. Pictured in the photograph are Charlotte (Annis) and Robert K. Plummer with two of their children, George N. and Eliza M.

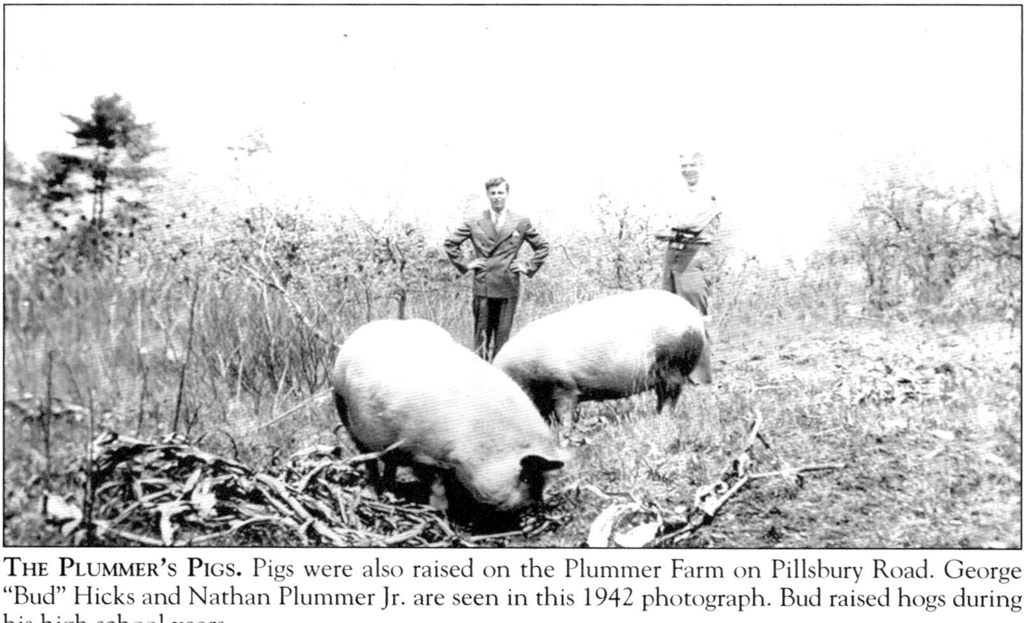

**THE PLUMMER'S PIGS.** Pigs were also raised on the Plummer Farm on Pillsbury Road. George "Bud" Hicks and Nathan Plummer Jr. are seen in this 1942 photograph. Bud raised hogs during his high school years.

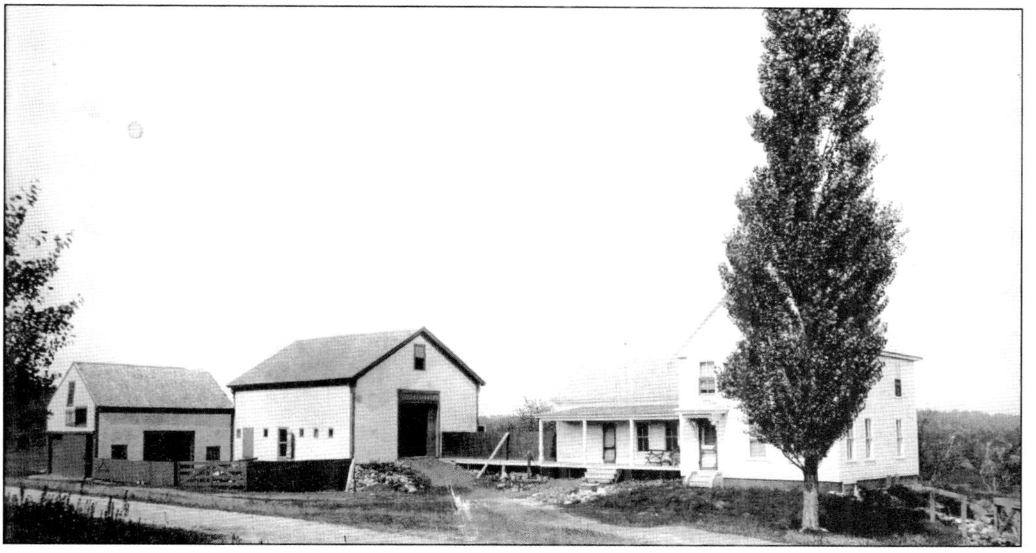

**THE PEABODY-HOLTON HOME.** Eldridge Peabody owned this home on the west side of Pillsbury Road c. 1850. He had four sons, who were wheelwrights, blacksmiths, and carpenters. The shop extended from the barn to the foot of the Woodbury's hill. A red board fence formed the barnyard between the barn and the road with a wide red gate in front of the blacksmith shop. The first flax mill in Londonderry was built on this farm, which stood on the corner of west Pillsbury Road and Holton Circle. The farm was recently destroyed in a controlled fire.

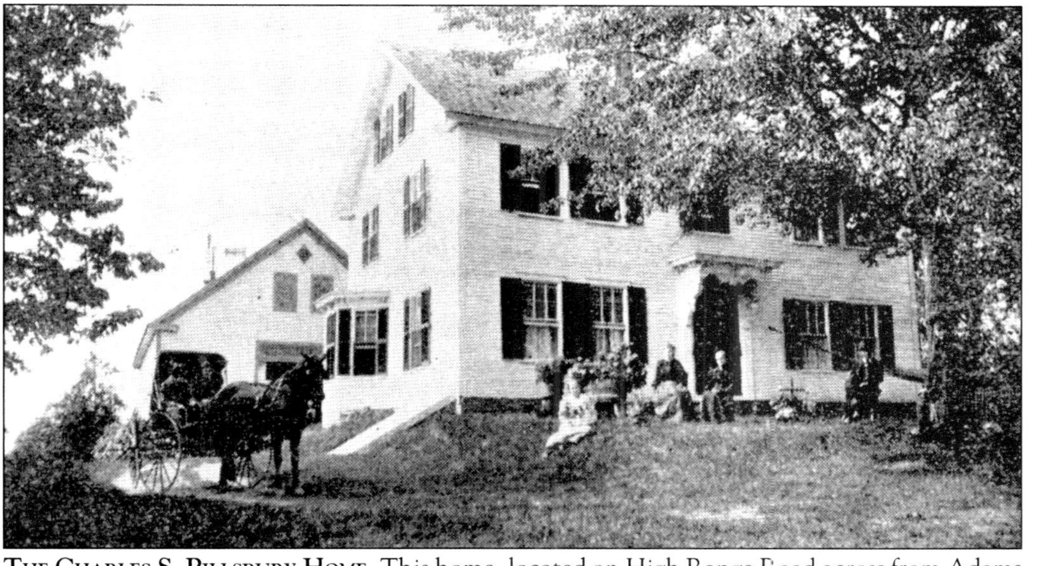

**THE CHARLES S. PILLSBURY HOME.** This home, located on High Range Road across from Adams Road, was built on the lot of James Gregg and Benjamin Kidder, two of the original settlers of the town. Charles S. Pillsbury bought the home when he moved to Londonderry in 1866. The home passed to his son Charles G., who married Alice Miller in 1894 and had two daughters, Vera (Pillsbury) Ralston and Grace (Pillsbury) Mack, wife of Wallace P. Mack Jr. The original barn still stands, but the home has burned. A home of similar style was built on the site.

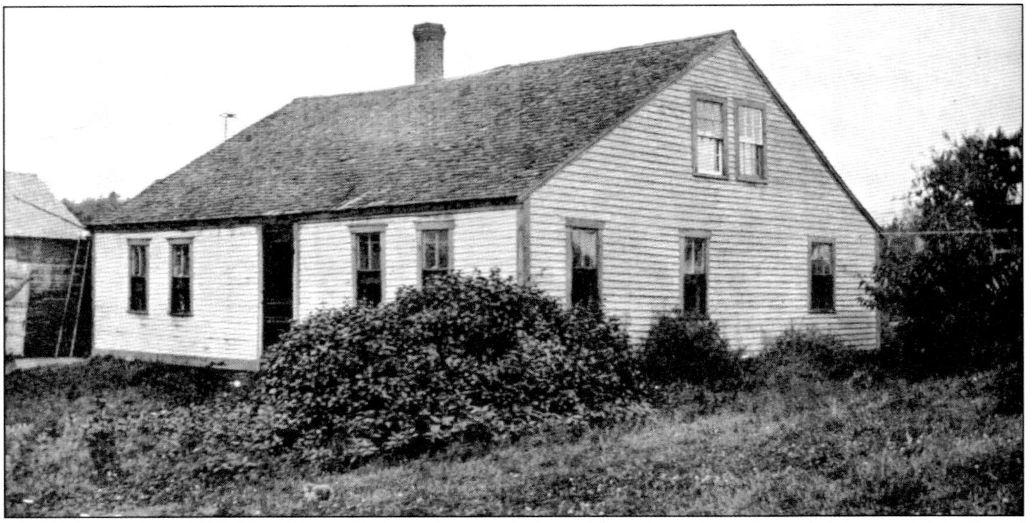

**The Towne Homestead.** Dr. G. T. Towne owned this farm on Boyd Road. Jabez Towne lived in the home and died at the age of 96. Across old Nashua Road was the Towne cemetery, where the Towne and Boyd families are buried. The home is no longer standing.

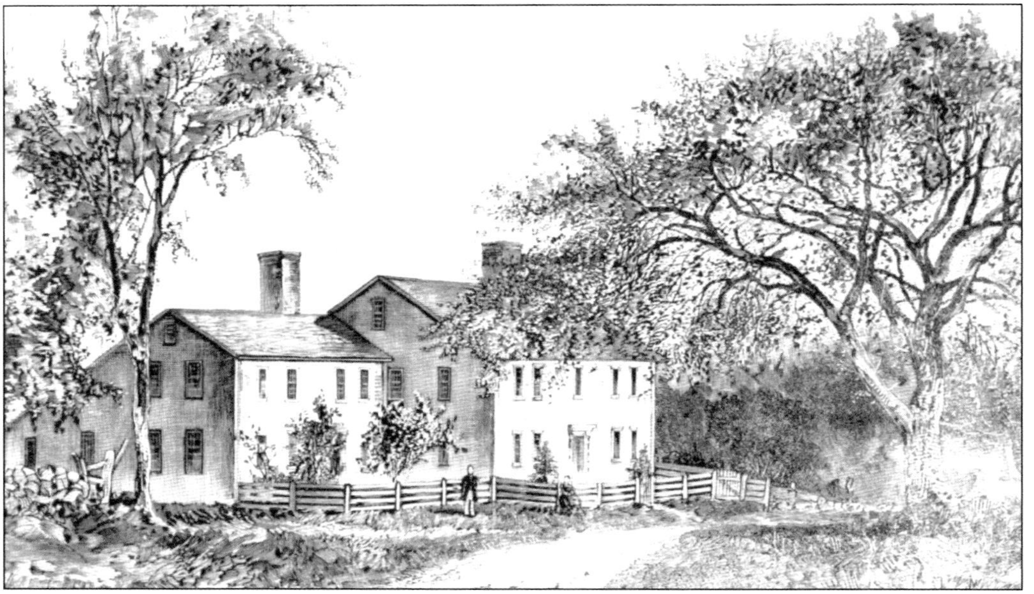

**The Patterson Homestead.** Peter Patterson, who came to Londonderry from Ireland in 1736, purchased this home on Adams Road from William and Elias Dickey. Peter was a weaver who traveled to Boston to sell Londonderry linen. The Patterson homestead manufactured Londonderry linen, which was considered the best in New England and was in high demand. Linen making, a skill brought over from Ireland, became the main industry of early Londonderry. Because many people claimed to sell linen made in the town, in 1731, the New Hampshire House of Representatives passed an act that required all linen made in Londonderry to have a seal stamped on the material.

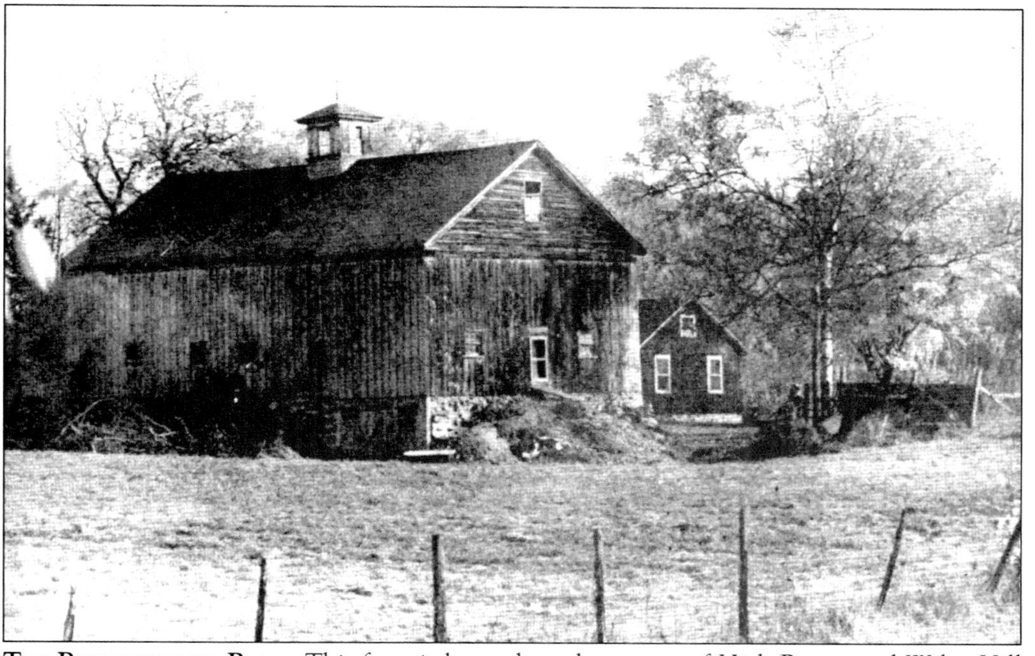

**The Butterworth Barn.** This farm is located on the corner of High Range and Wiley Hill Roads. The McKay family, who owned the property in the 1920s, used the dining room of the connected Colonial house (which has since burned) to operate a small store that sold flour by the barrel, cornmeal, and, to the delight of children, licorice sticks.

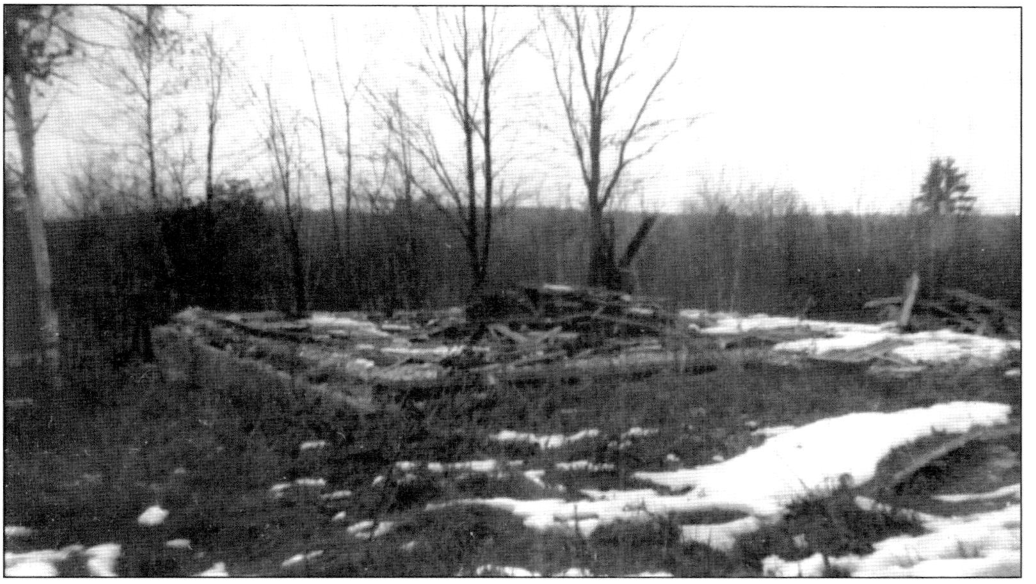

**The Site of Schoolhouse No. 5.** Located on Wiley Hill Road near the intersection with High Range Road, this brick schoolhouse was similar in design to Schoolhouse No. 4. Bricks for both schools, as well as for the Lowell Mills, were made near Wiley Brook, formerly Brickyard Brook, on Wiley Hill Road. Students brought small rugs to school and put them under their desks to keep their feet warm. The school was taken down in 1925.

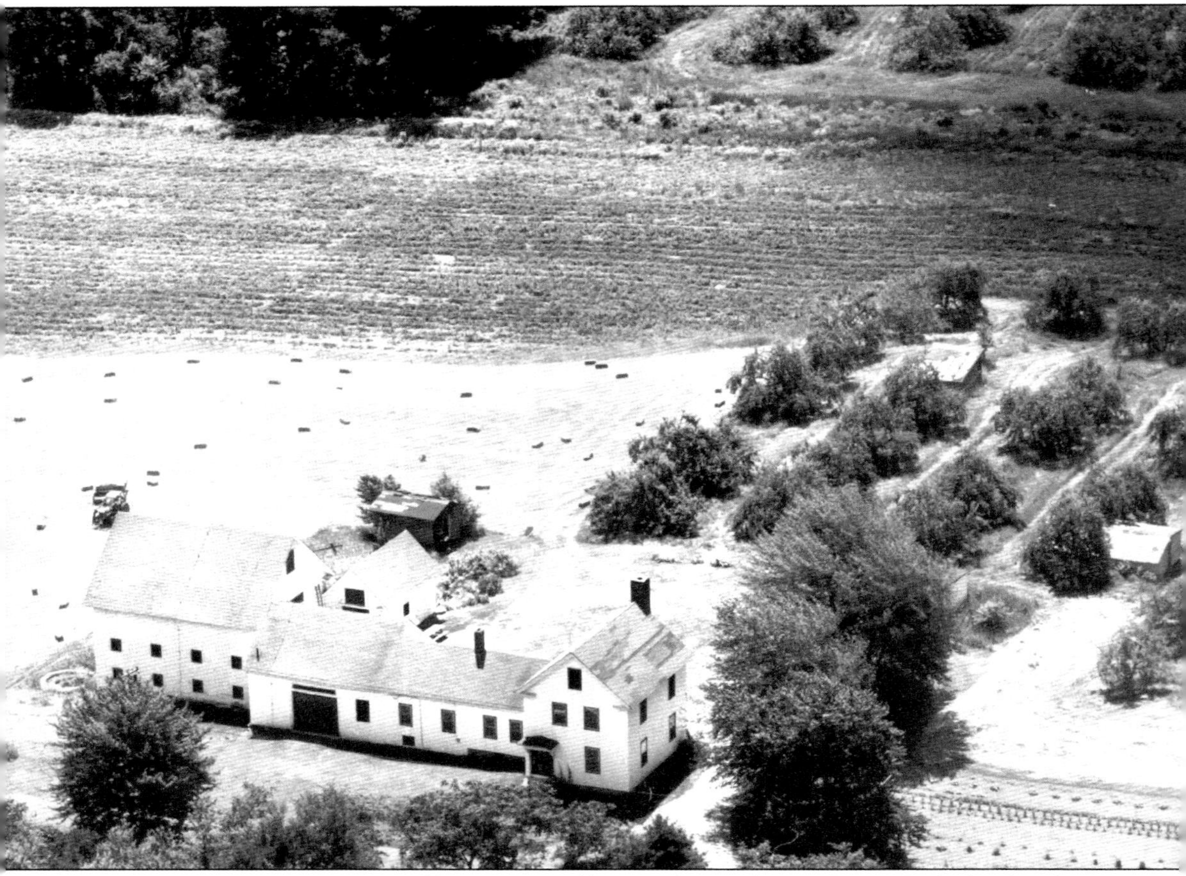

**BREEZY HILL FARM.** George Hill, a county jail keeper during the Civil War, built this farmhouse in 1850. Oxen transported the huge granite blocks that form the home's foundation from Milford. A blacksmith shop once stood between the house and the brook. Currently, the house is well known as Londonderry's sole bed and breakfast, which has been operated by Emily and Ron Foley since 1994. The name was taken from a nearby *c.* 1800 farm located farther east on Adams Road; that farm is no longer standing, but its cellar hole is still visible.

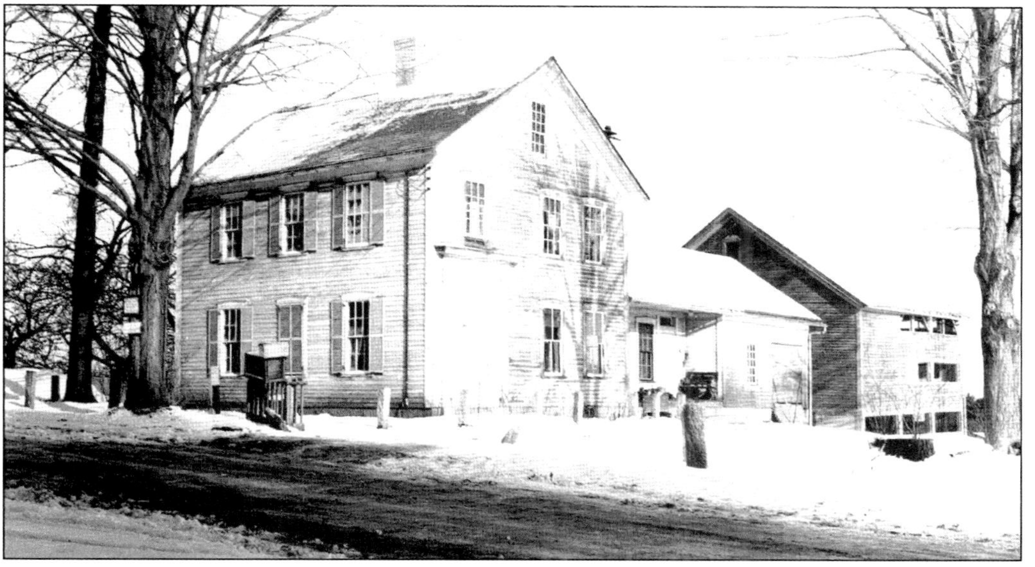

**THE CALDWELL-BLODGETT HOUSE.** The original lot of Samuel Houston, laid out in 1729 on the north side of High Range and Moose Hill Roads, was divided among the Bolles and the Caldwells, who built this home in 1892. George Blodgett, who had a poultry business, later owned it. Mrs. Blodgett was an avid gardener, and there were a greenhouse and a large flower garden on the south side of the home.

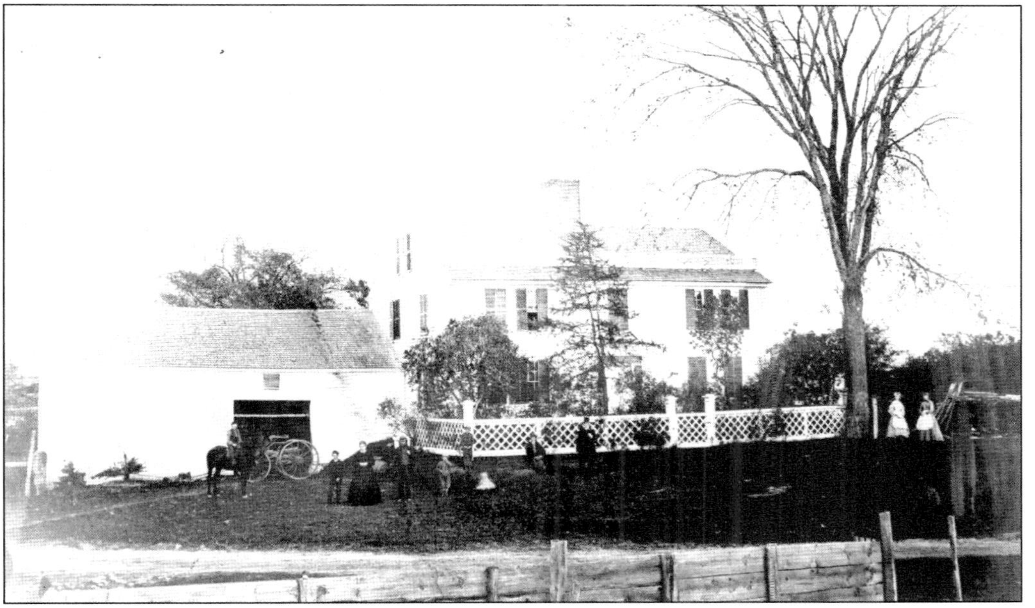

**THE HURD HOUSE.** At the corner of High Range and west Pillsbury Roads was the home of Charles Hurd, which Hurd purchased from Samuel Dickey in 1841. The large Colonial home, which is still standing, faces west, and the barn is across the road. It was a stopping place for stagecoach travelers. Charles Hurd lived in the home with his wife, Nancy Woodburn, at the time of this 1869 photograph. As happened to many of the large homes in this area after the stagecoach days, it became a summer boardinghouse.

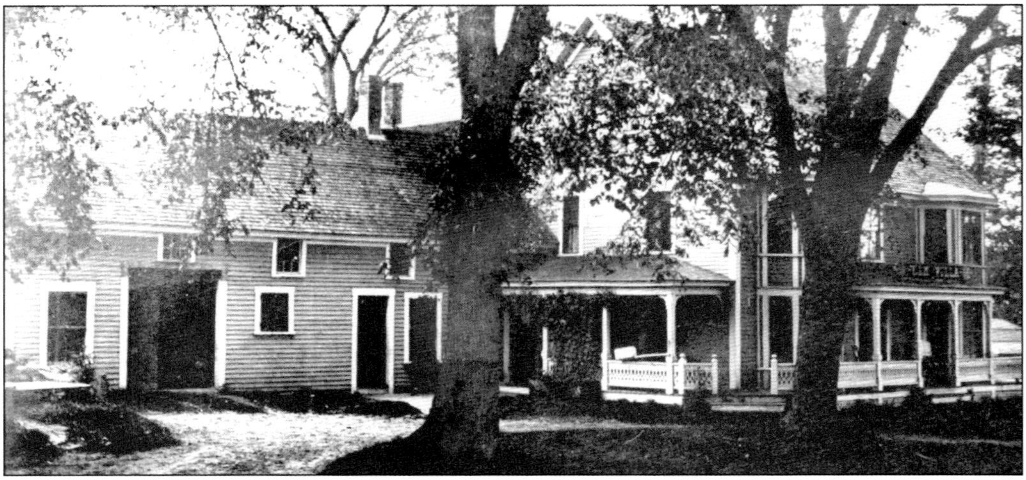

**The Lowd-Peabody Home.** William Lowd owned this large farm in the mid-1800s. In the early 1900s, Elwin Peabody lived here with his wife, Minnie, whom he married in 1885. They had two children, Mildred and Bertrand, who went into the undertaking business. Elwin was a carpenter, and he built a watering trough for horses to drink from as they passed along the road. Elwin's great-grandfather Jonathan was the first Peabody to settle in Londonderry in 1843. This home no longer exists; it was located on West Pillsbury Road near the old flax-retting pond.

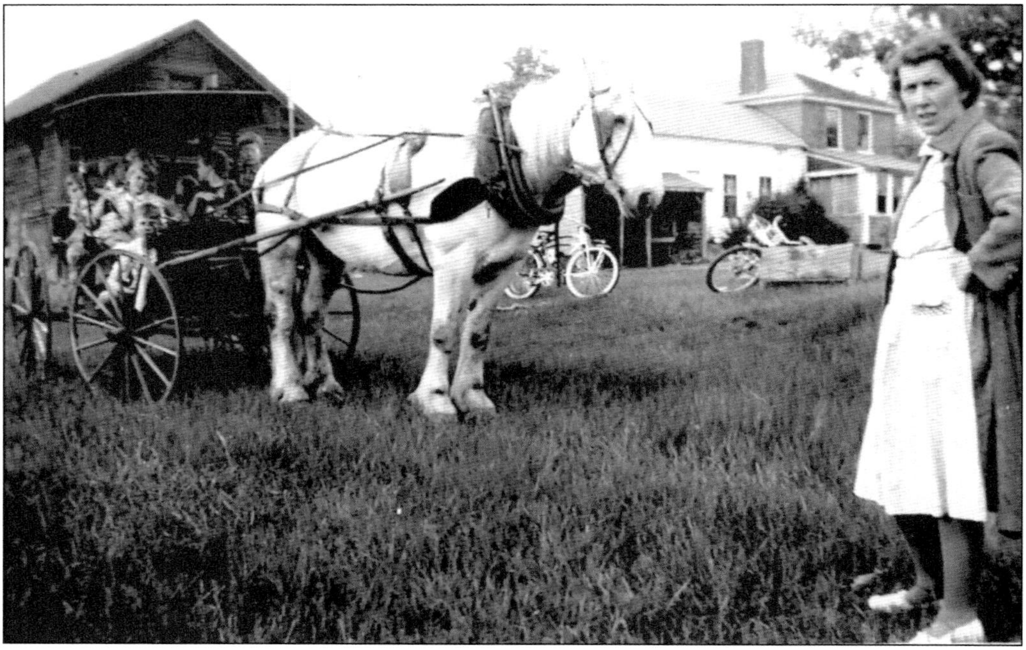

**The Hicks Home.** Hazel Plummer Hicks is pictured in this 1940 photograph along with the wagon and family horse, Tom. In the background is their brick home, built in the late 1800s using bricks from Brickyard Brook on Wiley Hill Road. Hazel married Daniel Hicks Sr. in 1923. Both were very involved in the community, Hazel as chairwoman of the school board and Daniel as the original commander of the American Legion Parmenter-Harrington Post No. 27 from 1917 to 1918 and as town clerk, tax collector, and selectman. They had seven children. This brick home still stands as a residence on High Range Road.

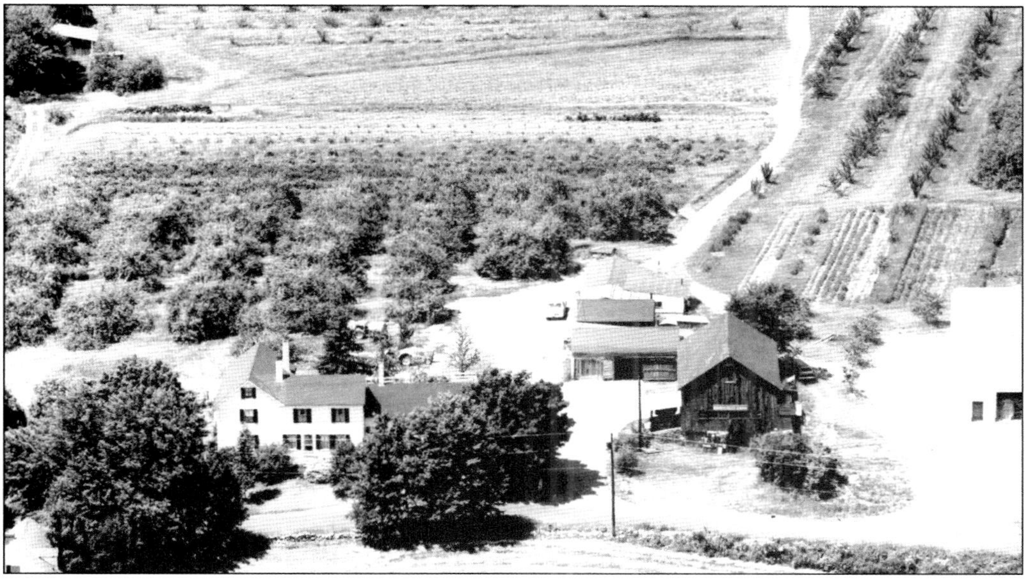

**Sunnycrest Farm.** In 1943, Alfred F. Conner, a teacher at Pinkerton Academy for 37 years, and his wife, Marjorie, bought this farm from Donald Northway. They raised chickens and field crops and took produce to the Manchester farmers' market. In 1966, a storage facility was built with a controlled atmosphere for apples. A cider mill and press were added in 1971. Sunnycrest Farm still operates today on High Range Road and is the only orchard in town with a bakery on the premises.

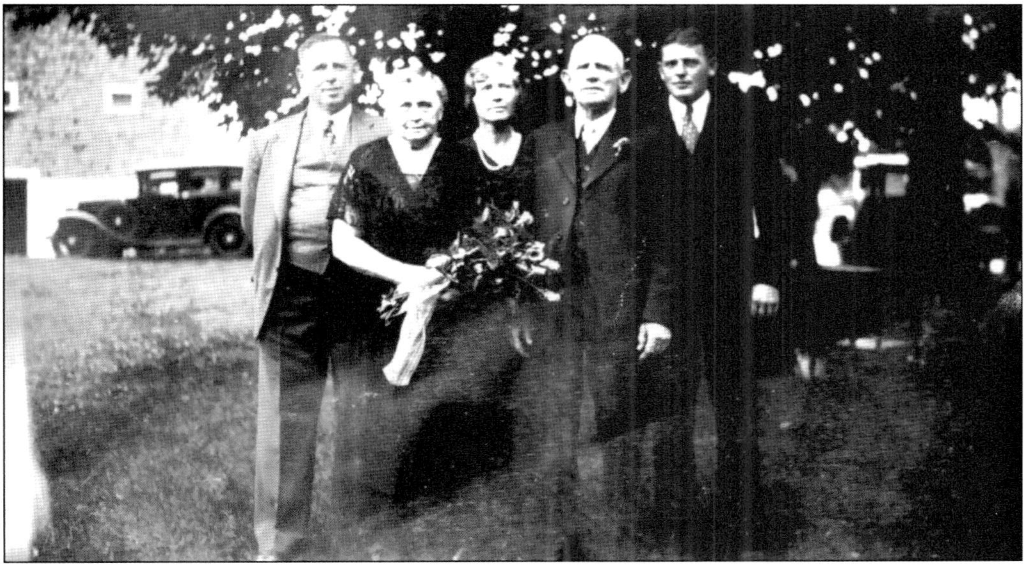

**The Parmenter Family.** This 1933 photograph was taken to celebrate the 50th wedding anniversary of Edward and Cordelia Parmenter, pictured with their three children, Ralph, Lottie, and Draper. The family home on High Range Road was later owned by Draper. Note the barn in the background. Draper was on the school board and served as a selectman and as a representative to the General Court. He was a member of the Grange for over 50 years and a charter member of the American Legion Parmenter-Harrington Post No. 27.

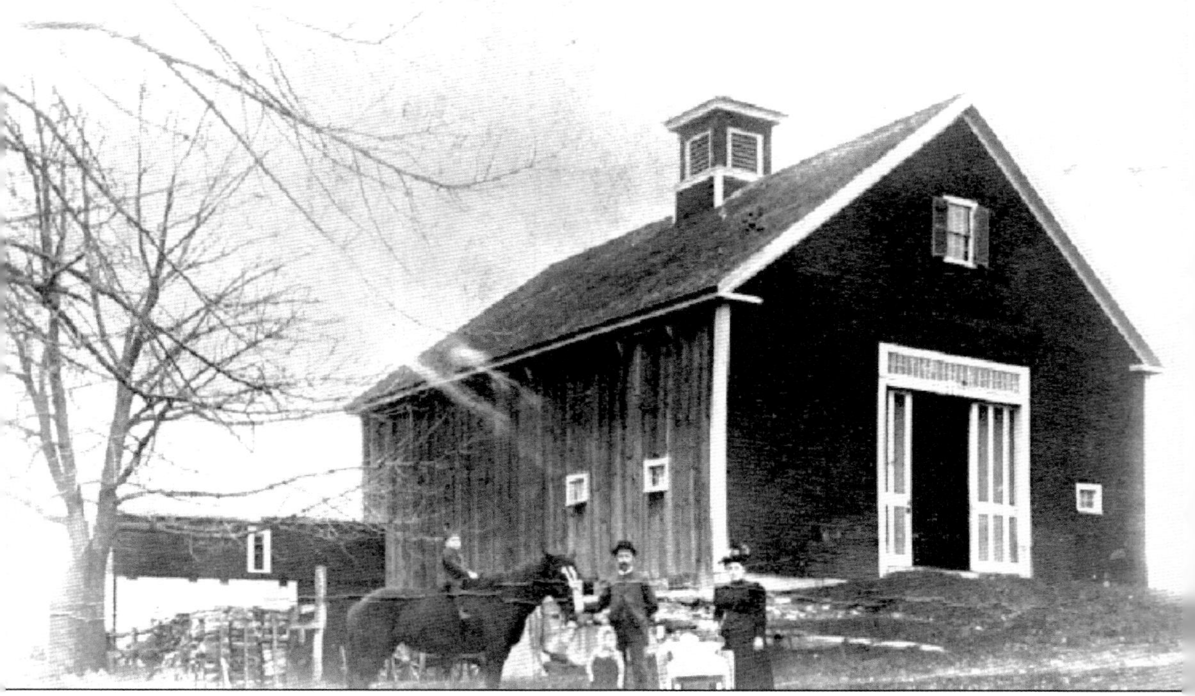

**THE PARMENTERS' BARN.** Located on High Range Road, the barn was built in 1859 in a traditional community barn raising. The Parmenter barn is actually part of the old homestead of John L. and Emeline G. Blood. This 1899 photograph shows their grandson, Wilbur L. Blood, and his wife, Bernice N. (Thompson) Blood, with their two children, Harland and Rosina, who were born on the homestead in 1893 and 1895, respectively. By 1998, the barn had fallen into disrepair and was scheduled for demolition. A civic-minded contractor donated the structure to the Londonderry Historical Society, which dismantled, moved, and reassembled the barn on its property on west Pillsbury Road. The Yankee post-and-beam construction with mortise and tenon joints is typical of dairy barns of the era.

*Nine*

# Breakneck Hill

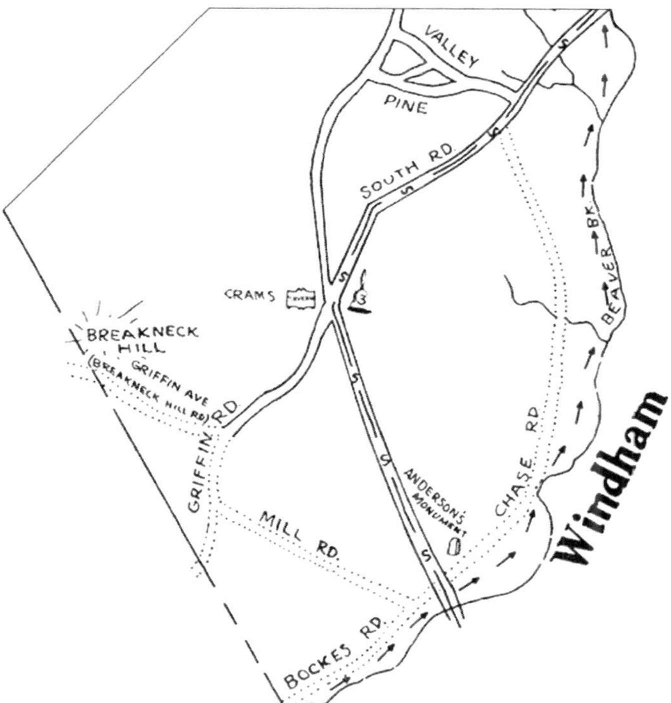


**South Central.** This area of Londonderry was where Schoolhouse No. 3 was located, at the intersection of South and Mammoth Roads.

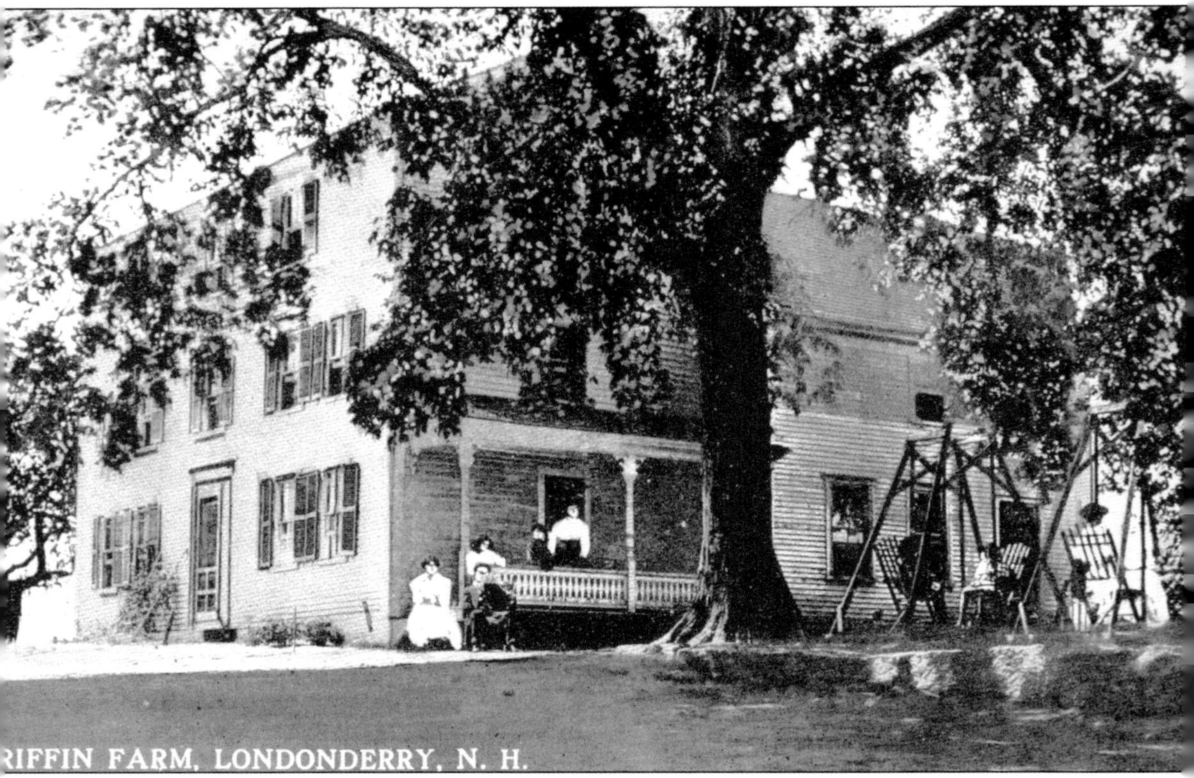


**THE GRIFFIN FARM.** In 1898, Frank Griffin and his wife, Margaret, moved to Londonderry and bought this farm on Griffin Avenue (Breakneck Hill). The original two-story Colonial home was remodeled into the three-story home seen in this photograph. The Griffins had 10 children.

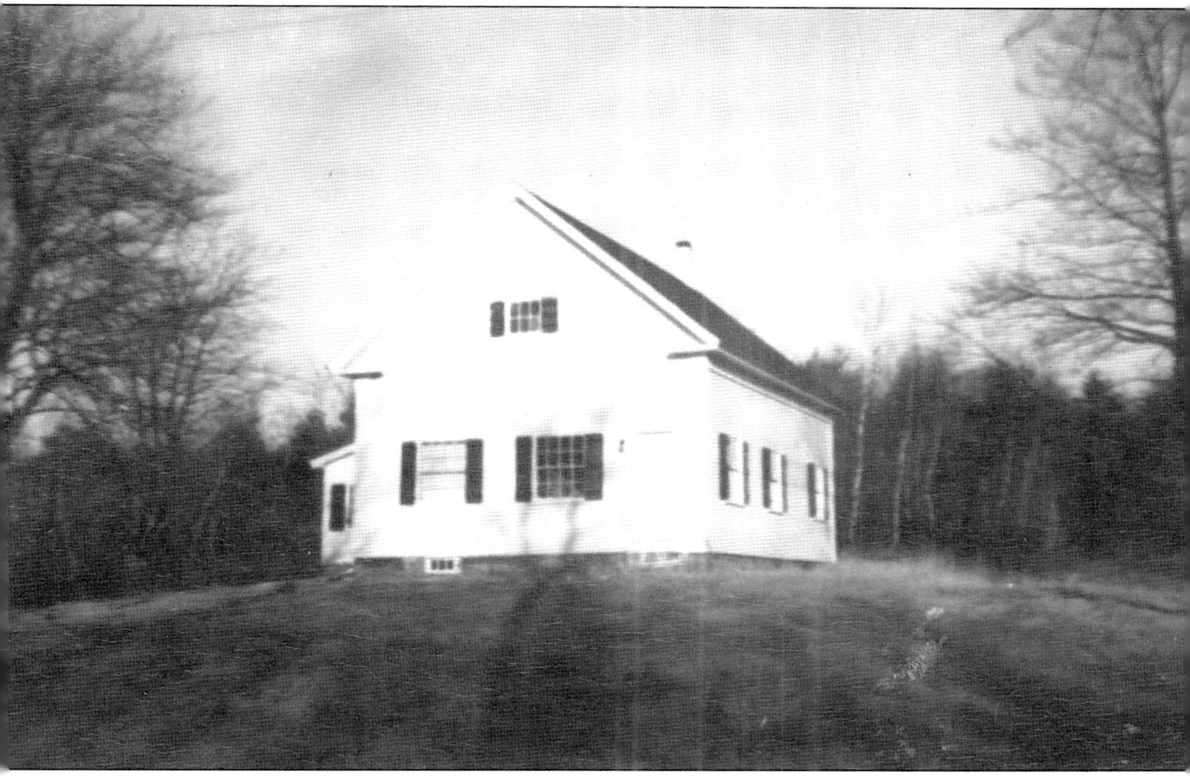

**Schoolhouse No. 3.** When Londonderry incorporated in 1827, it was divided into nine school districts. The average teacher's salary in the mid-1800s was $6 a month for women and $16 a month for men; this rose to $32 a month for women and $34 a month for men in 1900. Schoolhouse No. 3, located on Mammoth and South Roads, was closed in 1940 and became a private home.

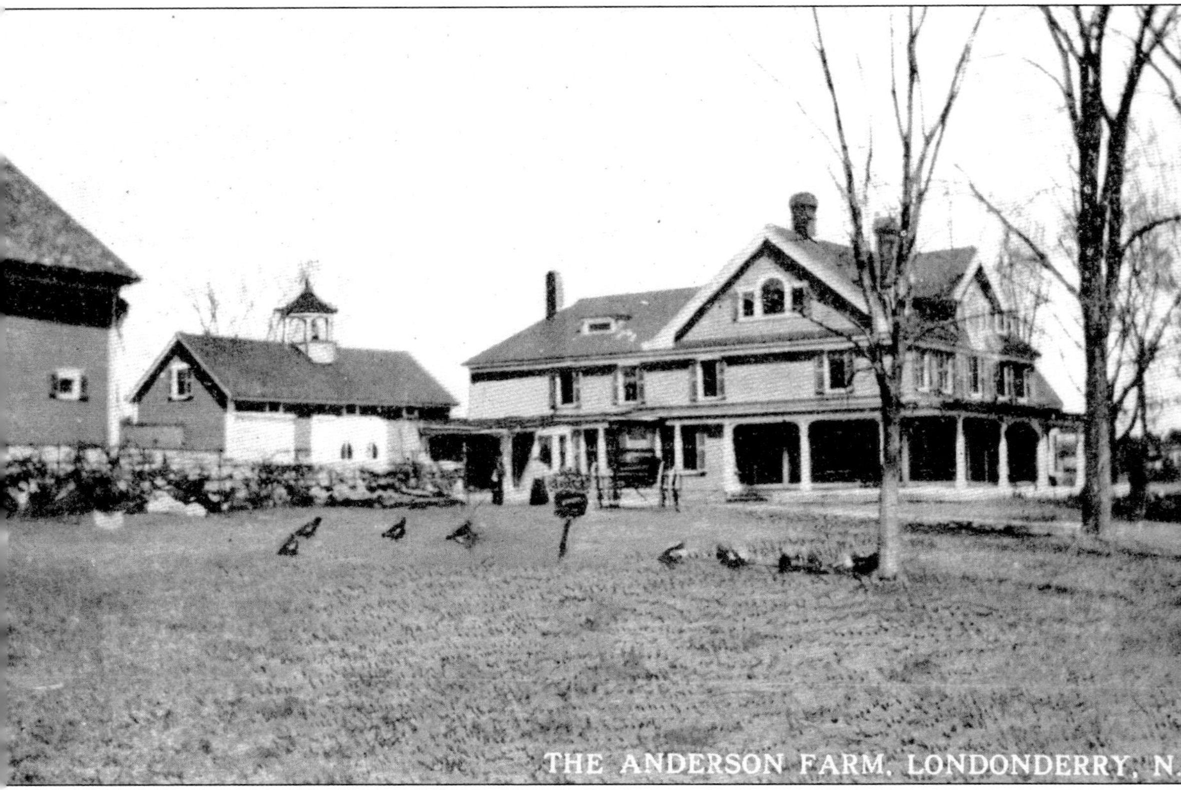


**THE ANDERSON FARM.** Family records date back to 1720, when Samuel Anderson lived in this home on the corner of Bockes and Mammoth Roads. Across Mammoth Road is a stone monument to the original owners of the Anderson land, with the names of Samuel, David, Frank, and William H. This farm still stands today.